ROUTLEDGE LIBRARY EDITIONS:
ACCOUNTING HISTORY

Volume 38

SHAREHOLDER USE AND UNDERSTANDING OF FINANCIAL INFORMATION

T0384483

SHAREHOLDER USE AND UNDERSTANDING OF FINANCIAL INFORMATION

T. A. LEE AND D.P. TWEEDIE

Routledge
Taylor & Francis Group

LONDON AND NEW YORK

First published in 1990 by Garland Publishing, Inc.

This edition first published in 2021
by Routledge
2 Park Square, Milton Park, Abingdon, Oxon OX14 4RN

and by Routledge
52 Vanderbilt Avenue, New York, NY 10017

Routledge is an imprint of the Taylor & Francis Group, an informa business

British Library Cataloguing in Publication Data
A catalogue record for this book is available from the British Library

ISBN: 978-0-367-33564-9 (Set)
ISBN: 978-1-00-304636-3 (Set) (ebk)
ISBN: 978-0-367-51793-9 (Volume 38) (hbk)
ISBN: 978-0-367-51795-3 (Volume 38) (pbk)
ISBN: 978-1-00-305522-8 (Volume 38) (ebk)

Publisher's Note
The publisher has gone to great lengths to ensure the quality of this reprint but
points out that some imperfections in the original copies may be apparent.

Disclaimer
The publisher has made every effort to trace copyright holders and would welcome
correspondence from those they have been unable to trace.

SHAREHOLDER USE AND UNDERSTANDING OF FINANCIAL INFORMATION

T. A. LEE AND D. P. TWEEDIE

GARLAND PUBLISHING, INC.
New York & London
1990

Library of Congress Cataloging-in-Publication Data

Lee, T. A. (Thomas Alexander)
(Private shareholder and the corporate report)
Shareholder use and understanding of financial information / T. A. Lee, D. P. Tweedie.
p. cm. — (Accounting history and thought)
Originally published as: The private shareholder and the corporate report, 1977.
Includes bibliographical references.
ISBN 0-8240-3321-3 (alk. paper)
1. Corporation reports—Great Britain. 2. Corporations—Great Britain—Finance—Decision-making. I. Tweedie, D. P. II. Lee, T.A. (Thomas Alexander) Private shareholder and the corporate report. III. Title. IV. Series.
HG4028.B2L43   1990
657'.3—dc20   89-28438

Printed on acid-free 250-year-life paper

Manufactured in the United States of America

ACKNOWLEDGEMENT

Due to pressure of work as UK technical partner of Peat, Marwick McLintock, David Tweedie has been unable to contribute to this introduction in the time-scale available to us for its production. I am most grateful to him, and to the ICAEW, for permission to reproduce our 1977 and 1981 studies in this Garland series. This introduction represents my personal views on financial reporting, and does not necessarily represent either the views of David, the original publishers of the studies (ICAEW), or ICAS of which I am a Council member.

INTRODUCTION

ECONOMIC REALITY, FAITHFUL REPRESENTATION AND ACCOUNTING NUMEROLOGY

A Further Study of the Use and Understanding of Financial Information

Prior to the mid 1970s much was postulated but little was known of the degree to which reported financial information was used and understood by those individuals for whom it was intended. Commentators on the state of accounting standards and practices suggested unsophisticated distinctions between expert and non-expert report users (for example, Chetkovich, 1955; Hicks, 1966; and Rappaport, 1963). And normative accounting theorists prescribed accounting solutions on the basis of argued but unevidenced user needs and decision models (for example, Chambers, 1966; Edwards and Bell, 1961; and Sterling, 1970).

The position with respect to accounting practice was little different in principle. Professional accounting bodies, apparently as a result of continuous criticism of the state of financial reporting practice, commissioned researchers to provide conceptual frameworks. However, these studies incorporated the prevalent tendency to prescribe postulated user groups, needs and situations (for example, AICPA, 1973; and ASSC, 1975). A similar approach was to be found in a government-sponsored study of financial reporting (Sandilands, 1975).

But all was not moving in the same direction. Some researchers were adopting an alternative approach to financial reporting developments—indicated instead that reporting prescriptions were of limited benefit unless they were more factually based. In other words, there was an increasing feeling that it was no longer acceptable to merely hypothesise the state of financial reporting needs, usage and understanding. Instead, work was needed to establish on a more functional basis than hitherto the shape of the reporter user community—particularly the nature and problems facing its definable individual groupings. A concern therefore grew to explore the world of the financial report user in terms of observed rather than assumed information needs, uses and issues.

The research that has been undertaken since the mid 1970s can be categorised into two main types. The first concerns the establishment of financial report users' information needs and preferences. It is largely survey-based, and opinion-orientated. But, nonetheless, it has considerable potential utility for accounting policy-makers and standard-setters (see, for example, Baker and Haslem, 1973; Benjamin and Stanga, 1977; and Chenhall and Juchau, 1977).

The second category of user study relates more to survey fact-finding about actual use and understanding of financial information (as distinct from user preferences for it). The most substantial and original work in this area appears to be that of David Tweedie and I, and the major findings from it (Lee and Tweedie, 1977 and 1981) are reproduced in this volume (but see also Lee and Tweedie, 1975a, 1975b and 1976 for the complete package of publications). Studies which have either extended, replicated or complemented the Lee and Tweedie work include those of Anderson (1981), Arnold and Moizer (1984), Day (1986), and Klaassen and Schreuder (1981).

My main purposed in this introduction to the Garland reproduction of the 1977 and 1981 ICAEW-sponsored reports by Lee and Tweedie is to put the findings of these studies into a contemporary context and, in so doing, to provide some further unreported data from them. In particular, my general message is that the findings contained in this volume are just as relevant in 1989 as they were in 1977 and 1981. And that, in itself, is a biting comment on the lack of improvement in financial reporting practices during the 1980s.

THE LEE AND TWEEDIE FINDINGS

It is not my intention to report the detail of the findings that are contained in the studies reproduced in this volume. Hopefully, the interested reader will explore these in context and depth for purposes of debate and, most importantly, for further research into the issues concerned. Instead, my main concern at this stage is to identify the main features of the studies that appear to me to highlight continuing major problems in financial reporting today.

The original pilot studies of private and institutional shareholders (Lee and Tweedie, 1975a, 1975b and 1976) were extensive and significant in their own right, although the intention with them was to provide a suitable basis for more detailed studies. They concluded that only those report users with accounting and/or financial expertise tended to thoroughly use annual financial reports (and other relevant information sources); and that only those individuals appeared to have sufficient understanding of the fundamentals of reporting practice to make meaningful use of financial information. The so-called less sophisticated report users were found to make little use of any major financial information source, and to have a poor understanding of reporting fundamentals.

The general conclusions of these early studies were replicated in greater detail in a further major study of private shareholders (Lee and Tweedie, 1977). This forms the first part of this volume, and its results confirm the existence of a very small group of private shareholders with the background and expertise to use and understand such major information sources as annual financial reports.

The final stage of the Lee and Tweedie research (Lee and Tweedie, 1981) focused attention on the use and understanding of financial information by institutional investors and stockbrokers—the so-called sophisticated and expert users of financial reports. These findings revealed extensive use being made by these experts of all sources of financial information, and a reasonable understanding by them of most reporting fundamentals surveyed.

It is impossible for me to do justice to the detail of these research results in the space available, but the following main points appear to be pertinent. First, the institutional expert appeared to make, and be able to make, far more thorough use of available financial information than did, or could, his private investor counterpart. The level of understanding of reporting fundamentals was of crucial importance in this respect—understanding apparently being a potential constraint or barrier to thorough and effective use of financial information.

Second, those individuals with the best understanding of reporting fundamentals appeared to make the most use of available financial information. Indeed, the overall conclusion was that, in the context of financial reporting, an exclusive world had been created in which accounting appeared to take place for accountants; and where only accountants could meaningfully use and understand reported financial information.

These seem to me to be the most significant findings of the studies. Far from the financial reporting function achieving its societal aim of accountability by management to owners and other interested parties, the reality appeared to be the existence of a closed reporting system—entry to which was dependent on a specific and detailed education and training. This does not appear to me to be a matter that can be justified. If these results are valid, financial reporting does not seem to be serving either the sectionalised interest of ownership (as required by legislation such as the UK Company Acts) or the broader public interest that has evolved in the 1970s and 1980s within an increasingly consumer-oriented world.

FURTHER FINDINGS

By the time the 1981 ICAEW study was published, David Tweedie and I were developing separate interests and specialisms (David particularly in the context of a new career in public accounting practice). One of the consequences of this separation has been our mutual frustration at not being able to pursue the research further. We both feel that the problems we identified in the 1970s persist to this day and require reemphasising. For this purpose, and with David's permission, there are certain data from the 1979 and 1981 ICAEW studies that have not been published previously, and that I believe reinforce the comments I have made in the previous section. They relate particularly to the differences in findings between the two groups of private shareholders and institutional investors. The following tables and explanations describe these differences.

Understanding differences

In both the 1977 and 1981 studies, respondents were questioned in a variety of areas concerning financial reporting fundamentals. In each case an index of understanding was constructed from a scoring of respondent's answers to specific questions. The indices ranged from much above average to much below average understanding, and were based in each case on the average score for the group as a whole. It is therefore possible to compare these indices, reconstructing that for institutional investors to eliminate from the relevant scores any points on a specific area not covered in the private shareholder study. The comparison is given in two forms in Tables 1 and 2 below. For purposes of these and later tables, PS is defined as private shareholders and II as institutional investors.

TABLE 1
Private Shareholders and Institutional Investor
Understanding Using Institutional Investor Scoring

UNDERSTANDING	PS	II
	%	%
Much below average	5	10
Above Average	1	11
Average	18	52
Below Average	12	15
Much below Average	64	12
	100	100
	===	===
Chi square value		136.55
Significance		0.000
Contingency co-efficient		0.452

Table 1 applies institutional scoring on understanding to the private shareholder responses—the strictest comparison of the results possible. It can be seen that only 24% of the private shareholders achieved an average institutional understanding of the reporting fundamentals concerned (mean score 22.43 out of 34), compared with 73% of the institutional investors. (In this case, the average category was split at 21 points—62% of the maximum score possible.) Indeed, only

6% of private shareholders compared with 21% of institutional investors, achieved 75% or more of the maximum score of 34. With results significant at a level of less than 0.001 using the chi square test (and the contingency co-efficient indicating a sizeable positive relationship between the data sets), they tend to support a general hypothesis that the institutional investors had a significantly higher understanding of the reporting fundamentals tested than did the private shareholder respondents. Table 2 provides an alternative and more detailed analysis of these findings, applying the less stringent private shareholders' scoring to the responses of the institutional investors, and separating the private shareholder responses between those with significant accounting experience and those with little or no such experience.

TABLE 2
Private Shareholder and Institutional Investor
Understanding Using Private Shareholder Scoring

UNDERSTANDING	PS			II
	Significant Accounting Experience	Little or No Accounting Experience	Total	
	%	%	%	%
Much above average	43	6	11	46
Above average	24	12	13	27
Average	33	53	50	23
Below Average	—	18	16	2
Much below average	—	11	10	2
	100	100	100	100
	===	===	===	===
Number of respondents	42*	250*	301	231
Chi square value		172.73		
Significance		0.000		
Contingency co-efficient		0.498		

*9 respondents gave no data on accounting experience and have been omitted from the analysis.

Cutting the range of scores at 24 (71% of the maximum of 34), the data in Table 2 reveal that only 6% of private shareholders with little or no accounting experience achieved a much above average understanding, compared with 43% of private shareholders with significant accounting experience and 46% of institutional investors responding. Indeed, 82% of private shareholders with little or no accounting experience had average or below average understanding, compared with 33% of private shareholders with significant accounting experience (none in the below average categories) and 27% of institutional investors (4% in the below average categories). With results using the chi square test significant at less than 0.001, and the contingency co-efficient describing a material positive relationship, the afore-mentioned general hypothesis is further supported.

Thus, within the private shareholder grouping surveyed, there was an identifiable minority with significant accounting experience that scored as well as the vast majority of the institutional investor grouping surveyed. Conversely, there was a much smaller minority of the institutional investor grouping that scored as badly as the poorest of the private shareholders. These results lead to a perhaps not unsurprising conclusion and recommendation. That is, the conventional classification of private shareholders as 'unsophisticated' in financial information terms, and institutional investors as 'sophisticated,' is too crude a distinction.

Both groups, on the basis of the evidence of these studies, contain sophisticated and unsophisticated members. In addition, I would argue that such classifications by accounting policymakers and researchers should take into account a range of ability in terms of using and understanding reported financial information.

Use differences

The above remarks are also supported by a relevant analysis of investor differences regarding use of reported financial information. Table 3 contains the broad analysis, and Table 4 provides a more detailed splitting of the private shareholder group between those respondents with significant accounting experience and those without such a background.

TABLE 3

Overall Analysis of Annual Report Readership

READERSHIP	PS	II
	%	%
Very thorough	5	26
Thorough	19	60
Less thorough	76	14
	100	100
	===	===
Number of respondents	301	229*
Chi-square value	202.64	
Significance	0.000	
Contingency co-efficient	0.526	

*2 chartists were omitted from the analysis.

The above results indicate the extent to which those institutional investors surveyed, with a better understanding of reporting fundamentals, read the annual report more thoroughly than did their private shareholder counterparts (24% of the latter compared with 86% of the former read the annual report at least thoroughly; results significant at less than 0.001 using the chi square test, and with a material contingency co-efficient). These findings can be examined in more detail in Table 4.

TABLE 4

Readership and Accounting Experience

READERSHIP	PS		II
	Significant Accounting Experience	Little or No Accounting Experience	
	%	%	%
Very thorough	10	4	26
Thorough	35	17	60
Less thorough	55	79	14
	100	100	100
	===	===	===
Number of Respondents	42*	250*	229**
Chi-square value	204.46		
Significance	0.000		
Contingency co-efficient	0.531		

*9 respondents gave no data on accounting experience and have been omitted from the analysis.
**2 chartists were omitted from the analysis.

Compared with the remainder of the group, a materially higher proportion of private shareholders with significant accounting experience read the annual report at least thoroughly—although this was considerably smaller than the equivalent proportion of institutional investors (results positively related, and significant at less than 0.001 using the chi square test).

Conclusions

These data confirm the overall findings of the 1977 and 1981 ICAEW studies that the provision of a package of financial information for accountability purposes appears, on the basis of the evidence available, to be usable in a meaningful way if the user concerned has sufficient accounting expertise to cope with the complexities of the reported data. Thus, I would specifically recommend that accounting policy-makers should distinguish between thorough users of financial reports (with reasonable understanding of accounting fundamentals) and other users making lesser use of reports and with less understanding of these fundamentals.

OTHER RESEARCH EVIDENCE

Since the 1977 and 1981 ICAEW studies, other research has been undertaken that bears upon the conclusions and recommendations of the latter. I review this research in no particular order of importance; merely to reflect that the shareholder studies should be read in the context of a broader programme of research that has taken place in the late 1970s and 1980s.

Use studies

First, in relation to either the perceived or actual value of financial information sources, there appears to be a remarkable consistency of results of other researchers with the results of the Lee and Tweedie studies—for example the importance to private shareholders of the annual financial report (Anderson, 1981; Chang and Most, 1977; Chenhall and Juchua, 1977; Klaassen and Schreuder, 1981; Wilton and Tabb, 1978; and Winfield, 1978); the ranking by private shareholders of individual parts of the annual report, particularly the use made of the chairman's report or its equivalent (Anderson, 1981; Klaassen and Schreuder, 1981; Wilton and Tabb, 1978; and Winfield, 1978); and the thorough use of all sources of financial information (including annual financial reports) by institutional users (Arnold and Moizer, 1984; and Day, 1986). Indeed, the strength of the consistency of these results has caused one researcher to question and seek an explanation of their incompatibility with the efficient markets hypothesis—that abnormal investment returns cannot be achieved through use of such late information as contained in the annual financial report (Hines, 1982). Whatever the explanation, however, it is clear that investors of all types appear to regard the annual financial report as an important information source. This makes the question of understanding reported financial information a vital one.

Readability

The last point, has, in my opinion, much to do with the readability of reported financial information. Early studies of the degree of reading difficulty associated with financial reports indicated that the average reader would be inconvenienced by the complexities of these documents (Soper and Dolphin, 1964; Smith and Smith, 1971; and Still, 1972). More recent research indicates that this remains the case, and that there has been little improvement over time—even in simplified financial statements of the type that David Tweedie and I recommended in our 1977 ICAEW study (see Courtis, 1986; and Lewis et al., 1986). I believe that, unless readability is taken on board as a serious issue by accounting policy-makers, it is difficult to envisage a speedy resolution to the understanding and use issues with respect to reported financial information.

Numerology

It would be remiss of me not to mention other research studies that have a considerable bearing on the issues of the use and understanding of reported financial information. They relate to what Sterling (1988b) describes as accounting numerology—the activity of producing accounting for the sake of producing accounting numbers, and without due regard to whether or not these numbers have any meaning in terms of faithful representations of real-world matters.

Sterling (1988a and 1988b) has sought to demonstrate that accountants tend to produce figures with no real-world meaning. Earlier, he identified the cumulative customs and habits of accountants as possible reason for this position (Sterling, 1977). And later, he challenged accounting educators to change this position by teaching accountants to faithfully represent economic reality (Sterling, 1988c). If Sterling is correct in his analysis (and there appears to be no contrary argument or evidence in the relevant literature), I believe it is unsurprising that non-accountants (such as those responding in the 1977 and 1981 ICAEW studies in this volume) demonstrate an inability to understand and use reported accounting numbers. If these numbers have no real-world meaning, it is logical to expect only accountants (as numerologists) to be able to interpret and use them.

The effects of custom and habit in accounting have also been demonstrated in recent times by researchers. First, Tweedie (1977) provides clear indications that the intuitions of non-accountants are to interpret accounting numbers in terms of faithful representations of real-world exchanges and states, and not in terms of meaningless accounting numerology. And, second, Lee (1984) reveals the habituation process of accounting education in which non-accountants abandon their intuitions about accounting numbers and assume, as trained accountants, the customs and habits of accounting numerology. These findings support the views and arguments of Sterling.

DEVELOPMENTS SINCE 1981

In 1981, David Tweedie and I published our final use and understanding study (Lee and Tweedie, 1981). Since then, as the previous sections have attempted to indicate, research has tended to confirm our usage findings, and provide explanations of our understanding findings (that is, in terms of readability and numerology). The position in practice has been little different in terms of financial reporting improvements.

First, financial reporting has become far more complex, and thus made the potential use of financial reports much more burdensome—particularly for the user with little or no accounting experience or knowledge. The minimum disclosure level for reporting has increased significantly due to regulation and legislation. Standardisation has expanded beyond all expectations (Zeff, 1989). The level of creativity, abstraction and manipulation in accounting and reporting has also increased materially (Griffiths, 1986). Specific examples of reporting problems include off-balance sheet financing (Tweedie and Kellas, 1987) and brands accounting (Tweedie, 1989).

In many countries, the lack of a conceptual framework makes life exceedingly difficult for accounting policy-makers and standard-setters to justify particular reporting practices. Criticism of the reporting package is consistent and continuous—such that suggestions have been made from the research committee of one professional body to abandon the current reporting model (McMonnies, 1988). The growing evidence clearly of a recycling and non-resolution of financial reporting issues (Brief, 1975; Lee 1977, 1979 and 1983; Mumford, 1979; and Sterling, 1979).

And the lack of progress to improvements in financial reporting has had repercussions in the world of accounting research—normative accounting research being proscribed in favour of positive accounting research (Watts and Zimmerman, 1979, 1986). And counter-claims and arguments being made in defence (Christenson, 1983; Kinney, 1989; Sterling, 1989; and Whittington, 1987). In addition, accounting education appears to be in a closed loop with practice, and much of the results of research (particularly of a fundamental and pure nature) appears not to have the potential to impact either practice or the classroom (Baxter, 1988; and Lee, 1989a).

I have described this apparently chaotic state in greater detail in a historical analysis of the world of accounting—to be published in the same series as this volume (Lee, 1989b). I believe such a world to be a state of accounting by accountants for accountants, with the closures that have taken place being those of an open social system that has become supra-human or autopoietic—that is, a system that acts in its own interests to remain viable and stable and that, as such, is beyond the direct control of its human participants. However, this does not mean that accounting researchers have no part to play in developing and improving the world of accounting. The results of their research are always available to such a system—to be used by it, as and when necessary, to maintain its long-term survival or evolution into a system of a different order. In this respect, I believe it is important to identify key issues for researchers to work on if this degree of influence is to be achieved.

A KEY ISSUE

A key issue that related to this review, and to the two volumes reproduced with it, appears to me to be concerned with the basic objective in financial reporting of representing economic reality (that is, exchanges, flows and states) in accounting terms. There is a growing awareness of the need to produce and communicate these representations as faithfully as possible. This can be seen in such recent conceptual studies as McMonnies (1988) and Solomons (1988) where the stated intention is to achieve relevant and reliable financial reporting, with reliability interpreted in terms of either faithfully representation, correspondence with economic reality, or substance over form.

The problem with these broad conceptual underpinnings to financial reporting is knowing what is meant by such matters as economic reality and faithful representation. As I have tried to demonstrate elsewhere (Lee, 1989b), accounting as a function has become increasingly abstract, and its representations no longer can be said to be faithful depictions of aspects of economic reality. This is due to the subjectiveness and fictions that are introduced to the calculational procedure; reducing it to what Sterling (1988b) has described as accounting numerology (the production of accounting data that particularly lack the scientific objectivity of observation, measurement and independent verification). In my view, there appears to be little point in accounting policy-makers adopting criteria such as representational faithfulness as a basis for financial reporting if it merely refers to accounting calculations producing bookkeeping fictions but purporting to describe economic reality (see the debate between Solomons, 1988 and 1989; and Lee, 1989c).

This appears to me to be a possible reason why non-accountants have considerable difficulty in using and understanding the reporting products of accountants. If these reports contain representations of an accounting reality created by accountants through the process of numerology (but appear to describe an economic reality), it should not be surprising that report users have such difficulty. These meta-abstractions in the form of accounting data do not and cannot faithfully represent economic reality. There can be no correspondence and no reliability in accounting in such circumstances. If accounting numbers have no economic meaning, users can presumably sense this even if they cannot fully articulate their difficulties. Thus, I would suggest that, in order to improve the use and understanding of financial reports, and the accounting data contained therein, accounting policy-makers and researchers require to delineate what they mean by the economic reality they are reporting, and the means by which they are attempting to faithfully represent it in accounting terms.

In particular, they require to differentiate, and understand the differentiation, between economic and accounting realities. They must understand the lack of economic meaning in the present set of accounting numbers; the potential economic meaning in alternative accounting numbers; and, thereby, the opportunity available to improve levels of use and understanding of financial information. Unless these things happen, I fear that the results that David Tweedie and I report in this volume will represent a permanent feature of the world of accounting. Report users will continue to be excluded from the world of accounting, and financial reports will be capable only of being used and understood by accountants. Such a ritualistic situation may have societal merit (as suggested by Gambling, 1987, in his view of accounting as a form of magic). It certainly does nothing to enhance the image of accounting as being a mature profession capable of producing financial information in accordance with scientific principles as suggested by Sterling (1979).

Professor T.A. Lee
University of Edinburgh

REFERENCES

Accounting Standards Steering Committee, *The Corporate Report*, Accounting Standards Steering Committee, 1975.

American Institute of Certified Public Accountants, *Objectives of Financial Statements*, AICPA, 1973.

R. Anderson, 'The Usefulness of Accounting and Other Information Disclosed in Corporate Annual Reports to Institutional Investors in Australia,' *Accounting and Business Research*, Autumn 1981, pp. 259–65.

J. Arnold and P. Moizer, 'A Survey of the Methods Used by UK Investment Analysts to Appraise Investments in Ordinary Shares,' *Accounting and Business Research*, Summer 1984, pp. 195–208.

H.K. Baker and J.A. Haslem, 'Information Needs of Individual Investors,' *Journal of Accountancy*, November 1963, pp. 64–69.

W.T. Baxter, *Accounting Research—Academic Trends Versus Practical Needs*, Institute of Chartered Accountants of Scotland, 1988.

J.J. Benjamin and K.G. Stanga, 'Differences in Disclosure Needs of Major Users of Financial Statements,' *Accounting and Business Research*, Summer 1977, pp. 181–92.

R.P. Brief, 'The Accountant's Responsibility in Historical Perspective,'*Accounting Review*, April 1975, pp. 285–97.

R.J. Chambers, *Accounting, Evolution and Economic Behaviour*, Prentice-Hall, 1966.

L.S. Chang and K.S. Most, 'Investor Uses of Financial Statements: An Empirical Study,' *Singapore Accountant*, Vol. 12, 1977, pp. 83–91.

R.H. Chenhall and R. Juchau, 'Investor Information Needs—An Australian Study,' *Accounting and Business Research*, Spring 1977, pp. 111–19.

M.N. Chetkovich, 'Standards of Disclosure and Their Development,'*Journal of Accountancy*, December 1955, pp. 48–52.

C. Christenson, 'The Methodology of Positive Accounting,' *Accounting Review*, January 1983, pp. 1–22.

J.K. Courtis, 'An Investigation into Annual Report Readability and Corporate Risk-Return Relationships,' *Accounting and Business Research*, Autumn 1986, pp. 285–94.

J.F.S. Day, 'The Use of Annual Reports by UK Investment Analysts,'*Accounting and Business Research*, Autumn 1986, pp. 295–307.

E.O. Edwards and P.W. Bell, *The Theory and Measurement of Business Income*, University of California Press, 1961.

T. Gambling, 'Accounting for Rituals,' *Accounting, Organizations and Society*, Vol. 12, No. 4, 1987, pp. 319–29.

I. Griffiths, *Creative Accounting*, Sidgwick and Jackson, 1986.

E.L. Hicks, 'Materiality,' *Journal of Accounting Research*, Autumn 1961, pp. 158–71.

R.D. Hines, 'The Usefulness of Annual Reports: the Anomaly Between the Efficient Markets Hypothesis and Shareholders Studies,' *Accounting and Business Research*, Autumn 1982, pp. 296–309.

W.R. Kinney, 'Commentary on the Relation of Accounting Research to Teaching and Practice: A "Positive View",' *Accounting Horizons*, March 1988, pp. 119–24.

J. Klaassen and H. Schreuder, 'Corporate Report Readership and Usage in the Netherlands,' *Maanblad voor accountancy en bedrigfshuishoudkunde*, Vol. 55, No. 2/3, 1981, pp. 101–17.

T.A. Lee, '"The History of Accounting": Three Reviews,' *Accounting and Business Research*, Winter 1977, pp. 58–61.

T.A. Lee, 'The Evolution and Revolution of Financial Accounting: a Review Article,' *Accounting and Business Research*, Autumn 1979, pp. 209–16.

T.A. Lee, 'The Early Debate on Financial and Physical Capital,' *Accounting Historians Journal*, Spring 1983, pp. 25–50.

T.A. Lee, 'Cash Flows and Net Realisable Values: Further Evidence of the Intuitive Concepts,' *Abacus*, December 1984, pp. 125–37.

T.A. Lee, Education, Practice and Research in Accounting: Gaos, Closed Loops, Bridges and Magic Accounting, *Accounting and Business Research*, Autumn 1989, (forthcoming).

T.A. Lee, *The Closure of the Accounting Profession*, Garland Publishing, 1989b.

T.A. Lee, 'What is Reality in Accounting?', *Accountancy*, 1989c, (forthcoming).

T.A. Lee and D.P. Tweedie, 'Accounting Information: An Investigation of Shareholder Usage,' *Accounting and Business Research*, Autumn 1975a, pp. 280–91.

T.A. Lee and D.P. Tweedie, 'Accounting Information: An Investigation of Shareholder Understanding,' *Accounting and Business Research*, Winter 1975b, pp. 3–17.

T.A. Lee and D.P. Tweedie, 'The Private Shareholder: His Sources of Financial Information and His Understanding of Reporting Practices,' *Accounting and Business Research*, Autumn 1976, pp. 304–14.

T.A. Lee and D.P. Tweedie, *The Private Shareholder and the Corporate Report*, Institute of Chartered Accountants in England and Wales, 1977.

T.A. Lee and D.P. Tweedie, *The Institutional Investor and Financial Information*, Institute of Chartered Accountants in England and Wales, 1981.

N.R. Lewis, L.D. Parker, G.D. Pound and P. Sutcliffe, 'Accounting Report Readability: The Use of Readability Techniques,' *Accounting and Business Research*, Summer 1986, pp. 199–213.

P.N. McMonnies, *Making Corporate Reports Valuable*, Kogan Page, 1988.

M. Mumford, 'The End of a Familiar Inflation Accounting Cycle,' *Accounting and Business Research*, Spring 1979, pp. 98–194.

D. Rappaport, 'Materiality,' *Price Waterhouse Review*, Summer 1963, pp. 26–33.

Sandilands Inflation Accounting Committee, *Inflation Accounting*, Cmnd.6225, HMSO, 1975.

J.E. Smith and N.P. Smith, 'Readability: A Measure of the Performance of the Communication Function of Financial Reporting,' *Accounting Review*, July 1971, pp. 552–62.
D. Solomons, *Guidelines for Financial Reporting Standards*, ICAEW, 1988.

D. Solomons, 'The Solomons Guidelines: A Reply to the Critics', *Accountancy*, August 1989, (forthcoming).

F.J. Soper and R. Dolphin, 'Readability and Corporate Annual Reports,' *Accounting Review*, April 1964, pp. 358–62.

R.R. Sterling, *Theory of the Measurement of Enterprise Income*, University of Kansas Press, 1970.

R.R. Sterling, 'Accounting in the 1980's,' in N.M. Bedford, ed., *Accountancy in the 1980's—Some Issues*, Council of Arthur Young Professors, University of Illinois, 1977, pp. 1–44.

R.R. Sterling, *Toward a Science of Accounting*, Scholars Book Co., 1979.

R.R. Sterling, 'Confessions of a Failed Empiricist,' *Advances in Accounting*, Vol. 6, 1988a, pp. 3–35.

R.R. Sterling, 'The Subject-Matters of Accounting,' *unpublished paper*, University of Utah, 1988b.

R.R. Sterling, 'Commonsense and Uncommon Nonsense,' *unpublished paper*, University of Utah, 1988c.

R.R. Sterling, 'Positive Accounting: An Assessment,' *unpublished paper*, University of Utah, 1989.

M.D. Still, 'The Readability of Chairmen's Statements,' *Accounting and Business Research*, Winter 1972, pp. 36–39.

D.P. Tweedie, 'Cash Flows and Realisable Values: The Intuitive Concepts? An Empirical Test,' *Accounting and Business Research*, Winter 1977, pp. 2–13.

D.P. Tweedie, 'Brands, Goodwill and the Balance Sheet,' *Accountancy*, January 1989, pp. 20–22.

D.P. Tweedie and J. Kellas, Off-Balance Sheet Financing,' *Accountancy*, April 1987, pp. 91–95.

R.L. Watts and J.L. Zimmerman, 'The Demand For and Supply of Accounting Theories: The Market for Excuses,' *Accounting Review*, April 1979, pp. 273–305.

R.L. Watts and J.L. Zimmerman, *Positive Accounting Theory*, Prentice-Hall, 1986.

G. Whittington, 'Positive Accounting: A Review Article,' *Accounting and Business Research*, Autumn 1987, pp. 327–36.

R.L. Wilton and J.B. Tabb, 'An Investigation into Private Shareholder Usage of Financial Statements in New Zealand, *Accounting Education*, May 1978, pp. 93–101.

R.R. Winfield, *Shareholder Opinion of Published Financial Statements*, paper presented at the Accounting Association and New Zealand 1978 Conference, University of Otago, New Zealand, pp. 1–12.

S.A. Zeff, 'Recent Trends in Accounting Education and Research in the USA: Some implications for UK Academics,' *British Accounting Review* June 1989, pp. 159–76.

THE PRIVATE SHAREHOLDER
AND
THE CORPORATE REPORT

A report to the Research Committee of
The Institute of Chartered Accountants
in England and Wales

T. A. Lee
(*Professor of Accountancy and Finance,
University of Edinburgh*)

D. P. Tweedie
(*Lecturer in Accountancy,
University of Edinburgh*)

THE INSTITUTE OF CHARTERED ACCOUNTANTS
IN ENGLAND AND WALES
CHARTERED ACCOUNTANTS' HALL, MOORGATE PLACE,
LONDON EC2P 2BJ
1977

This book is set in Times New Roman (327) 10 pt on 12;
Tables and quotations in 9 pt on 10.
Typeset by Chapel River Press, Andover.
Printed and bound by Biddles Ltd., Guildford.

Contents

Preface

Despite popular belief to the contrary, accountancy can hardly be described as dull. Particularly during the last five or six years in the United Kingdom, the practising accountant has been faced with a constant stream of comment, criticism, debate and recommendation with regard to the way in which he conducts his function, especially that of financial reporting. Unfortunately, some of the criticism has been destructive in its nature, but the greater part has been constructive. Never at any time has it been uninteresting. It has caused accountants, and their professional societies, to consider as never before the foundations upon which their practice lies. As a result accountancy may have lost some of its credibility in the short-term, but, without doubt, the radical changes which are gradually taking place will ensure its long-term viability.

It is within this context of change that our monograph has been prepared. It is concerned with one of the most familiar aspects of accountancy – that of company financial reporting. This vital function has been subjected to the greatest amount of criticism in recent years, particularly with regard to its apparent inability to meet the assumed needs of a variety of decision makers involved in the financial affairs of companies. Much of the criticism has been concentrated on the correspondence of financial reports to the needs of the best known of these groups, shareholders, and the general feeling appears to be that financial reports are generally ignored by these persons.

Given the latter point, and also given the recent suggestions in *The Corporate Report* and the Sandilands report on *Inflation Accounting* (both of which explore the needs of shareholders and others), it is vital that evidence can be presented to support the popular view that financial reports are little used by shareholders. In particular, we believe it is important to find out whether or not such persons understand financial reports; what matters they are able to understand (and therefore those they do not understand); whether they use financial reports; whether they make use of sources of information about companies other than financial reports; and the type of shareholders who have most (and least) understanding and who make most (and least) use of financial reports. We further believe that this anatomy of the shareholder-user of financial reports will provide those concerned with improving the quality of reported information with guidelines with which to aid them in meeting the information needs of shareholders.

This monograph contains findings from a research project funded by The Institute of Chartered Accountants in England and Wales (ICAEW) in which we attempted to examine each of the areas mentioned above. It follows our earlier pilot study, and both sets of findings fully confirm the overall impression that financial reports are poorly used and understood. However, we say this with an important caveat – the findings relate solely to the private shareholder. We fully intended at the outset of the ICAEW-sponsored study to examine the financial report behaviour of both private and institutional shareholders. However, our results are such that their strength confirms an impression gained in the pilot study that the private shareholder has unique problems in his use and understanding of financial reports. Consequently, we decided that it was important to highlight these separately from those of the institutional shareholder, in order to prevent any misunderstandings occurring as to the information needs of each group.

We fully intend to present evidence of the institutional aspect of this general problem, and are presently in the process of conducting the necessary investigation. Meanwhile, we present our private shareholder findings which are related to the reporting problems of more than 90% of the total shareholder population in the United Kingdom. We have not attempted to generalise on our findings but we are confident they are strong enough, when combined with those of the pilot study, to warrant serious attention. Taking both studies together, nearly 700 private shareholders have been surveyed and we believe this to be sufficient to be used in the solution of a major problem already under consideration following *The Corporate Report* and other similar recent publications – that is, the need to report relevant financial information to private shareholders in such a form that it can be both used and understood by them. The present system, as our evidence shows, is at fault in this respect, and something must be done to improve the situation. If it is not then the needs of many thousands of individual investors will be ignored. It is wrong in our opinion to concentrate, as so many writers do, on the so-called sophisticated investor and assume that if he is catered for that is all that really matters. We would point out that to the individual private shareholder an investment of £500 may be as important to him as an investment of £500,000 is to an institutional investor. Both deserve appropriate information to monitor and decide upon their investments, and we hope this study provides sufficient data to justify greater attention than before to the needs of the individual private shareholder.

T. A. Lee

D. P. Tweedie

Acknowledgements

There are many individuals and bodies we wish to thank in connection with this study. Without their help we would not be in the present position of presenting this monograph.

First, to the Research Committee of The Institute of Chartered Accountants in England and Wales for supporting the study in such a generous and helpful way.

Secondly, to the chairman and board of directors of the survey company for giving us access to its share register. Access to shareholders could not have been achieved without this cooperation.

Thirdly, to all shareholders who gave us so much of their time as well as their statements on financial reporting.

Fourthly, to Jim Eckford, Simon Jenking, Robin Leith, Keith Millward, Janet Roberts, Stephen Samuels, Brian Shepherd and Gary Steel who conducted the interviews of shareholders. The research would have taken considerably longer without their efforts on our behalf.

Fifthly, to Debbie Hathorn and Chris Nash for not only producing the final manuscript but also helping on much of the secretarial work involved in the project.

And, finally, to our wives for their forbearance in allowing us to complete this study in the time we set ourselves to do it.

There may be errors of omission or commission in the pages which follow. None of the above can be blamed for this.

T. A. Lee and D. P. Tweedie

July 1977

Abstract of Results
and Main Conclusions

Introduction

In 1973, private shareholders were the largest single group of investors, holding 42% of the quoted ordinary shares issued by U.K. companies. (*Source: Royal Commission on the Distribution of Income and Wealth.*) As such they pose a challenge to those reporting financial information. Can these shareholders cope with the increasing complexity of modern financial statements, or have the technicalities of current accounting practice resulted in these shareholders becoming ever more confused by the accountant's reports?

The research study described in this monograph was initiated to consider this question and provides useful evidence of an apparent failure of communication between the reporting accountant and the private shareholder. Given the complexity and length of the study, however, we feel it is important that the reader initially is given a summarised abstract of its content and the main conclusions to be drawn from it.

The Background to the Study

A major objective of corporate financial reports is to convey information about a company's profit or loss and state of affairs to those interested in its economic progress and performance. For communication between the company and those interested in its financial welfare to be effective, however, the report must be both understandable to and read by its recipients. Unfortunately, little is known of the extent to which such reports are used and understood, except in terms of investigations of aggregate share price movements following the release of published data. Given the increasing complexity and detail of reported information, it appeared to us important to investigate in depth the related problems of report use and understanding.

The research programme had three main aims. First, it sought to discover whether or not financial reports were understood by private shareholders; secondly, it attempted to assess whether or not these shareholders read such reports; and finally, it considered the question of whether any particular types of shareholder were, in relation to others, less able to understand or less interested in reading the reports.

A pilot survey completed prior to the commencement of this study (and reported in *Chapter 1*), had given some insights into the possible outcome of part of the investigation. For example, it was found that, although 68% of the respondents examined in the pilot study claimed that they understood reported information, simple test questions revealed that few of them, in fact, did understand such data. It was also discovered that, on the whole, respondents did not make extensive use of the major financial statements. Indeed, the chairman's report was the most widely and frequently used section of the annual financial report.

Research Method

Armed with the findings from the pilot study, we initiated the main study to which this monograph relates. By means of interviewing 301 private share-holders in a very large public company, we were able to examine the problems of use and understanding in detail. As *Chapter 2* reveals, the respondents were taken from various locations in the U.K. The majority were male, had relatively small shareholdings in the survey company, and had less than 20 items in their portfolios. Few respondents were in accounting or related occupations (only 14% having a significant experience of accounting matters), although 69% made their own investment decisions without help or advice from experts. A follow-up survey of non-respondents revealed they had very similar backgrounds and characteristics to those of the respondents.

Understanding of Reported Information

The first objective of the study was, as explained above, to assess the level of the private shareholder's understanding of the corporate report. While once again a high proportion of the respondents (74%) believed that they understood reported information (see *Chapter 3*), tests on five specific areas of reporting practice revealed that the confidence of many of these respondents in their ability to comprehend financial reports was misplaced. Questions on the general nature of financial reporting (its objectives, legal responsibility and the general nature of reported data); the nature and contents of the main financial and related statements in the annual report; accounting terminology; accounting valuations and the meaning of financial ratios revealed that in many areas the respondents were largely ignorant of the methods and terminology used by accountants in reporting to them (see *Chapter 4*).

Discovering the overall understanding of the respondents as a group, while illustrating the communication problems in financial reporting would not, however, assist with the accomplishment of the third objective; namely, to discover the level of understanding of the individual shareholder. What was needed, therefore, was a measure of the overall understanding of the individual respondent. This was accomplished (see *Chapter 5*) by constructing an index of understanding for each shareholder by means of a points score attributed to the answers given to the questions in four of the five areas of reporting practice. (The questions on the general nature of financial reporting were not considered to be critical to the appreciation and use of information contained in financial reports and were, therefore, omitted from the index.)

Use of Reported Information

Before turning to look at the individual shareholder, however, it was considered more appropriate to complete the overall picture by considering the use made of financial information by the respondents as a whole. *Chapter 6* shows that the chairman's report was again the most widely read section of the corporate financial report, with 52% of the respondents reading it thoroughly. 39% paid the same degree of attention to the profit and loss account but the other sections of the report (including the auditor's report) typically were poorly used; most being read only briefly for interest.

Having established in detail the particular parts of the annual report which respondents in total tended to use or ignore, it was now possible to discover the reading pattern of the individual shareholder. It was found, for example, that only 5% of the respondents read every section of the report thoroughly, while a similar percentage did not read any section. On the basis of their reading pattern of the annual report, the shareholders were divided into two readership groups – thorough readers and less interested readers. The criteria for the division of the shareholders into these categories is explained in *Chapter 6*, but basically to be a thorough reader the shareholder should have read the profit and loss account and balance sheet thoroughly and, *on average*, have read all other sections of the report at least briefly.

Shareholders, of course, may not simply rely on the company's annual financial report for information, they may use other sources. In *Chapter 7* the use of other forms of financial information was examined. Financial press reports, which were read thoroughly by 54% of the respondents, were the most extensively used. It was suspected that shareholders who did not read the company's annual report thoroughly might, instead, use the alternative sources. This was not found to be the case. Those who read the annual report thoroughly also used the other sources tested in the survey more extensively than the less interested reader of the annual report. This could have been due to one of two reasons.

First, the less interested shareholder may not have read all sources of financial information because he could not understand them or, secondly, the shareholder may simply not be interested in financial information.

The objective of examining the individual shareholder's use and understanding of the annual report, however, gave some indication of which of these explanations seemed the more likely to be correct.

The Individual Shareholder's Use and Understanding of the Annual Report

The measures of individual shareholder understanding of reporting practice and intensity of reading of the annual report provided two important elements in the search for insights into the problems of financial reporting. It was now possible to assess whether those who read the annual report thoroughly were also those who understood reporting practices; that is, were understanding and use of accounting statements related? The evidence presented in *Chapter 8* indicates that this was indeed the case. Thorough readers of the annual report tended to be those with a higher level of understanding of reporting practices than others. So it appears possible that to read accounting statements thoroughly the shareholder has to have a good knowledge of accounting. But, perhaps, knowledge of accounting was more widely distributed amongst the responding shareholder groups. Further analysis, however, revealed that this was not the case. Those respondents who had relatively high levels of understanding were generally those in accountancy-related occupations or those who had a significant degree of accounting experience. The degree of accounting experience was, therefore, almost inevitably related to the annual report reading pattern of the shareholders. Those with significant experience of the subject were far more likely to read the annual report intensively than those who had no such experience.

As far as interest and depth of reading of the annual report was concerned, those respondents who made their own investment decisions were, indeed, more likely to read the report more thoroughly than those who made their investment decisions with help from an expert. The proportion of the former reading the annual report thoroughly, however, was well below that of the shareholders with significant accounting experience. Interest, it appeared, was not enough. The major influence on the reading of the annual report seemed to be knowledge of accounting – that is, the impression was given that shareholders had to be trained in accounting if they were to be able to read accounting reports.

The problems facing accountants when communicating financial data to laymen were amply illustrated in *Chapter 9* which examined in detail the understanding of each particular group of shareholders. The analysis highlighted the inability of the non-accountant to understand accounting terminology, valuation methods and financial ratios. It pinpointed the need for a new approach to financial reporting as far as the layman was concerned.

The shareholders themselves were quite willing to suggest solutions to the problem (see *Chapter 10*). 53% of respondents advocated simpler and less technical financial reports. In general, most support for the simplified reports came from those who had a poor understanding of reporting practices and from those who were defined as less interested readers of the present annual report. In other words, the majority of respondents who, apparently, were unable to use or understand the existing form of financial report appeared to be looking for less complex statements to provide them with relevant information.

Overall Conclusions

The overall conclusion from this study is that available financial information about companies is generally little used or understood by private shareholders. This is probably an expected conclusion but *it does mean that reporting accountants are failing to communicate adequately with a very large number of individuals, and that existing financial reports have become documents which are prepared by accountants for accountants*. In order to cope with this serious problem, it is suggested (in *Chapter 11*) that attention be paid by the accountancy profession to the ideas of simplifying existing statements, defining accounting terms used in financial reports, providing explanations of and comments on financial results as reported, and seeking alternative systems of reporting which may prove more meaningful to the 'unsophisticated' user of financial reports.

CHAPTER 1

Introduction

'The purpose of accounting is to communicate economic messages on the results of
business decisions and events, insofar as they can be expressed in terms of quanti-
fiable financial data, in such a way as to achieve maximum understanding by the
user and correspondence of the message with economic reality'.[1]

This particular interpretation of the general scope and aims of accounting
can be applied relatively easily to the corporate financial reporting function,
and emphasises the need to ensure that potential users of financial data not
only use but also understand it. In other words, financial reporting is nothing
if it is not an exercise in communication.

This particular overview of reporting does not appear always to have been
appreciated in the past by accountants and legislators. The traditional means
of seeking improvements in financial reports have usually involved either
changes in the measurement process or increased disclosure and explanation
of financial data. Little or no attention appears to have been given to the
needs and problems of the financial report user; at least until very recently.

The Financial Report User

The structure of companies, particularly with regard to the inevitable separation of ownership from management in the larger entities, underlies the
relatively obvious need for regular reporting by boards of directors to their
shareholders. This has been recognised with reasonable consistency in the
UK ever since the first major enactment regulating company behaviour – the
Joint Stock Companies Act 1844. Thus, over the last 130 years, successive
Companies Acts, supported more recently by Stock Exchange regulations and
professional accountancy recommendations and requirements, have resulted
in the present system of financial reporting to shareholders. This includes,
where relevant, annual reports containing both qualitative and quantitative

1

data of a predominantly historic nature; relatively similar interim reports, usually in summary form and mainly quantitative in content; and occasional financial reports relating to such matters as acquisitions and mergers with other companies (as well as new issues of share and loan capital) and containing summaries of largely historic data in addition to certain predictive data. The dominant language used is that of accounting and finance and, consequently, all such reports are relatively complex and technical in nature.

The quantity and quality of the reported data have improved considerably over a long period of time, with the Companies Act 1948 proving to be an important milestone in the development of the annual report, and the Statement of Intent of the Institute of Chartered Accountants in England and Wales in 1969 providing a more recent one. The initial report of the Scope and Aims Working Party of the Accounting Standards Steering Committee[2] in 1975 will no doubt prove to be yet another, as will the report of the Sandilands Committee on Inflation Accounting.[3] However, despite these undoubted improvements in UK financial reporting, the role of the report user has been relatively ignored, or assumed without further investigation.

In the U.K., company legislation defines the primary report user as the shareholder, without distinguishing between different types; all shareholders, irrespective of size of holding, occupation, or accounting and financial experience, are legally entitled to receive the same information. Debenture-holders are also recognised to be legally entitled to receive annual reports. (Recent publications of professional accountancy bodies have, however, recognised other important report user groups.[4] Nevertheless, it appears reasonable to suggest that shareholders are a primary group, and this text concentrates on their needs.)

Despite the legal and professional recognition of shareholders as major recipients of financial reports, there is little evidence that either legislators or accountants have attempted to examine whether or not shareholders use such information and, if they do, whether or not they understand it. The only evidence which does exist is the relatively superficial comments by accountants who suggest that, typically, there are three types of shareholder report users – those with little or no knowledge of accounting; those who are fairly knowledgeable about accounting matters; and those who can be regarded as professionals in this area.[5] This type of separation has led to a not infrequent suggestion that company financial reports should be directed at the knowledgeable professional user rather than the inexperienced individual. For example, Mautz and Sharaf have suggested that financial reporting standards should be determined in relation to the professional analyst rather than investors at large.[6] Similarly, Rappaport has advocated the establishment of materiality principles in relation to the financial analyst rather than the average prudent investor.[7] The following statement by Leach appears to underlie this approach:

'In recent years there have been enormous changes in public interest in and understanding of financial statements. The informed user of accounts today is no longer solely the individual shareholder but equally the trained professional acting for institutional investors and the financial news media'.[8]

Thus, there appears to be a tendency to regard financial reports as being primarily for the consumption of the suitably qualified user; that is, one with qualifications and experience to use and fully understand reported financial data. This is a somewhat awkward situation to be in – the law demanding that all shareholders receive the same information, thereby assuming that all shareholders are equally equipped to use and understand it. Yet, at the same time, it is freely acknowledged that reported data are highly complex and technical, and may only be of use to the professional analyst. This dilemma has been usefully summed up as follows:

'Understandability does not necessarily mean simplicity, or that information must be presented in elementary terms, for that may not be consistent with the proper description of complex economic activities. It does mean that judgment needs to be applied in holding the balance between the need to ensure that all material matters are disclosed and the need to avoid confusing users by the provision of too much detail. Understandability calls for the provision, in the clearest form, of all the information which the reasonably instructed reader can make use of and the parallel presentation of the main features for the use of the less sophisticated'.

'The information presented should be complete in that it provides users, as far as possible, with a rounded picture of the economic activities of the reporting entity. Since this is likely to be complex it follows that corporate reports as we define them are likely to be complex rather than simple documents'.[9]

If financial reports are useful only to the sophisticated investor then this poses several important questions. Investment by shareholders in companies involves a great many individual shareholders, therefore what should be done for those who cannot possibly have the qualifications and/or experience to make proper use of financial reports? Are they to become merely passive investors, not relying on formal information in their investment decision making, and simply following share price trends established by the relatively few institutional investors who can employ the expertise necessary to maintain large portfolios? Or are they to become more active but not very knowledgeable investors relying on the interpretive and analytical skills of experts such as stockbrokers? Or can something be done to recognise the data deprivation caused by their inability to use and understand the present types of financial report?

There is a definite trend of decreasing private investment in companies over recent years – Moyle reveals that personal holdings (expressed as a percentage of total share capital) in the equity capital of 290 UK companies fell from 65.8% in 1957 to 47.4% in 1969,[10] and the Royal Commission on the Distribution of Income and Wealth reports that personal holdings had fallen further to 42% by 1973. This can be seen more fully in Table 1 below.

TABLE 1

The Pattern of Ownership of Quoted Ordinary Shares in UK Companies

CATEGORY OF OWNERSHIP	*Percentage of Total Ordinary Shares in Issue*
	%
Persons, executors and trustees resident in UK	42
Charities and other non-profit making bodies	5
Insurance companies	
— long term funds	14
— general funds	2
Pension funds	12
Investment trust companies	7
Unit trusts	3
Banks and other financial institutions	3
Non-financial companies	4
Public sector	3
Overseas	5
	100

Source: The Royal Commission on the Distribution of Income and Wealth; figures taken as at 31 December 1973

Nevertheless, institutional investment can involve a relatively small number of very large holdings, causing private investment to consist of a relatively large number of small holdings. For example, an examination of the 1974/1975 annual reports of the top 100 manufacturing companies[11] reveals that; of the 15 companies disclosing relevant data, private shareholders in 4 of them held between 81% and 90% of total shareholdings, and in the remaining 11 companies, the comparable figures were between 91% and 100%. Yet, in each of the 15 companies, institutional investors held more than 50% of the share capital. Thus, even from this limited evidence, it appears that a great many private shareholders are receiving financial reports, and it consequently appears rather doubtful to concentrate attention on producing reports for a relatively few institutional investors who happen to hold, in aggregate, majority holdings in the larger companies. In this situation, it appears reasonable to suggest that the needs of large organisations must not be allowed completely to dominate the equally important needs of the individual. For this reason, this study is concerned with the role of financial reporting as it affects the private shareholder. A further study is now being undertaken to investigate the comparable situation of the institutional shareholder.

Evidence of Shareholder Behaviour

Little is known of individual shareholder behaviour *vis-à-vis* available financial information – that is, what sort of information he uses in his investment activities (if he uses any at all); the use to which it is put; and the degree to which it is understood. This contrasts sharply with the amount of research time which has been devoted to studying the effects of information on aggregate shareholder behaviour and, particularly, the relationship between the movement of share prices and the release of reported information.[12] In general, these studies have found evidence to suggest that investors do make use of accounting data and this can be detected in share price movements. However, this use is limited, as evidenced by Ball and Brown:

'Of all the information about an individual firm which becomes available during a year, one half or more is captured in that year's income number. Its content is therefore considerable. However, the annual income report does not rate highly as a timely medium since most of its content (about 85 to 90%) is captured by more prompt media which perhaps include interim reports. Since the efficiency of the capital market is largely determined by the adequacy of its data sources, we do not find it disconcerting that the market has turned to other sources which can be acted upon more promptly than annual net income'.[13]

Benston, in a similar study, could also state:

'Thus, as measured in this study, the information contained in published accounting reports is a relatively small portion of the information used by investors'.[14]

Other studies have revealed that, at least in the United States, shareholders do make some use of reported information – for example, Brown and Kennelly,[15] Kiger[16] and May[17] each suggesting that interim financial reports do appear to have some influence on share prices. However, these are American studies and relate to the aggregate use and influence of reported data on shareholder behaviour. So far as can be reasonably determined no

5

research has been undertaken previously into the use of financial reports by individual private and institutional investors in the UK – that is, what, how, why and when they use available information. Neglect of this type of research is surprising as it is a major means of determining the adequacy or inadequacy of the existing information sources *vis-à-vis* investor needs, and of finding out what investors really need by way of relevant data in order to make rational investment decisions.

It is surprising also because of the changes which have taken place in financial reporting in recent years without apparent examination of shareholder needs. In other words, changes have been effected with implied assumptions that they are useful and relevant to investors of all kinds. For example, in the period since 1967, the following events have taken place in corporate annual financial reporting:

(1) The Companies Act 1967 increased the disclosure of mainly quantitative historic data in the annual financial statements and directors' report.[18]

(2) Since 1971 there has been a steady flow of *Statements of Standard Accounting Practice* from the main professional accountancy bodies, aimed at minimising the inherent flexibility in accounting practice and disclosing, for the benefit of report users, the practices actually adopted when producing annual financial statements.[19]

(3) Additional financial statements have been recommended for inclusion in the annual reports of mainly quoted companies: first, inflation-adjusted historic cost financial statements designed to reflect the effect of changes in the purchasing power of money on the financial results of companies;[20] and, secondly, sources and application of funds statements which give the user an overview of the financial management of corporate resources.[21]

Further, the Accounting Standards Steering Committee has recently advocated the publication of certain additional financial statements as supplements to the existing statements.[22] These include statements of value added, employment, money exchanges with government, transactions in foreign currency, future prospects, and corporate objectives. These are recommended on the basis of a variety of information needs which are postulated in the report concerned.

Even more recently, the Sandilands Committee on Inflation Accounting has advocated the abandonment of historic cost and current purchasing power accounting and, instead, has recommended the use of a form of current replacement cost accounting; this being argued on the basis of the need for realistic measurement procedures to reflect the effects of inflation, rather than on the basis of specified user needs.[23]

It is this advocacy of improvements and changes in financial reporting, by reference to procedures rather than user needs, and more by supposition than by empirical testing, which raises doubts as to the value and relevance of the resultant data. No matter how sound the proposals and recommendations may appear to be in relation to presumed information needs, and no matter how well the material is measured and presented, it will be useless if it is not used. Equally, it is extremely dangerous if it is used by persons who do not fully appreciate the meaning of its message. Therefore, it appears to be timely to conduct research into shareholder use and understanding of existing information in order to establish whether or not it is satisfactory and, if not, what might replace it. The remainder of this text is thus concerned with reporting on this research – firstly, at the pilot stage and, secondly, at a more detailed state (the latter work being financed by The Institute of Chartered Accountants in England and Wales – ICAEW).

The Research Strategy

This is a study of shareholder use and understanding of financial information. It is recognised that there are other important user groups, such as lenders, creditors and employees, but it was felt that shareholders constitute the primary user group given their involvement in and inevitable separation from company activity. Of the two main shareholder groups (private and institutional shareholders) the former appear to be less likely to use and understand financial information. Institutional investors usually employ suitably qualified experts to obtain, analyse and interpret available data, whereas private individuals can be presumed usually to lack the necessary skills and experience to make best use of financial reports. In addition, it was also felt that little is known of private shareholder behaviour and, given that they appear to be an increasingly neglected group vis-à-vis financial reporting, it appeared to be logical to examine their behaviour before proceeding to the presumably more sophisticated institutional group.

The matters to which the research was directed were four in number – that is, the parts of the annual financial report which private shareholders read, coupled with the thoroughness of such reading; the other sources of financial information which private shareholders read, and, again, the thoroughness of such reading; whether or not private shareholders *believe* they understand

7

reported accounting information, and find it relevant to their investment decisions; and whether or not private shareholders do, *in reality*, understand such information.

The research was conducted in two stages – a pilot survey and a more detailed survey.

In the case of the pilot study, the data were collected by means of a postal questionnaire; in the case of the main study, an interview questionnaire was used.

The Pilot Study

Before proceeding to undertake the ICAEW research project using the interview technique, it was believed to be necessary to conduct a pilot study in which the questionnaire could be tested and research hypotheses formulated. This was done by obtaining access to the share register of a medium-sized engineering company, Matthew Hall and Co. Ltd., and sending a postal questionnaire to each named private shareholder in the register. There were 1974 shareholdings listed and, after elimination of nominee and institutional holdings, 1594 shareholders were circularised. 374 completed questionnaires were returned; a 23.5% response rate. The data were coded and computed and three main papers produced – two of which gave a straightforward univariate analysis of shareholder use[24] and understanding[25] of financial information, with the third[26] giving a multivariate analysis necessary to test six specific hypotheses concerning use and understanding. The results were successful in the sense that they were significant enough to warrant initial conclusions and the need for further research. They were usually statistically significant when chi square tests were applied, and they confirmed the reasonableness of the research approach, the questions posed, and the hypotheses tested. It is not proposed to comment in detail on the results obtained in the pilot study (this can be done by referring to the papers cited above) but the following appear to be the major findings which are relevant to the more detailed research work which will be described in later sections of this text. These findings are confined to the shareholder group which responded to the questionnaire; they should not be interpreted in a wider context until confirmed or rejected by more extensive results. Nevertheless, they provide interesting insights into shareholder behaviour in this area of corporate and investment activity:

(1)   First, in relation to shareholder use of financial information:[27]
       'Many of the respondents appear to skim through the annual report – the

8

chairman's report being the most widely read section. Those shareholders with some form of training in accounting read the report more carefully than those without any such experience and paid particular attention to the profit and loss account. Those with no knowledge of accounting were more inter-ested in the chairman's report than any other section, and this was confirmed when these respondents rated the chairman's statement the most useful part of the annual financial report for investment decision making purposes. Those with accounting or financial experience rated the profit and loss account and balance sheet as the most useful sections.

Financial press reports were considered to be the most important of the sources of information other than the annual financial report. Shareholders even rated the financial press as being slightly more useful than the published profit and loss account. Six monthly interim accounts were only considered to be of moderate to slight importance – one third of the respondents considered these reports to be of no use to them for investment decisions, although those with accounting experience rated them more highly than those without accounting experience.

The economic prospects of a company were considered to be the most important item of information contained in both the annual report and the other sources of information'.

(2)   Secondly, in relation to shareholder understanding of financial information:[28]

'While over two thirds (68%) of respondents stated that they understood accounting information, tests on various aspects of the reporting process revealed that actual knowledge was well below the respondents' perception of their comprehension. Indeed, under half of the shareholders knew (i) the usual method of valuing plant and machinery in the financial statements (47.9%); (ii) where responsibility for the financial statements lay (41.2%); and (iii) the approximate nature of accounting income and values (40.2%). In only one of the four tests of comprehension of the reporting process (that concerning the present objectives of annual financial statements) did a majority (59.3%) of the respondents show that they understood present practice . . . What is possibly even more startling is the finding that, in each of the four tests of understanding, almost half of the respondents who stated that they understood accounting information and found it relevant for investment decision making, gave an answer revealing their ignorance of reporting practices . . .

In all four of the tests of comprehension, those respondents with some experience of accounting matters revealed a greater knowledge of reporting practice than did those with no such experience . . . Similarly, those at present employed in accountancy, investment or financial management also revealed a greater knowledge of the reporting process than those in other occupations or in retirement . . .

It should be noted at this stage, however, that accounting education or experience appears to be no guarantee of knowledge of reporting practice'.

9

(3) Thirdly, in relation to both use and understanding:[29]
'Interest in financial information appears to be consistent. Shareholders who read thoroughly the annual report examine other sources of information more thoroughly than do less interested readers of annual reports. The latter shareholders, therefore, do not appear to compensate for their lack of attention to annual reports.

Those shareholders who read annual reports thoroughly are more likely to believe they understand reporting practices, and more likely to find these reports relevant to their investment decisions, than those who are less interested in reports.

Thorough readers of annual reports tend to have a greater understanding of reporting practices than less interested readers.

Thorough readers of annual reports appear to have a reasonably accurate belief in their relative ability to understand reporting practices, although their actual comprehension is not at a high level'.

Thus, it appears from this preliminary research that the complexities of financial information, and particularly the highly technical language of accounting, make much of the quantitative aspects of company and other reports seemingly unsuitable sources of knowledge for the typical private shareholder lacking the expertise to make best use of them. Given that thorough readers of annual reports appear to be likely to be thorough readers of other sources of financial information, it is worrying to find that training or experience with accounting is apparently related to the use and understanding of such reports. In fact, there is more than a suspicion from the evidence of this study that such background experience and/or training may be necessary before private shareholders become thorough readers of annual reports and similar published data. Thus, if the provider of financial information wishes to communicate effectively to all shareholders, it may be necessary to present less complex data to encourage those with little or no accounting background to read financial reports more thoroughly. In addition, there appears to be a considerable premium on the analytical and interpretive skills of experts such as financial advisors and journalists upon whom the private shareholder may largely rely in his investment decision making.

The pilot study results therefore were material enough to warrant further confirming research of a more detailed nature. In particular, it was felt to be important to examine the use and understanding of financial reports in much greater depth, and with a different group of shareholders, in order to come to more definite conclusions regarding these matters. The following chapters will describe this work at length, beginning with an explanation and description of the research methodology and survey respondents.

10

REFERENCES

[1] J. R. Jordan, 'Financial Accounting and Communications', in *Accounting: a Book of Readings* (G. G. Mueller and C. H. Smith, eds.), Holt Rinehart and Winston, 1970, p 139.

[2] *The Corporate Report*, Accounting Standards Steering Committee, 1975.

[3] *Inflation Accounting*, Cmnd. 6225, HMSO, 1975.

[4] For example, as in *The Corporate Report*, and in *Objectives of Financial Statements*, AICPA, 1973.

[5] See, for example, M. N. Chetkovich, 'Standards of Disclosure and Their Development', *Journal of Accountancy*, December 1955, pp 48-52; and E. L. Hicks, 'Materiality', *Journal of Accounting Research*, Autumn 1961, p 160.

[6] R. K. Mautz and H. A. Sharaf, *The Philosophy of Auditing*, American Accounting Association, 1961, p 191.

[7] D. Rappaport, 'Materiality', *Journal of Accountancy*, April 1964, p 42.

[8] R. G. Leach at the press conference launching *The Corporate Report*, July 1975.

[9] *The Corporate Report*, *op cit*, pp 28-9.

[10] J. Moyle, *The Pattern of Ordinary Share Ownership: 1957-1970*, Cambridge University Press, 1971, p 18.

[11] Taken from *The Times 1000*, 1975-76.

[12] For example, G. J. Benston, 'Published Corporate Accounting Data and Stock Prices', *Empirical Research in Accounting: Selected Studies*, 1967, pp 1-54; and R. Ball and P. Brown, 'An Empirical Evaluation of Accounting Income Numbers', *Journal of Accounting Research*, Autumn 1968, pp 159-77.

[13] Ball and Brown, *op cit*, pp 176-7.

[14] Benston, *op cit*, p 28.

[15] P. Brown and J. W. Kennelly, 'The Informational Content of Quarterly Earnings: An Extension and Some Further Evidence', *Journal of Business*, July 1972, pp 403-5.

[16] J. E. Kiger, 'An Empirical Investigation of NYSE Volume and Price Reactions to the Announcement of Quarterly Earnings', *Journal of Accounting Research*, Spring 1972, pp 113-26.

[17] R. G. May, 'The Influence of Quarterly Earnings Announcements on Investor Decisions as Reflected in Common Stock Price Changes', *Empirical Research in Accounting: Selected Studies*, 1972, pp 1-38.

[18] See, for example, *The Companies Act 1967: Some Requirements and Implications*, The Institute of Chartered Accountants of Scotland, 1967.

[19] See, for example, 'Disclosure of Accounting Policies', *Statement of Standard Accounting Practice 2*, 1971.

[20] 'Accounting for Changes in the Purchasing Power of Money', *Provisional Statement of Standard Accounting Practice 7*, 1974.

[21] 'Statements of Source and Application of Funds', *Statement of Standard Accounting Practice 10*, 1975.

[22] *The Corporate Report*, *op cit*, pp 47-60.

[23] *Inflation Accounting*, *op cit*, p 160.

[24] T. A. Lee and D. P. Tweedie, 'Accounting Information: An Investigation of Private Shareholder Usage', *Accounting and Business Research*, Autumn 1975, pp 280-91.

[25] T. A. Lee and D. P. Tweedie, 'Accounting Information: An Investigation of Private Shareholder Understanding', *Accounting and Business Research*, Winter 1975, pp 3-17.

[26] T. A. Lee and D. P. Tweedie, 'The Private Shareholder: His Sources of Financial Information and His Understanding of Reporting Practices', *Accounting and Business Research*, Autumn 1976, pp 304-14.

[27] Lee and Tweedie (Usage), *op cit*, p 288.

[28] Lee and Tweedie (Understanding), *op cit*, p 11.

[29] Lee and Tweedie (Private Shareholder), *op cit*, p 314.

11

CHAPTER 2

Research Methodology
and Survey Respondents

The purpose of this chapter is to indicate to readers the means by which the survey research was conducted, in addition to the characteristics of the private shareholders who participated in it. Much of the description will also provide an introduction to the background factors which were used as variables in the cross-analyses made with data derived from the survey.

As in the earlier pilot study, it was decided that the required data-gathering should be undertaken by means of a survey of private shareholders. However, the pilot study had revealed that a postal survey gave limited data because of the need to reduce the size of the questionnaire to a level which ensured an acceptable response rate. Consequently, the method of approach adopted in the main study was an interview questionnaire – that is, a face to face meeting with private shareholders who had previously agreed to be interviewed. The questionnaire used for this purpose has been reproduced in full in Appendix 1. It was realised that due to the inconvenience of personal interviews, the survey response rate might well be lower than that commonly experienced in postal surveys. In any case, due to the amount of data which it was realised would be generated from each interview (as well as the time necessary to undertake each interview), the number of respondents had to be limited. In this case, provided the responding group of shareholders was a reasonably representative one, it was felt that approximately 300 interviews would be as much as could be handled without undue burdens of time and cost.

The Survey Company

The pilot study had utilised the share register of a medium-sized public company, and questionnaires had been sent to each of its 1594 private shareholders. The 23.5% response rate which was achieved may appear to have been low, but it seems reasonable to suggest that the survey results were obtained from shareholders with more than just a passing interest in the financial reporting function. In any case, as all the private shareholders had been sent questionnaires (which were unidentifiable to preserve confidentiality), there was little that could be done to improve the response rate.

Nevertheless, criticisms of the pilot study results would remain if the research was left at that stage. Consequently, it was necessary to expand the questionnaire to produce much more detailed results, and to involve a different group of shareholders in a different type of company. For this purpose, the company chosen is one of the largest in the U.K. – herewith designated as XYZ.

According to its 1975 financial report, it had an issued ordinary share capital of £43,545,330 comprising 217,726,650 20p ordinary units. At the time of writing, XYZ had a total ordinary share capitalisation of £127,370,090, and its total shareholdings, again according to its 1975 report, were 39,428, of which 82% comprised holdings of under 2500 20p units. In other words, this is a very large company with a great many individual holdings. In terms of size, therefore, it is markedly different from the company used in the pilot study.

The Survey Response

With 39,428 individual shareholdings from which to sample, the initial problem was to reduce the sampling frame to manageable proportions. This was done, in the first instance, by limiting the choice to named private shareholders living in or around Edinburgh, Glasgow, Liverpool, London and Newcastle. This had to be done in order to reduce to a minimum the time and cost of interviewing – the researchers and their interviewers mainly being based in Edinburgh and Liverpool. In addition XYZ's origins, as well as its existing operations, are largely located in Edinburgh and Newcastle; with Glasgow also reflecting its predominantly Scottish structure; and Liverpool and London representing its interests in other parts of the U.K.

Letters seeking interviews were sent to 2002 named private shareholders who, using random number tables, had been selected from XYZ's share register as it existed at 27 April 1975. The selection was made only from shareholders in the five locations mentioned in the previous paragraph. 339 agreements were received, of which 301 were eventually used – 300 being the number beyond which time, cost and computational limiting factors suggested it was not prudent to exceed. Expressed as a percentage of the original requests for interview (and minus 56 shareholders who could not respond because of illness or death, or because no forwarding address was available; and minus 38 shareholders who had agreed to be interviewed but were not required), this resulted in a total response rate of 15.7%. This may appear low but it was to be expected, given the nature of the subject being researched and the method of research. In addition, it can be argued that these respondents would tend to be the more interested and, possibly, the most informed of all those sampled. In order to ensure there were no significant differences between respondents and non-respondents, however, a sample of the latter were later sent a brief questionnaire to ascertain their background factors for purposes of comparison with those of the respondents. This analysis is described at the end of this chapter. Appendix 2 reproduces the questionnaire issued for this purpose.

Background Factors

In order to construct an aggregate profile of the 301 respondents, the following background factors were sought: location; sex; size of shareholding in XYZ; total number of shareholdings held; occupation; accounting and related experience; investment decision making; reading of financial press. In other words, these were factors which described where the respondents were located; the size of their share portfolios; the extent to which they could be said to have knowledge of accounting and financial matters; whether or not they relied on expert help and advice when making investment decisions; and whether or not they read the financial press regularly.

There may well be other factors which could have been used for purposes of this profile, and there may well be a case for examining the factors actually sought in much greater depth than has been possible in this study. However, because of their personal and private nature, it was decided to reduce this aspect of the interviews to a minimum in order to maximise the overall response rate. In any event, as subsequent analyses will reveal, many of the factors examined revealed insignificant differences in responses to individual reporting matters covered in the questionnaire.

The following sections discuss each of the background factors utilized in this study. *It should be noted that the relevant tables and appendices are expressed as percentages of 301 responding shareholders. This practice has been adopted throughout the text unless, for some reason, the number of response varies from 301. In these cases the number of analysable responses will be stated specifically in the table or appendix concerned.*

14

Location of Respondents

Table 2 outlines the various locations of the survey respondents.

TABLE 2
Location of Survey Respondents

	%	%
Original Location of Company		
Edinburgh	37	
Newcastle	11	
	—	48
Other Locations		
Glasgow	16	
Liverpool	21	
London	15	
	—	52
		100

As can be seen from these figures, the 301 respondents were located relatively equally between the original areas of production of XYZ (that is, Edinburgh and Newcastle) and other locations. Alternatively, they reveal that 53% of respondents were located in Scotland, with the remaining 47% located in England. There therefore appears to be a reasonable spread of location, taking into account XYZ's past and present operational structure. However, in each of the cross-analyses made of survey data with the location variable, it was found that, when chi-square tests of significance were applied, differences in location were significant at levels which suggested relatively consistently that the location of respondents had little to do with differences in response to financial reporting matters. For this reason, it was decided not to incorporate such analyses into the study.

Sex of Respondents

As in the pilot study, the respondents were predominantly male – 71% in this case (see Table 3).

TABLE 3
Sex of Survey Respondents

	%
Male	71
Female	29
	100

Intuitively, this is not unexpected as it appears reasonable to suppose that married men, particularly, still take responsibility for financial matters. The cross-analyses of the main data of the survey with this background factor revealed consistently (again using chi-square tests of significance) that male shareholders read financial reports more thoroughly and understood them much more than did female shareholders. This confirmed similar analyses in the pilot study.[1] However, as this did not appear to provide any interesting conclusion relevant to the matters under review in this study, it was decided not to pursue any further the issue of differences according to such a static variable. Instead, attention was concentrated on variables which were flexible in nature.

Shareholdings in XYZ

As previously stated, 82% of the shareholdings in XYZ are of a size of less than 2500 20p ordinary units or, alternatively, 500 £1 units. As can be seen from Table 4 below, 85% of respondents came into this category. The largest group of shareholders (46%) fell into the 101-500 £1 unit category and, more specifically, as Appendix 3 (giving the analysis in much greater detail) reveals, 30% of respondents were in the 101-200 £1 unit category.

TABLE 4

Shareholdings in Survey Company held by Respondents

Share Units Held (expressed in £1 units)	%
0 — 100	39
101 — 500	46
501 +	15
	100

Thus, most of XYZ's private shareholders appear to own relatively small holdings, and this is reflected in the distribution attributable to respondents. Lest it should be thought that these shareholders are of no importance, several points should be noted: (a) all the survey respondents came from a group of shareholders who held (at 27 April 1975) 96% of the total shareholdings in XYZ and 23.6% of its total ordinary share capital; (b) at 27 April, 1975 a holding of £100 1 units had a market value of £267 and a

16

holding of 500 £1 units had a market value of £1335; (c) the latter figures are not insignificant sums, particularly to the individuals to whom they relate.

As it was felt that size of shareholding may have had some influence on the degree of interest in financial reports, it was decided to include this variable in later cross-analyses.

Respondents' Portfolios

This particular topic is one where there is a danger of intrusion into the personal affairs of respondents, and only the most general question was asked of them – that is, how many individual shareholdings they held. Admittedly it would have been useful to obtain much more detailed data in this connection, but it was felt that obtaining this might have antagonised respondents, and thereby reduced the overall response rate. Table 5 outlines the distribution obtained.

TABLE 5
Number of Shareholdings held by Survey Respondents

	%
1 − 5	22
6 − 10	21
11 − 20	26
21 +	31
	100

The figures reveal a relatively even spread of holdings, with a bias towards larger portfolios – for example, the largest category (31% of respondents) covers portfolios of 21 or more items. Indeed, 57% of respondents held more than 10 items in their portfolios. Most respondents therefore appear to hold a number of investments, and many hold substantial portfolios. This comment has to be tempered because of lack of data regarding the values attributable to portfolios but, when coupled with the market value data obtained in the previous section with regard to XYZ shares, it appears that many respondents may be holding portfolios of some significant value. Indeed, a cross-analysis of respondents' shareholdings in XYZ with the size of their portfolios revealed that the larger the shareholding, the larger was the spread of investment (results significant at a level of less than 1%).

17

It was felt that this portfolio variable would be useful in further analysis, and it re-appears in later parts of the text where appropriate.

Respondents' Occupations

In the pilot study it was found that respondents' occupations were a key variable with regard to both financial report usage[2] and comprehension.[3] For this reason, it was included in the interview study. Table 6 gives the broad analysis of findings, and Appendix 4 provides a much more detailed summary.

TABLE 6
Occupations of Survey Respondents

	%
In accountancy, investment, banking or financial management	16
In non-financial management	22
Housewives	11
Others	51
	100

84% of respondents were in what can loosely be described as 'non-accounting or non-financial' occupations, and, more specifically, 62% were in occupations which had little or nothing to do with financial or accounting matters on a day to day basis. For this purpose, it appears reasonable to assume that the non-financial managers (22% of respondents) would in some way come into contact with accounting matters on a regular basis. This does not appear to be the case with architects, doctors, lawyers, teachers, and so on.

Thus, although this particular group of respondents is largely of a non-accounting nature, any significant differences in response by these groups have been looked at in depth later in the text.

Respondents' Accounting Experience

As with occupation, this particular background factor revealed significant response differences in the pilot study,[4] and, in any case, provides an alternative view of accounting background to that covered by respondents' occupations – that is, respondents with apparently relevant occupations need not necessarily be those with the most relevant experience.

TABLE 7
Accounting and Related Experience or Knowledge of Survey Respondents

	%
Significant	14
Little	24
None	59
Unknown	3
	100

Table 7, supported by a more detailed Appendix 5, largely confirms the occupation distribution in Table 6. Only a small proportion (14%) of the survey respondents have had what could be described as a significant experience of accounting and related matters. 59% of respondents had no such experience at all.

These findings support the non-accounting orientation of the respondents and, in conjunction with the occupation variable, will be used in subsequent cross-analyses.

Respondents' Investment Decisions

TABLE 8
Taking of Investment Decisions by Survey Respondents

	%	%
Decisions taken on own initiative		69
Decisions taken on own initiative but with help from an expert	8	
Decisions made by an expert on investor's behalf*	23†	
	—	31
		100

*

	%
Decisions made by the following experts:	—
stockbrokers	16
bankers	3
accountants	1
solicitors	2
others	3
	—
	25†
	—

† 5 respondents (2% of 301) relied on two experts

19

Given that the previous two sections, coupled with similar findings in the pilot study, indicate private shareholder populations lacking expertise in accounting and related matters, it could be presumed that the shareholders concerned would tend to rely on expert advice and help in their investment decisions. Table 8 appears to reject that hypothesis very firmly.

In fact, almost 7 out of every 10 respondents (69%) stated they made their own investment decisions without help or advice from experts, and a further 8% made their own decisions supported by some advice. This is a surprising finding which will be investigated still further later in the text, but it is not unreasonable at this stage to attempt to ascertain who these respondents are. Table 9 outlines these subsidiary findings.

TABLE 9
Occupation, Accounting Experience and Investment Decisions

RESPONDENTS' OCCUPATIONS		INVESTMENT DECISIONS		
		Taken entirely on own	Taken with help from an expert	Total
	n	%	%	%
Accountancy, investment, etc.	48	81	19	100
Non-financial management	65	81	19	100
Housewives	34	50	50	100
Others	154	65	35	100

Chi square = 15.16; 3 degrees of freedom; significance = 0.00

ACCOUNTING EXPERIENCE		INVESTMENT DECISIONS		
		Taken entirely on own	Taken with help from an expert	Total
	n*	%	%	%
Significant	42	86	14	100
Little	72	68	32	100
None	178	66	34	100

Chi square = 6.15; 2 degrees of freedom; significance = 0.05

* 9 respondents (3% of 301) did not indicate their accounting experience and have been omitted from this analysis

Cross-analyses of respondents' occupations and accounting experience with the data in Table 8 are shown in Table 9, and indicate that those respondents with accounting (or related) or non-financial management occupations tend to make their own investment decisions when compared with those in other occupations (81% and 81%, respectively, of the former groups as against 50% and 65%, respectively, of the latter). Similarly, those respondents with significant accounting or related experience also tend to make their own decisions compared with those with little or no such experience (86% as against 68% and 66%). In other words, and not surprisingly, those respondents with knowledge or experience to make their own decisions appear to do so to a greater extent than those respondents lacking such attributes.

The investment decision making variable will be used in later cross-analyses although, because of its stated relationship to the occupation and experience variables, it will not be used as extensively as the latter. To do so would simply duplicate findings about what is largely the same group of respondents.

Financial Press Readership

The remaining background factor sought in this study concerns readership of the financial press, and has obvious connections with the extent to which respondents make use of financial comment and analysis to guide them in their investment decisions. Table 10 outlines these findings, and Appendix 6 gives a detailed analysis of the same data.

TABLE 10
Financial Press Read Regularly by Survey Respondents

	%
Three or more sources read	16
Two sources read	31
One source read	39
No source read	14
	100

It is encouraging to find that 86% of respondents read at least one financial press source, with 47% reading two or more. However, 1 in every 7 respondents (14%) did not read any source. The *Financial Times* appears to be the most popular source (36% of respondents reading it regularly), although the

21

most popular combination appears to be the *Telegraph* and the *Sunday Times*.

This variable will be used in subsequent cross-analyses but, because it can be used to confirm findings in another part of the survey relating to financial press readership, it will not be used as extensively as others.

Summary on Background Factors

It is somewhat difficult to come to any measured conclusion about the 'typical' respondent in this study, but the following appears to be a reasonable summary. Such a respondent is more likely to be male rather than female; have a holding of less than 500 £1 ordinary share units in XYZ; have a total portfolio of 10 or more items; be in a non-accounting, non-financial occupation and therefore have little or no experience of accounting or related matters; make his own investment decisions without expert help; and read regularly at least one financial press source. Of all these variables, by far the most significant in relation to financial report usage and understanding are occupation and experience, as later chapters will reveal.

Respondents and Non-respondents

In order to ensure that the survey respondents were representative of the group of shareholders sampled, it was necessary to ascertain the main background characteristics (outlined in the previous sections) pertaining to the non-respondents. For this purpose a brief questionnaire covering these matters was sent to 400 randomly selected non-respondents – that is, 25% of these non-responding shareholders sampled who could have responded. Allowing for 14 non-responses due to illness, change of address, etc., 139 replied to it prior to the closing date for acceptance – a 36% response rate. Table 11 summarises the results, the data being expressed as percentages of 139 replies in the case of non-respondents, and 301 in the case of respondents. Four background factors used in this study were covered – that is, number of shareholdings held, occupation, accounting experience, and investment decision behaviour. As later chapters will evidence, these were found to be the most significant factors in relation to use and understanding of financial information. The data in Table 11 largely confirm the representativeness of the survey respondents in relation to the sample frame from which they were drawn.

TABLE 11
Respondents and Non-Respondents

BACKGROUND VARIABLES	Respondents	Non-respondents	Significance
	%	%	
Number of Shareholdings			
1 — 5	22	36	
6 — 10	21	20	
11 — 20	26	23	
21 +	31	21	
	100	100	0.02
Occupation			
In accountancy, investment, banking, etc.	16	11	
In non-financial management	22	17	
Housewives	11	16	
Others	51	53	
Unknown	—	3	
	100	100	0.20
Accounting Experience			
Significant	14	14	
Little	24	29	
None	59	57	
Unknown	3	—	
	100	100	0.60
Investment Decisions			
Taken on own initiative	69	63	
Taken with help from an expert	31	37	
	100	100	0.20

So far as size of investment portfolio was concerned, it appears that respondents tended to have larger portfolios than non-respondents. (22% of the respondents having 1 to 5 items, compared with 36% of non-respondents; and 31% of the former group having more than 20 items, compared with 21% of the latter group). Using the chi-square test, these differences were significant at the 2% level, indicating that the size of shareholders' portfolios could well be one factor in explaining why some responded to the request for inter-

23

view whilst others did not – that is, shareholders with smaller portfolios tending not to respond compared with those with larger ones.

The analyses of the remaining background factors produced few material differences between respondents and non-respondents. For example, 16% of respondents were in accountancy or related occupations, compared with 11% of non-respondents; 14% of respondents had significant accounting experience, compared with an identical percentage of non-respondents; and 69% of respondents made their own investment decisions, compared with 63% of non-respondents. None of these analyses were significant at a low enough level to suggest that there was any convincing connection between the variables for the respondents and non-respondents. In other words, it appears from the evidence that respondents and non-respondents were likely to have relatively similar occupation, experience and decision backgrounds, and this was confirmed in the results achieved. The overall conclusion, therefore, is that respondents were generally representative of the total sample. Only in the case of portfolio size was there a significant difference – respondents tending to have larger portfolios than non-respondents.

The Interviews

It would be inopportune to continue with the detailed analysis of the survey findings without mentioning the method of the interviewing. The questionnaire, which is reproduced in Appendix 1, formed the basis for each interview, and these were conducted mainly by graduating students in accounting at the Universities of Edinburgh and Liverpool. The remaining interviews were conducted by lecturers in accountancy in these Universities.

The interviews were arranged by telephone or letter, and usually took between 1 to 1½ hours to complete. The overall time taken to cover the interviewing stage of the research project was 3 months.

Each interviewer was thoroughly briefed prior to interviewing, and provided with the required questionnaires and interview cards (necessary for questions with a limited choice of answers). The questionnaires were then returned to the researchers for coding, computation and analysis. The analysis was undertaken by the writers at the University of Edinburgh's Regional Computing Centre, and the program used was the Statistical Package for the Social Sciences.

Approach to Analysis

In the pilot study the approach to analysis was to examine the use made of financial and other reports[5] prior to examining shareholder understanding of financial reporting practice.[6] The final stage was the cross-analysis of use and understanding to ascertain, inter alia, whether or not thorough users of reports were able to understand them.[7] From these examinations, it was quite clear that shareholder comprehension was the key factor from which all subsequent examinations and analyses could be made. For this reason, the remainder of the text will be structured as follows:

(1) An examination of the *overall levels of understanding* of survey respondents (Chapters 3, 4 and 5). This is concentrated on five specific areas of financial reporting practice, and particularly indicates, in aggregate only, whether respondents' understanding in each area is reasonable, vague or non-existent. The results are aggregated into an overall index of understanding, revealing the comprehension distribution of respondents, which is then available for use in further analyses.

(2) A review of the *reading behaviour* of survey respondents in relation to annual financial reports and other sources of financial information about companies (Chapters 6 and 7). The main aim of this section is to ascertain, again in aggregate, those respondents who can be classified as thorough readers and those who can be classified as less interested readers of annual reports. This distribution of respondents is then available for use in further analyses. A secondary, though not unimportant objective of this section, is to establish the relative importance to, and influence on, respondents of the various sources of financial information.

(3) An analysis of those respondents who *understand and read* sources of financial information (Chapter 8). In other words, having constructed in aggregate terms, in Chapter 5, an index of comprehension related to average understanding, and having identified, in Chapter 6, thorough and less interested readers of financial information (again in aggregate), Chapter 8 attempts to relate these two factors, as well as to use the previously-mentioned background factors to identify those respondents who understand and use financial information.

(4) An analysis of the *specific areas of financial reporting practice* which are or are not understood by survey respondents (Chapter 9). This is an attempt to investigate the usage and comprehension problems of financial reporting in much greater detail, in order to identify those areas where understanding is strongest or weakest. It is also an attempt to identify those respondents who have difficulty in understanding specific areas of financial reporting practice.

(5) A survey of *improvements and amendments* to the existing system of financial reporting (Chapter 10). Having identified in previous chapters those respondents who use and can understand financial information (as well as those who do not), and having pinpointed certain of the problem areas, this chapter looks at ways in which the existing system might be improved. This is based, in part, on the respondents' own suggestions.

REFERENCES

[1] T. A. Lee and D. P. Tweedie, 'Accounting Information: An Investigation of Private Shareholder Usage', *Accounting and Business Research*, Autumn 1975, p 282; and T. A. Lee and D. P. Tweedie, 'Accounting Information: An Investigation of Private Shareholder Understanding', *Accounting and Business Research*, Winter 1975, p 12.

[2] Lee and Tweedie (Usage), *op cit*, p 282.

[3] Lee and Tweedie (Understanding), *op cit*, p 11-12.

[4] Lee and Tweedie (Usage), *op cit*, p 282; and Lee and Tweedie (Understanding), *op cit*, p 11-12.

[5] Lee and Tweedie (Usage), *op cit*, pp 280-91.

[6] Lee and Tweedie (Understanding), *op cit*, pp 3-17.

[7] T. A. Lee and D. P. Tweedie, 'The Private Shareholder: His Source of Financial Information and His Understanding of Reporting Practices', *Accounting and Business Research*, Autumn 1976, pp 304-314.

CHAPTER 3

Understanding Financial Information

As mentioned in Chapter 1, the trend in financial reporting has been towards the production of increasingly more technical and, inevitably, more complex statements, such that the concept of adequate disclosure of accounting and other financial information now appears to be related more to the professional analyst's needs than to those of the non-professional investor. Thus, as Hendriksen[1] has correctly stated:

'Wise investment decisions cannot be made, except by chance, by persons uninformed in accounting and business technology and procedures'.

This is a crucial problem in financial reporting for, as the analysis in Chapter 2 reveals, there are numerous private shareholders, yet (at least from survey evidence) few appear to have the employment background or experience of accounting and related matters to enable them to be informed enough to make wise investment decisions. In addition, a considerable number of these shareholders make their own investment decisions without any form of expert help or advice.

Unfortunately, the tendency in financial reporting over the years appears to have been towards ensuring the adequacy and relevance of disclosed information *vis-à-vis* what is usually described as the informed reader of financial reports; presumably to the detriment of the so-called unsophisticated user. Two further quotes from Hendriksen[2] underline this development: first,

'The type and amount of disclosure depend, in part, on how expert the reader can be expected to be in interpreting accounting data. He should not be expected to be an expert accountant, yet he should have some knowledge of accounting and business'.

And secondly:
'The non-professional investor should not be discouraged from attempting to become informed on financial matters, but the special needs of the professional analyst should also be kept in mind'.

It is a matter of debate as to the extent to which the non-professional investor has been discouraged and the professional investor satisfied by reporting developments in recent years. However, the main requirement would appear to be an obligation to evidence the degree to which financial reports are actually understood by private shareholders, who, typically, appear to lack the relevant background to cope with the complexities of present-day financial reports. Once levels of actual understanding amongst private shareholders have been established, attention can then be paid to ascertaining precisely the individuals who lack understanding, as well as the specific reporting areas where such a lack of understanding exists. With this evidence to hand, it should be easier to identify ways by which the existing system of financial reporting can be improved so as to meet the needs of both the professional analyst and the non-professional investor.

This chapter therefore aims to provide some evidence on aggregate levels of understanding which can be used as a starting point for further explanation of the private shareholder comprehension problem.

Assessing Actual Understanding

The 301 survey respondents were asked to indicate their perceived understanding of reported accounting information, and were then tested in five specific areas in order to construct an aggregate profile of comprehension for the group as a whole. The questions asked can be found in the questionnaire in Appendix 1, and were related entirely to the existing system of financial reporting. Such a system has been in operation for many years and, for this reason and despite increased disclosure of information, should be reasonably familiar to private shareholders. The questions asked of respondents are therefore free of the added complexities of recent suggestions and recommendations,[3] and the survey results should be read in that context.

It is extremely difficult to devise adequate tests relating to shareholder comprehension of financial reporting practice, particularly within the structure of an interview questionnaire. The pilot study had concentrated on two areas only:[4] (a) the conceptual framework of financial reporting (reporting objectives, legal responsibility for reports, and the general nature of reported data); and (b) the main valuation bases appropriate to particular assets. It was felt, however, that this did not adequately provide a broad enough comprehension frame, although it provided extremely interesting and useful results.[5] Consequently, the comprehension tests in the main study were expanded to include three further areas where understanding hopefully

28

should exist; (c) the general contents of specific financial statements; (d) accounting terminology commonly used in financial reports; and (e) financial ratios.

It was hoped that these additional tests would provide a more comprehensive and searching analysis of respondents' understanding of financial reporting practice, and the following chapter will deal with each in turn prior to establishing an overall index of understanding for the responding group as a whole.

Perceived Understanding of Respondents

Although it may have only a limited significance to the study of *actual* comprehension, it is useful to establish at the outset exactly what respondents *believed* to be their level of understanding of financial reporting practice. Table 12 summarises their views on this matter, and Appendices 7 to 12, inclusive, provide cross-analyses of these views with the five main background variables thought to be relevant for this purpose.

TABLE 12
Perceived Understanding of Reported Accounting Information

	%	%
Respondents indicating that they understood reported accounting information:		
and found it relevant to their investment decisions	39	
and found it irrelevant to their investment decisions	35	
	—	74
Respondents indicating that they did not understand reported accounting information		26
Respondents giving other answers		—*
		100

* 1 respondent fell into this category

3 out of every 4 respondents (74%) believed they understood reported accounting information, although only 53% of such a group also stated they found it relevant to their investment decisions. The figure for perceived

understanding is surprisingly high given the relative lack of accounting sophistication amongst the total responding group, thereby providing an adequate reason for establishing the actual level of understanding attributable to respondents. It is also somewhat disturbing to find that only 4 out of every 10 respondents (39%) indicated that they found reported data relevant to their investment decisions. Chapters 6 and 7 will pursue this point in depth to establish how extensively annual reports are used by respondents, as well as the extent to which other sources of financial information are read by them.

The analysis of perceived understanding by background variables (Appendices 7 to 12 inclusive) reveals several interesting points worthy of mention. First, it appears (Appendix 7) that the size of shareholding in XYZ has little relationship to perceived understanding – in other words, it was not found that respondents with the larger holdings had different perceptions of their level of comprehension compared with those with smaller holdings. Indeed, the figures for each shareholding group are remarkably similar to each other, and to the overall situation in Table 12. This lack of difference in results appears to be confirmed by the rejection of the null hypothesis at the 47% level.

Analysis of the size of respondents' portfolios produced differences in perception which are significant at the 1% level (Appendix 8). Thus it appears that for respondents with large portfolios the level of perceived understanding is greater than for those with smaller portfolios, particularly with regard to understanding and investment decision relevance (49% of respondents in the largest portfolio group down to 27% in the smallest portfolio group).

Appendix 9 also contains significant differences in perception, in this case in relation to respondents' occupation (significant at a level of less than 1%). Indeed, the differences are marked – those in accountancy or related occupations almost unanimously believing they have an understanding of reported data (98%), and two-thirds (67%) of the same group also believing it to be relevant to their decisions. Non-financial managers (who may in some way have contact with accounting data) also produced a much higher level of perceived understanding (83%) when compared with housewives (65%) and other occupations (65%). The conclusion from this appears to be that perceived understanding, and relevance to decisions, is much higher for those respondents in accountancy and related occupations than for others covered in the survey.

The above finding is confirmed in the cross-analysis with the accounting experience variable (Appendix 10), and the results are again significant at a level of less than 1%. All respondents with significant accounting experience believed they understood reported data, compared with 84% of those with little experience and 65% of those with no experience. Similar differences are to be found in relation to relevance of reported data for investment decisions (60% as against 44% and 32%, respectively).

Not surprisingly, Appendix 11 shows that those respondents making their own investment decisions have a higher level of perceived understanding (79%) than do those who rely wholly or partly on advice from experts (63%). In addition, 45% of the former group find reported data relevant to their decisions compared with only 25% of the latter group. These results are significant at a level of less than 1%, and tend to confirm the difference between the two groups – those not making decisions entirely on their own either not understanding the data supplied to them or understanding it but finding it irrelevant.

Appendix 12 contains the final cross-analysis of perceived understanding; on this occasion with data relating to regular readership of the financial press. Again, the results are significant at a level of less than 1%. The overall impression from this tabulation is that the greater the readership of the financial press, the higher the level of perceived understanding – for example, only 44% of those respondents who did not read the financial press at all believed they understood reported data compared with 81% of those who regularly read three or more items. The same distinct trend can also be noted in relation to those who find such data relevant to their decisions – only 12% of the group not reading any financial papers finding it relevant compared with 58% of the most widely read group.

In conclusion, therefore, it would appear that perceived understanding of reported accounting information is highest amongst those respondents who have the largest portfolios; are in accountancy or related occupations; have significant accounting or related experience; make their own investment decisions without help from experts; and read extensively in the financial press. In addition, these respondents were also more likely than others to find accounting information relevant to their decision making. Only in relation to the size of shareholding in the survey company does there appear to be little or no material differences in perception – a small clue to suggest that the size of individual investments does not influence interest (or lack of it) in accounting information. It is now appropriate to examine the respondents' actual levels of understanding in the following chapter.

REFERENCES

[1] E. S. Hendriksen, *Accounting Theory*, Irwin, 1970 (revised edition), p 561.
[2] Ibid.
[3] For example, as in the Accounting Standards Steering Committee's *The Corporate Report*, 1975, and the Sandilands Committee's *Inflation Accounting*, HMSO, 1975.
[4] T. A. Lee and D. P. Tweedie, 'Accounting Information: An Investigation of Private Shareholder Understanding', *Accounting and Business Research*, Winter 1975, pp 3-17.
[5] Ibid., pp 11-13.

CHAPTER 4

Assessing Actual Understanding of Financial Information

Establishing respondents' perceived understanding of reported accounting information provides little evidence of levels of actual understanding. Consequently, further analysis cannot be undertaken until the latter is evidenced and documented. The aim of this chapter is to provide such evidence.

As stated in Chapter 3, five main areas were identified for purposes of measuring respondents' actual levels of understanding of financial reporting practice. These areas were (a) the general nature of the financial reporting function; (b) the content of individual financial statements; (c) the terminology commonly used in financial statements; (d) the traditional valuation bases used for accounting measurement purposes; and (e) the meaning of commonly used financial ratios. It was believed that these were representative of reporting practice, generally, and reported accounting information, particularly. In no way is it assumed either that these areas are the only one that could have been covered, or that this was the only way of assessing respondents' understanding. However, given the time and cost constraints, it appears to be a reasonable approach to the problem. The following sections deal with each of the above areas in the order stated.

General Nature of Reporting

The purpose of testing respondents' reactions to this particular matter lies in the philosophy that there is little point in understanding the detailed workings of a particular system if there is no understanding of its general purpose or nature. For example, motorists should not only be able to drive a motor vehicle, but they must also be aware of the uses to which it can be put, the legal and other responsibilities which are related to it, and the care which must be given to it – that is, if the vehicle is to be used properly and effectively.

This approach applies equally to financial reporting – report users should understand the objectives, responsibilities and general nature of reported data, as well as the meaning of individual datum.[1] Understanding of financial information must be improved if there is also an appreciation of its conceptual (and practical) foundations. For this reason, respondents were asked to state, first, the person or persons legally responsible for producing and presenting annual financial statements to shareholders; secondly, the present-day main objectives of such statements; and, thirdly, the general nature of accounting data reported in the same statements (that is, whether or not it could be regarded as accurate).

Before commenting on the research results obtained in this area of shareholder comprehension, it is important to specify what were regarded as reasonable, vague or incorrect responses. So far as legal responsibility was concerned, responses indicating company boards of directors were classified as reasonable answers. All others were classified as incorrect, unless they were coupled with the correct response (in which case, they were usually reclassified as vague answers). Answers relating to reporting objectives were somewhat more difficult to classify but those specifying accountability, or the provision of data for investment decision making, were taken as reasonable responses. Vague understanding was attributed to responses indicating reported data which could be used to justify dividends or to those giving vague descriptions of shareholder accountability. In addition, responses including a reasonable answer coupled with an incorrect one were reclassified as vague. All other responses were regarded as incorrect. Finally, with regard to the nature of accounting data, reasonable responses were regarded as those indicating its approximate nature. Those respondents stating such data was either accurate or inaccurate were classified as having no understanding. The vague category was created for those responses indicating that reported data was partly approximate and partly accurate.

The overall response to these questions is contained in Table 13, and the more detailed supporting data are contained in Appendices 13 to 15, inclusive.

The overall impression to be gained from the results in Table 13 is that the respondents, as a group, were not particularly conversant with the general nature of financial reporting practice – in each of the three areas covered, the majority response indicated either a vague or an incorrect understanding. Legal responsibility was reasonably understood by 46% of respondents, and a similar result (49%) was achieved with regard to the accuracy of reported data. Objectives of financial statements was the least well understood area –

34

only 27% of respondents showing a reasonable understanding, with a further 23% having a vague understanding.

TABLE 13
Actual Understanding of the General Nature of Reported Financial Statements

LEVEL OF UNDERSTANDING	*Legal Responsibility for Financial Statements*	*Objectives of Financial Statements*	*Accuracy of Reported Data*
	%	%	%
Reasonable	46	27	49
Vague	6	23	1
None	48	50	50
	100	100	100

Although an understanding of these matters is not entirely necessary to an understanding of the detailed data in financial reports, it is somewhat disappointing to find so many respondents having little or no appreciation of them. More specifically, it is disturbing to find 18% of respondents (54 out of 301) state that company secretaries are legally responsible for financial statements; 30% (90 out of 301) state that financial statements are intended to indicate the overall values of companies to which they relate; and 47% (141 out of 301) state that reported accounting data accurately reflects financial progress and position.

Nature of Financial Statements

This section deals with respondents' understanding of the general nature of the contents of five main financial statements – the chairman's report, directors' report, profit and loss account, balance sheet, and auditor's report. Each is contained in company annual financial reports, and it is reasonable to suggest that shareholders ought to understand, at least in general terms, the nature of their content – that, for example, the chairman's report usually contains a review of the past year's financial results and, possibly, a statement of future prospects; the directors' report contains certain legally prescribed information; the profit and loss account describes profits realised from company trading and operations; the balance sheet is a statement of company assets, liabilities and capital; and the auditor's report contains an explicit opinion on the quality of reported data.

Because of the relatively open-ended nature of the questions asked in relation to each of these statements, a number of differing responses were received. The details of these are contained in Appendices 16 to 20, inclusive, and readers should refer to these in order to appreciate the range of answers given. However, for purposes of sensible analysis, it was necessary to categorise the answers into groupings indicating reasonable, vague and no understanding. Each of the Appendices notes how this was done, and the overall results are given in Table 14.

TABLE 14
Actual Understanding of the Nature of Individual Parts of the Annual Financial Report

LEVEL OF UNDERSTANDING	Chairman's Report	Directors' Report	Profit and Loss Account	Balance Sheet	Auditor's Report
	%	%	%	%	%
Reasonable	74	14	26	37	41
Vague	22	47	48	21	20
None	4	39	26	42	39
	100	100	100	100	100

By far the best understood statement was the chairman's report, with 3 out of every 4 respondents (74%) having a reasonable understanding of the nature of its content. In fact, only 4% had no understanding of this point. Somewhat surprisingly, given the technical language in which it is written,[2] the auditor's report was the next best understood statement – 41% of respondents having a reasonable understanding of it, and a further 20% having a vague understanding. The directors' report was poorly understood by the group as a whole, and only 14% of respondents could be stated as having a reasonable understanding of its content. Slightly better results were obtained with the profit and loss account and balance sheet. However, with the former, 3 out of 4 respondents (74%) had either a vague or no understanding, and with the latter, the corresponding percentage was 63%.

The most obvious conclusion to be derived from these results is that, at least for this group of private shareholders, understanding of the general contents of the main financial statements appears to be strongest for those of a predominantly non-quantitative nature – that is, the chairman's report and the auditor's report. Quantitative statements were very much less understood, and this is particularly disturbing in relation to the profit and loss account and balance sheet which are intended to be the main financial statements in the annual report. A common error was the confusion between these two statements – that is, the balance sheet being described as a profit and loss account, and vice versa.

Accounting Terminology

Financial reports of all kinds are prepared in a highly technical language – largely that of the accountant. Therefore, because specialist terms are used, there is a danger that the messages contained in the reports will not be understood by their recipients because of the language used.[3] The situation becomes even more confused when it is realised that some of the terminology is also used in every-day life, in numerous contexts, with differing meanings attributed to it – for example, asset, profit and reserve are familiar every-day terms. Consequently, an attempt was made in this study to examine the terminology problem by testing respondents' understanding of six commonly used reporting terms – profit, depreciation, current assets, equity capital, reserves, and accrued charges. These are all terms to be found in company financial reports, and are certainly to be found in that of the survey company, XYZ.

As in the previous section, the nature of the items tested led to numerous answers. These were analysed into suitable groupings and put into reasonable, vague and no understanding categories. These can be found in Appendices 21 to 26, inclusive, and Table 15 summarises the results.

TABLE 15
Actual Understanding of Terminology used Widely in Reported Financial Statements

LEVEL OF UNDERSTANDING	Profit	Depreciation	Current Assets	Equity Capital	Reserves	Accrued Charges
	%	%	%	%	%	%
Reasonable	34	26	18	22	33	34
Vague	39	56	25	33	21	7
None	27	18	57	45	46	59
	100	100	100	100	100	100

37

The pattern of comprehension evidenced in the previous two sections tends to be repeated in relation to accounting terminology – a minority of respondents having a reasonable understanding of each of the terms. Indeed, only one third (approximately) of the respondents had a reasonable understanding of each of the terms, profit, reserves, and accrued charges, with depreciation, current assets, and equity capital being reasonably understood by only 26%, 18% and 22%, respectively, of respondents. Although it is somewhat difficult to come to overall conclusions regarding the response to each term, it is reasonably clear that profit and depreciation were the terms most understood by the responding group as a whole – only 27% and 18%, respectively, having no understanding of these terms. The worst understood terms were current assets (57% of respondents having no understanding) and accrued charges (59% of respondents having no understanding). Equity capital and reserves were, on the whole, poorly understood by the group.

Thus it appears that profit and loss account items were much better understood by respondents than were balance sheet items, perhaps indicating a greater familiarity with profitability data. (This point will be pursued in Chapter 6 dealing with readership of financial statements). It is quite clear, however, that a majority of these respondents had, in relation to each of these terms, little or no understanding of their meaning. It is also clear that many respondents attributed definitions which may be appropriate to such terms when used in a non-accounting context but which are somewhat inappropriate in relation to financial reporting. For example, 19% defined profit as cash generated from trading; 15% felt current assets were assets held at the time of reporting; and 31% believed reserves to be comprised of money set aside for contingencies or specific purposes. It is a matter of some concern to evidence such misconceptions, particularly at a time when the present system of financial reporting is likely to change considerably, following the recommendations of the Sandilands Committee,[4] and when significantly more attention will require to be paid to the precise definitions of reported profits and reserves.[5]

Accounting Valuation Bases

One of the most vexed and crucial areas of financial reporting concerns the measurement of assets, generally, and valuation bases, particularly.[6] It therefore appears to be vital that users of financial reports appreciate the measurement bases for financial reporting in order that they do not come to any false conclusions regarding the meaning of asset valuations – for example, it has already been shown in this chapter that 30% of respondents believed the main objective of reporting to be to indicate the overall values of companies. In addition, and in light of possible future amendments to asset valuation bases (that is, the change from historic cost to current values), it is useful to assess respondents' present state of knowledge *vis-à-vis* the existing system.

It is reasonable to presume that the existing system is normally structured as follows – fixed assets being based on original costs minus any accumulated depreciation thereon; and current assets being based on the lower of original costs and estimated net realisable values.[7] Respondents were therefore tested in these two general areas – fixed assets represented by plant and machinery, and current assets represented by stock and work in progress and quoted investments; each of these items appearing in the financial reports of the survey company, XYZ. The results are summarised in Table 16, and the more detailed data are contained in Appendices 27 to 29, inclusive, in which the responses obtained have been determined as indicating either reasonable, vague or no understanding.

TABLE 16
Actual Understanding of Traditional Accounting Valuation Bases

LEVEL OF UNDERSTANDING	Plant and Machinery	Stock and Work in Progress	Quoted Investments
	%	%	%
Reasonable	70	35	21
Vague	3	4	5
None	27	61	74
	100	100	100

Responses to these questions tended to produce relatively black or white answers – very few respondents in each of the asset groups revealing a vague understanding. By far the best response was achieved in relation to plant valuation – 70% of respondents stating it to be based on historic cost with a deduction for accumulated depreciation. This contrasts sharply with the corresponding reasonable answers for the other two assets – 35% for stock and work in progress and only 21% for quoted investments. The reason for this difference is hard to evidence but it may be due to the fact that the respondents were familiar with such matters as motor vehicle depreciation in a

39

non-accounting context. This is also supported in the response to the definition of depreciation in Table 15 – only 18% having no understanding of that term.

So far as plant valuation responses are concerned, there is little indication that respondents thought current values were being used in reports – only 10% came into this category. However, this was not the case with current assets – 37% believing stock and work in progress to be on a current value basis (30% indicating realisable value), and 52% believing investments to be on a realisable value basis. There therefore appears to be a fairly large group of these shareholders who link sale values with current assets. This is not the case with fixed assets and, interestingly, it is in the latter area where the Sandilands proposals for changes to current value are largely concentrated.[8]

Financial Ratios

The final area of comprehension testing concerned financial ratios. In many ways, an understanding of these data by shareholders may be more vital than an understanding of the greater detail of accounting and financial reporting. They are derived from basic reported information and express relationships which can be compared over time and between entities for the benefit of investors and others. Several are important enough indicators of company progress and performance to be disclosed in annual financial reports, and to be quoted extensively in the financial press.

Such is the case for the price-earnings ratio (usually current share price to latest earnings per share); dividend yield (latest dividend per share to current share price); and dividend cover (number of times dividends covered by available profits). Each of these ratios is included in the *Financial Times* quotations list, and data for each are contained in the annual report of the survey company, XYZ. For this reason, respondents' comprehension of each ratio was tested. Table 17 contains the overall results, and Appendices 30 to 32, inclusive, describe the detailed data after it has been classified into reasonable, vague and no understanding answers.

So far as these respondents are concerned, there was little or no understanding of the most widely-quoted financial indicator – the price-earnings ratio. 7 out of every 10 respondents (70%) had no understanding of it, and only 15% had a reasonable understanding. Dividend yield was better understood, with 57% having a reasonable or vague understanding. Dividend cover was best understood (36% of respondents having a reasonable understanding) although 55% had no understanding. Thus, it appears that respondents' understanding of these indicators was, on the whole, poor, with dividend ratios being better understood than the profit ratio. It is disappointing to see these matters so poorly appreciated, given that they can be used without reference to the technical detail of formal financial reports.

TABLE 17
Actual Understanding of Financial Ratios

LEVEL OF UNDERSTANDING	Price Earnings Ratio	Dividend Yield	Dividend Cover
	%	%	%
Reasonable	15	14	36
Vague	15	43	9
None	70	43	55
	100	100	100

Summary

The overall conclusions from this analysis are reasonably straight-forward. First, a high level of reasonable understanding did not exist in any of the main areas covered. In fact, the majority of respondents in response to each question had little or no understanding, with the exceptions of the chairman's report (where 74% of respondents had a reasonable understanding) and plant and machinery valuation (where the corresponding figure was 70%).

Secondly, complete lack of understanding was most evident in relation to accounting terminology, valuation bases and financial ratios. In addition, for financial statement content, the lack of understanding varied from 4% (for the chairman's report) to 42% (for the balance sheet). Lastly, stock and quoted investment valuations had high lack of understanding results (61% and 74%, respectively) and price-earning ratio had a similar 70% lack of understanding response.

In their present state these results are difficult to evaluate further. Therefore, in the following chapter, an attempt is made to establish (a) in which areas understanding can be said to be greatest and worst; and (b) what the overall level of understanding was for the respondents as a whole. Meanwhile, the overall impression is of a fairly low level of understanding in this particular group of private shareholders.

REFERENCES

[1] The need to establish reporting objectives has been widely recognised in a number of recent publications – for example, Arthur Andersen and Co., *Objectives of Financial Statements for Business Enterprises*, 1972; Accounting Objectives Study Group, *Objectives of Financial Statements*, AICPA, 1973; Accounting Standards Steering Committee, *The Corporate Report*, 1975; and Report of the Inflation Accounting Committee, *Inflation Accounting*, HMSO, 1975.

[2] See, for example, comments about this problem in T. A. Lee, *Company Auditing: Concepts and Practices*, Gee and Co., 1972, pp 30-32; and J. G. Chastney, 'True and Fair View – history, meaning and the impact of the 4th Directive', *Occasional Paper No. 6*, ICAEW, 1975, pp 14-23.

[3] For example, in two recent studies, evidence was produced to support the claim that comprehension of financial reports was likely to be difficult and readership likely to be significantly restricted – F. J. Soper and R. Dolphin, 'Readability and Corporate Annual Reports', *The Accounting Review*, April 1964, pp 358-62 and J. E. Smith and N. P. Smith, 'Readability: A Measure of the Performance of the Communication Function of Financial Reporting', *The Accounting Review*, July 1971, pp 552-61. It has even been suggested that, in relation to company employees, the typical UK chairman's report may be difficult or impossible to comprehend – M. D. Still, 'The Readability of Chairmen's Statements', *Accounting and Business Research*, Winter 1972, pp 36-9.

[4] *Inflation Accounting, op cit*, pp 161-5 and 168-192.

[5] For example, in relation to the separation of operating and holding gains, and the recommendation to treat the latter as increases to reserves rather than as distributable profits – *ibid*, pp 162-4.

[6] See, for example, T. A. Lee, *Income and Value Measurement: Theory and Practice*, Nelson, 1974.

[7] See, for example, the various editions of The Institute of Chartered Accountants in England and Wales' *Survey of Published Accounts* for general evidence of this point, as well as more specific evidence in *Valuation of Stock and Work in Progress*, Institute of Chartered Accountants of Scotland, 1968, and P. N. McMonnies, 'Depreciation: Its Meaning, Purpose and Accounting Treatment', *The Accountant's Magazine*, February 1969, pp 73-85.

[8] *Inflation Accounting, op cit*, pp 169-177.

CHAPTER 5

Further Assessment of Actual
Understanding of Financial Information

The results analysed in Chapter 4 were reasonably clear with regard to the overall lack of understanding of financial reporting practice of many of the respondents. This chapter attempts to determine more precisely their actual levels of understanding in relation to group average.

The means by which this has been done is necessarily of an approximate nature and open to judgment, but appears to be the best that is available.[1] The main emphasis has been on the construction of an index of understanding which can be used to determine different levels of understanding. It is based on points scores attributed to respondents' answers to the questions asked in each of the five areas of financial reporting practice analysed in Chapter 4. Responses classified as indicating reasonable understanding were given a points score of 2; those indicating vague understanding were given a points score of 1; and those indicating no understanding were given a points score of 0. Thus, the maximum possible scores for each of the five areas were as follows: general nature of financial reporting – 3 questions, maximum score = 6; nature of financial statements – 5 questions, maximum score = 10; accounting terminology – 6 questions, maximum score = 12; accounting valuation bases – 3 questions, maximum score = 6; and financial ratios – 3 questions, maximum score = 6. This gave a total maximum score for understanding of 40.

Understanding Scores

Appendix 33 outlines the overall analysis of understanding in each of the five reporting areas covered. The above-mentioned points have been applied

43

to the responses which previously had been categorised as indicating reasonable, vague or no understanding. From this tabulation, it can be seen that the conclusions reached in Chapter 4 are largely confirmed – that is, for each of the areas, with the exception of that dealing with the nature of financial statements, the distribution is skewed by the respondents' lack of knowledge. This is particularly the case with accounting terminology (coefficient of skewness = 0.39) and financial ratios (coefficient of skewness = 0.54). In fact, the considerable lack of knowledge of respondents in the financial ratios area is most noticeable – 50% achieving scores of 0 or 1 out of 6. With regard to the nature of financial statements, the distribution is skewed by the respondents' understanding of these matters, but not significantly (coefficient of skewness = −0.17). These results can be seen more clearly in Table 18.

TABLE 18
Understanding Scores for Individual Financial Reporting Matters

UNDERSTANDING SCORE RANGE*	General Nature of Reporting	Nature of Financial Statements	Accounting Terminology	Accounting Valuation Bases	Financial Ratios
	%	%	%	%	%
Upper range	14	21	13	14	12
Middle range	32	59	41	29	28
Bottom range	54	20	46	57	60
	100	100	100	100	100

* Respondents' scores were expressed as a percentage of the maximum possible score in each area – see Appendix 33. For each of the five areas, with the exception of Nature of Financial Statements, the scores have been cut at the 33 and 67 percentiles. For the latter area, the cut was made at the 30 and 70 percentiles due to the 10 point scale involved.

The data in Table 18 have been constructed from that in Appendix 33. By grouping the points score scales into (approximately) a bottom third, a middle third, and a top third, the response rates can be examined in aggregate. The conclusions to be drawn from this data are as follows:

First, in each of the five areas, only a small minority of respondents achieved scores of more than two thirds of the maximum possible (ranging from 12% for financial ratios to 21% for the nature of financial statements).

Secondly, lack of understanding is the predominant feature of the table. With the sole exception of the nature of financial statements, almost half of the respondents failed to achieve a score of more than one third of the maximum possible.

Thirdly, the area concerning the nature of financial statements was the best understood by respondents as a whole (only 20% obtaining less than one third of the maximum possible score). This is the only area in which there appears to have been a general appreciation of the matters covered. In each of the other areas, there was a relatively obvious lack of appreciation by respondents.

Constructing the Index of Understanding

Having established, in general terms only, levels of understanding in each of the five reporting areas covered in the survey, the next stage was to aggregate the points score data still further and, from this, to construct an overall index of understanding which could reveal those respondents with an understanding above and below an average for the group as a whole.

Prior to this being done, two relevant matters had to be considered – first, whether all five reporting areas, and their related points scores, should be included in the index; and, secondly, whether any of the areas so included should be weighted on account of their relative importance. The first point related to the possible inclusion in the index of matters which were not a proper test of respondents' understanding of financial reporting practice and which, as a consequence, could distort the index. The second point concerned whether some of the individual areas covered were more significant tests of financial reporting practice than others. As with the previous point, lack of adequate weighting could unduly distort the index. The first question was dealt with before considering the other.

The five areas of reporting practice were examined critically with a view to establishing whether any were inappropriate for inclusion in the index. From this examination, it was felt intuitively that the area dealing with the general nature of financial reporting (that is, objectives, legal responsibility, and data accuracy) was one in which a lack of understanding was not absolutely critical to the appreciation and use of information contained in financial reports. The remaining four areas, however, appeared to be fundamental to such an appreciation and use. For this reason, it was decided to test the relationship of responses in the five areas to each other to ascertain whether or not the above-mentioned intuitive separation was valid – that is, whether or not respondents' understanding or lack of understanding of the general

45

nature of financial reporting was repeated consistently in their responses to the other four areas tested.

For this purpose, the test applied was Spearman's coefficient of rank correlation. This was believed to be superior to Kendall's tau because of the large number of responses which related to relatively few individual points scores. In order to conduct the tests of correlation, an overall index of understanding was constructed from the points scores achieved by respondents in each of the five reporting areas covered in the survey. The points scores of respondents in each of these areas were correlated with each other, as well as with the overall index, and Table 19 summarises the results.

TABLE 19

Significance of Relationship between Various Parts of the Index of Understanding

	PART 1		PART 2		PART 3		PART 4		PART 5		INDEX	
	r	α	r	α	r	α	r	α	r	α	r	α
PART 1	—	—										
PART 2	.04	.54	—	—								
PART 3	.14	.01	.52	.00	—	—						
PART 4	.19	.00	.40	.00	.45	.00	—	—				
PART 5	.21	.00	.44	.00	.50	.00	.41	.00	—	—		
INDEX	.37	.00	.74	.00	.82	.00	.69	.00	.73	.00	—	—

PART 1 = understanding of general nature of reporting; PART 2 = understanding of nature of financial statements; PART 3 = understanding of accounting terminology; PART 4 = understanding of accounting valuation bases; PART 5 = understanding of financial ratio; INDEX = overall index of understanding containing each of the previously-mentioned parts. Each based on points scores outlined in Appendix 33

r = Spearman's coefficient of rank correlation; α = significance level

The overall conclusion to be drawn from the correlation analysis is that, with the sole exception of responses to the general nature of financial reporting, the areas were significantly and positively correlated to each other and the overall index (the level of significance in all such cases being at a level of less than 1%). The correlation coefficients (again with the exception of the general nature of reporting) varied from 0.40 to 0.52, indicating a consistent if not particularly strong positive relationship. The corresponding coefficients with the overall index were much stronger – ranging from 0.69 to 0.82. The considerably weaker positive relationships between responses to the general nature of financial reporting and responses to the other areas and the overall index (ranging from 0.04 (admittedly only significant at the 54% level) to 0.37) appear to justify the exclusion of responses to this area from the overall index. In other words, there appears to be evidence to suggest that the understanding attributable to the general nature of financial reporting is somewhat different from that attributable to the other four areas, and has therefore been omitted from the amended index of understanding used in subsequent analyses.

It was somewhat easier to resolve the other index problem relating to the weighting of points scores in the four areas of the index. There appeared to be little evidence to suggest that any one area was more important to private shareholders' understanding of reporting practice than the others. All appeared to be equally important and, for this reason, no extra weighting was employed in the index, except so far as had been predetermined in the interview questions – 5 being asked in relation to the contents of financial statements; 6 being asked in relation to accounting terminology, and 3 each being asked in relation to valuation bases and financial ratios. However, this apparent weighting is not as substantial as the figures suggest. 5 questions covered the general nature and content of financial statements; 6 questions covered the terminology contained in these statements; and the remaining 6 questions covered data contained in or derived from financial statements. This appears to have produced a reasonable balance between the different areas covered.

The Index of Understanding

The four areas to be represented in the index gave a maximum possible score of 34. Respondents' scores were aggregated, and an overall distribution obtained ranging from a score of 0 to a score of 33. The mean score was 15.17, with a standard deviation of 6.71, and a coefficient of skewness of 0.25 (indicating a distribution skewed by the respondents' lack of understanding).

Because it was important, for purposes of further analysis, to concentrate on those respondents with the greatest and the least understanding, the overall distribution required to be regrouped into appropriate categories relating to what were considered to be above average, average, and below average understanding. To do this, the index was, first, decomposed into three segments – the top 25% of respondents, the middle 50%, and the bottom 25% (top referring to those with high scores, and bottom to those with low scores). It was then possible to decompose the data still further by introducing distribution categories covering the top and bottom 10% of respondents. Thus, the overall distribution was broken at the following percentiles: 11, 24, 74, and 90. It was not possible, because of the particular cumulative frequency achieved, to break at the 10, 25, 75 and 90 percentiles. The resultant distribution is shown in Table 20.

TABLE 20
Overall Index of Actual Understanding of Financial Reporting

OVERALL UNDERSTANDING SCORE*	%	%
Much above average understanding 24-33	11	
Above average understanding 21-23	13	
	—	24
Average understanding 11-20		50
Below average understanding 7-10	16	
Much below average understanding 0-6	10	
	—	26
		100

* maximum possible score obtainable from the four reporting areas covered in the index was 34.
Mean = 15.17; standard deviation = 6.71; skewness co-efficient = 0.25.

24% of respondents had an understanding above the average determined for the group as a whole, and 26% were below that average. 11% fell into the much above average category, and 10% into the much below average category. Having established this analysis of understanding for the group as a whole, it can then be used for later cross-analyses, particularly as against readership of financial information and the relevant background character-istics of respondents (see Chapter 8). Meanwhile, the initial comparison is with perceived understanding, as analysed in Chapter 3.

Perceived and Actual Understanding

Having evidenced in Chapter 3 that 74% of respondents believed they understood reported accounting information, it is reasonable to compare their perceived understanding against their actual level of understanding, as measured by its relationship to the average for the group as a whole. In other words, to test the following hypotheses (*these will be labelled H throughout*

48

the remainder of the text, and will be given numerical subscripts in series –
that is, $H_1, H_2 \ldots \ldots H_n$):

H_1 Those respondents who believed they understood reported accounting information had an actual understanding at least equivalent to the average achieved by the group as a whole.

H_2 Those respondents who believed they understood reported accounting information had a significantly better understanding of such matters compared with those respondents who believed they did not understand it.

H_3 Those respondents who believed they understood reported accounting information and found it relevant to their investment decisions, and those who believed they understood it but found it irrelevant, had similar levels of actual understanding.

The aim of testing these hypotheses was to ascertain whether or not respondents' perceived and actual understanding were reasonably compatible, as well as provide an insight as to whether or not respondents who found reported information to be irrelevant did so for reasons other than that they did not understand it. The results achieved are given in Table 21.

TABLE 21
Perceived and Actual Understanding of Survey Respondents

PERCEIVED UNDERSTANDING		LEVEL OF ACTUAL UNDERSTANDING					
		Much above average	Above average	Average	Below average	Much below average	Total
	n*	%	%	%	%	%	%
Understand and find relevant	116	15	26	47	10	2	100
Understand and find irrelevant	107	13	9	56	14	8	100
Do not understand	77	1	—	44	30	25	100

Chi square = 74.21; 8 degrees of freedom; significance = 0.00

* 1 respondent failed to indicate his perceived understanding of reported accounting information, and has been omitted from this analysis.

Note: For purposes of further testing of hypotheses H_2 and H_3, the above figures were suitably aggregated (both vertically and horizontally), and the resultant data were found to be significant at a level of less than 1% in both cases. This further strengthens the comments made in the text.

The results in Table 21 are significant at a level of less than 1%, and reveal substantial differences. 88% of those respondents who found reported information to be both understandable and relevant had an actual understanding of the matters tested equal to or above the average level of the responding group as a whole, and 41% were above such an average. This compares with equivalent figures of 78% and 22%, respectively, for those finding the information understandable but irrelevant, and 45% and 1%, respectively, for those finding it incomprehensible.

Thus, there is relatively clear evidence that those respondents with a perceived understanding of reporting matters were likely to have an actual understanding at the average or above average levels. Hypothesis H_1 therefore appears to be reasonably valid, although it must be noted that 12% and 22%, respectively, of the two perceived understanding groups had a below average understanding, and 2% and 8%, respectively, were much below average. Similarly, hypothesis H_2 appears to be largely supported by these results – respondents in the two perceived understanding groups having a substantially better understanding than those respondents with a perceived lack of understanding – 55% of the latter having a below average rating, and 25% being much below average.

So far as hypothesis H_3 is concerned, there does appear to be some differences between respondents who found reported information relevant and those who found it irrelevant. 41% of the former group had a level of understanding rated above average, compared with only 22% of the latter group. Similarly, the below average data reflect differences – 12% and 22%, respectively. Thus it appears that actual understanding is substantially higher for the relevance group, and that hypothesis H_3 is not fully validated by this evidence.

Overall, therefore, respondents' perceived understanding (or the lack of it) appears to be borne out by the results achieved from the specific understanding tests, although by no means absolutely and in every case. It should also be noted that these comparisons have been made in relation to the responding group's average understanding rather than to any preconceived notions that the researchers or the reader may have about what constitutes an average of reasonable understanding of these matters.

Summary

This chapter has presented evidence, within the context of the survey interviews and questions, that respondents' understanding of financial reporting matters is fairly consistently at a relatively low level, with the nature of financial statements being the best understood area by the group as a whole, and financial ratios being the worst understood. There appears to be a marked difference between the nature of understanding relevant to the general nature of financial reporting and that relevant to the remaining areas tested. For this reason, responses relating to the former matter were excluded from the overall index of understanding which was constructed in order to ascertain those respondents with a better or worse than average understanding for the group as a whole. The first analysis of this index revealed that, on the whole, respondents' perception of their understanding was matched by the reality of the situation – with the exception of those who found accounting information irrelevant to their investment decisions (their actual understanding being substantially less than that of respondents who found such information relevant to their decisions).

The next stage of comprehension analysis is to find out precisely who the respondents were who had above or below average understanding. This will be undertaken in Chapter 8, but, before it can take place, it is necessary to examine the reading behaviour of respondents in general, and to establish, in particular, who were the thorough readers of financial information, in order to provide more meaningful explanations of why comprehension differences existed. The readership analysis is contained in Chapters 6 and 7.

REFERENCE
[1] A. N. Oppenheim, *Questionnaire Design and Attitude Measurement*, Heinemann, 1966, pp 100-102.

CHAPTER 6

Assessing Annual Report Usage

The Corporate Report states that annual financial reports:

'should seek to satisfy as far as possible, the information needs of users: they should be useful'.[1]

To be useful to the private shareholder, however, they must be both understandable and contain relevant information. Respondents' understanding of the annual report and of reporting practice have been examined in Chapters 4 and 5. This chapter considers whether the present form of annual report provides private shareholders with relevant data; whether the information needs of the equity investor group identified in *The Corporate Report*[2] are confirmed by evidence from this survey; and, finally, whether the annual report is read by respondents – an acid test of its usefulness.

Useful Financial Information

As an introductory question to the interview, respondents were asked which pieces of financial information about companies they considered to be important to them as shareholders. Their answers are summarised in Table 22.

It is quite clear that data concerning company profitability were considered to be the most vital pieces of financial information. Not only did over one half of the respondents mention profits or earnings, but a further 9% indicated that profit trends were relevant (1 respondent mentioned both matters). Thus, more than 60% of the interviewees considered profit information to be important to them. This is not particularly surprising given the objectives of the business enterprise – *The Corporate Report* evidencing that chairmen of 166 of the largest 300 United Kingdom listed companies considered their primary objective was to make profits for the benefit of a number of groups.[3] The private shareholders in this survey clearly appeared to be in sympathy with this general objective.

TABLE 22

Financial Information Considered Important by Survey Respondents

	%
Profits/earnings	52
Dividend information	36
Future prospects	18
Sales/turnover	12
Capital base of the company (shares, reserves)	12
Share price	12
Profits trend	9
Assets	9
Cash/liquidity	7
General trend information	6

Dividend data was the next most popular response and, when considered in conjunction with share price information, showed, not unexpectedly, that returns on investment may be very important to these particular shareholders – 41 % mentioning one or other of these items.

Company future prospects came third in frequency of response but well below that predominant number of answers mentioning profit or dividend data. Few other pieces of financial information appeared to be important to many respondents – even data on company liquidity and solvency were not mentioned by the vast majority, despite the gloomy economic climate at the time of interviewing.

Respondents' Reading of the Annual Report

Each respondent was presented with a card on which was shown eight main sections of the annual report, and was asked to state the attention he paid to each section. The responses received are shown in Table 23.

The pattern of user attention revealed by respondents is similar to that in the pilot survey.[4] The chairman's report was the most widely read section of the report – only 7 % of respondents failing to read it. The two most important quantitative sections of the annual report (the profit and loss account and the balance sheet) were read thoroughly by far fewer respondents. Indeed, the profit and loss account, which contains data considered by many respondents to be most important to them, was only read thoroughly by 39 % of the group as a whole – some 13 % fewer than paid similar attention to the chairman's report. The reading of the balance sheet was even less. Almost one quarter of the respondents did not read it at all, and only 29% read it thoroughly. A similar percentage studied the directors' report carefully, but the other sections of the annual report were only read thoroughly by, at most, one fifth of the respondents.

TABLE 23
Parts of Annual Reports Read by Survey Respondents

PART OF ANNUAL REPORT	Read Thoroughly	Read Briefly For Interest	Not Read At All	Total
	%	%	%	%
Chairman's report	52	41	7	100
Profit and loss account	39	46	15	100
Balance sheet	29	48	23	100
Directors' report	27	48	25	100
Notes to accounts	21	42	37	100
Statistical data	19	44	37	100
Sources and application of funds statement	18	39	43	100
Auditor's report	16	36	48	100

As in the pilot study, the impression has been given that most respondents merely glanced through the annual report, with the greatest attention being paid to the chairman's summary of the year's main features and his views on prospects for the future – that is, it was the only section of the annual report read thoroughly by more than one half of the respondents. Few of these private shareholders read the complete report carefully, with only 5% reading every section thoroughly. A similar proportion did not read any section at all. Even the sources and application of funds statement (produced by the survey company, XYZ, for many years) was totally ignored by 43% of respondents.

9% of respondents claimed to undertake an analysis of financial statements. Some of this analysis simply consisted of comparing the current year's figures with the previous year's results. About 4% of the sample appeared to use ratio analysis, the results being compared by about 1% of respondents in each case with data of the previous year; for several years; and with other companies.

While the results so far may not be encouraging for reporting accountants attempting to communicate with the private shareholder (since, in most cases, the typical respondent in this survey appears to read most sections of the annual report briefly for interest) Table 23 reveals further rather disturbing aspects of the pattern of private shareholder readership of the annual report. Almost one half of the respondents failed to read the auditor's report and, while in most cases such a report is unqualified, it is disquieting to discover that, typically, 48% of respondents may not be in a position to detect a qualification, and may therefore fail to realise that a fundamental disagreement concerning measurement, valuation or presentation may exist between the auditor and the board of directors. Only 34% of those reading the profit and loss account thoroughly, and 41% of those studying the balance sheet with equal care, paid similar attention to the auditor's report. Indeed, the fact that many may have taken the directors' presentation for granted can be gauged by the fact that 32% and 29%, respectively, of those respondents reading thoroughly the profit and loss account and balance sheet did not read the auditor's report at all. A knowledge, therefore, that financial statements have been audited may be sufficient in itself to reassure these respondents that everything is in order. (A further possibility is that some respondents may be in the habit of glancing at the auditor's report to check that it is unqualified, and did not consider this to be a reading of the report.)

Further evidence that the data in the balance sheet and profit and loss account may be being taken at its face value by respondents is evidenced by the fact that almost two fifths of the group as a whole did not read the notes to the accounts. Modern reporting practice has led to these notes containing a wealth of detail about such methods as the treatment of extraordinary items, the valuation of assets and liabilities, the determination of certain categories of profits, as well as any changes from previous practice. It is disquieting, therefore, to discover that only 39% and 47%, respectively, of respondents who took the trouble to read thoroughly the profit and loss account and balance sheet, examined the notes supporting these statements with equal care. It should, however, be noted that few of those thoroughly reading the two main quantitative statements ignored the notes completely. Only 14% of those reading the profit and loss account thoroughly, and a mere 9% of those paying similar attention to the balance sheet, did not read the notes at all.

The annual report was read in different ways by respondents from different backgrounds. All respondents, with the exception of those whose comprehension of reporting practice was much above average (as revealed in the comprehension index in Chapter 5) tended to concentrate their attention on the chairman's report. Those with much above average comprehension of reporting practice appeared to be more concerned with the profit and loss

55

account, 64% of this group reading it thoroughly, 55% reading the chairman's report and 52% reading the balance sheet with an equal degree of care. Even this group, however, tended to neglect the auditor's report – only 24% reading it thoroughly. Respondents with much below understanding tended to rely (as far as they read anything thoroughly) on the more descriptive parts of the annual report. 27% examined the chairman's report thoroughly and 17% paid similar attention to the directors' report. Only 17% read the profit and loss account thoroughly, and a mere 7% paid similar attention to the balance sheet. 63% of the group failed to read the latter statement at all, and 50% did not read the profit and loss account.

Respondents with a significant experience of accounting tended to read the annual report more intensively than those who had no such experience. The general nature of the attention paid to particular sections of the report, however, was similar for both groups. 69% of those with significant experience read the chairman's report thoroughly while 60% and 50% read the profit and loss account and balance sheet, respectively, with the same degree of attention. These three sections were also those read most thoroughly by respondents with no experience of accounting, although the proportion reading each section was lower than for those with experience of accounting – 48% of the former group reading thoroughly the chairman's report, 32% the profit and loss account, and 24% the balance sheet.

The auditor's report was the section least well read by the 'inexperienced' group, and only 12% read it thoroughly. However, even respondents with significant experience of accounting tended to ignore the auditor's report – 31% read it in detail. Only the sources and application of funds statement received less attention (26%) from this group. It is interesting, too, to note, that this group, who should have been most aware of the importance of notes to the accounts, tended to ignore this data – only 33% reading them thoroughly.

Finally, those respondents making their own investment decisions read all sections of the annual report more thoroughly than those seeking advice in making investments. The pattern of reading of this group was similar to the others. The most intensively read section of the annual report was the chairman's report (60% reading it thoroughly), followed by the profit and loss account (46%) and balance sheet (36%).

Perceived Importance of Sections of the Annual Report

While the responding shareholders may have read certain sections of the annual report more thoroughly than others, this could have been due more to interest than to a desire to use these sections to determine present and potential profitability, liquidity or solvency prior to making an investment decision. The respondents were therefore presented with the afore-mentioned eight sections of the annual report, and were asked to rank them on a five point scale of influence related to their investment decisions – that is, 1 = maximum influence; 2 = considerable influence; 3 = moderate influence; 4 = slight influence; and 5 = no influence. The means and standard deviations of the respondents' answers are shown in Table 24.

TABLE 24
Survey Respondents' Views on the Degree of Influence of Parts of Annual Report on Their Investment Decisions

RANKING	Part of Annual Report	Mean*	Standard Deviation
Of considerable to moderate influence			
1	Profit and loss account	2.90	1.48
2	Chairman's report	2.94	1.47
Of moderate to slight influence			
3	Balance sheet	3.27	1.47
4	Directors' report	3.81	1.18
5	Sources and application of funds statement	3.98	1.16
Of slight to no influence			
6	Statistical data	4.10	1.15
7	Notes to accounts	4.11	1.11
8	Auditor's report	4.20	1.12

* Respondents who did not answer a particular part of this question were deemed to have considered that section of the report to be of no influence. The rank correlation between 'no answers' and 'no influence' was 0.91. All other categories of response, with only one exception (of slight influence), were inversely related to the 'no answers'. 14 respondents did not read any part of the annual report and were omitted from this analysis.

The data evidenced that, while more respondents thoroughly read the chairman's report than the profit and loss account, the latter statement was considered to be of marginally more influence on their investment decisions. 50% considered the profit and loss account to be of at least considerable influence (categories 1 and 2), and 19% rated it as being of maximum influence. The corresponding figures for the chairman's report were very similar – 46% and 20%, respectively. The chairman's report and the profit and loss account were the only two sections of the annual report to be considered to be of considerable to moderate influence on the respondents' investment decisions.

Three sections of the annual report fell into the moderate to slight influence category. Of these, the balance sheet appeared to exert most influence over the respondents' decision-making. The reason for the balance sheet being of much less influence than the chairman's report and profit and loss account appeared to be that, while 36% of respondents considered it to be of at least considerable influence, one third considered it to be of no influence at all. (25% and 24%, respectively, considered the profit and loss account and chairman's report to be of no influence on their investment decisions.)

The five remaining sections of the annual report were each considered by a large proportion of the respondents to be of no influence whatsoever on their investment decisions. For example, 59% held this view about the auditor's report; 55% had a similar opinion about statistical information; and even the notes to accounts were rated in a similar way by 53% of respondents. The sources and application of funds statement does not appear to be used by many respondents for investment purposes (48% stated that it had no influence on their decisions) and the information contained in the directors' report did not influence 41% of the group as a whole.

Similar results can be observed in Appendix 34 which describes the results of a question seeking to ascertain which sections of the annual financial report were considered to be *relatively* more important than others. Some sections of the annual report were considered to be equally important. In cases such as this the same ranking was given to each section concerned – for example, if two sections were considered to be most important they would both be given rank 1, the next section following would be given rank 3 and so on. Consequently, some columns in the appendix will aggregate to more than 100%. Correspondingly, other columns will amount to less than 100%.

The only difference in ranking the sections of the annual report on the basis of the means of relative importance and influence on investment decision making occurred with statistical data which was accorded last place in relative importance. It is interesting to note from the appendix that, once again, the profit and loss account, chairman's report and balance sheet occupy the dominant places in relative importance. Few respondents considered the other sections of the annual report to be of prime importance, whereas approximately 40% believed that the chairman's report and profit and loss account were the most important sections. A much lower, but not inconsiderable, proportion (18%) believed that the balance sheet was relatively more important than other sections. The appendix also shows the lack of importance of the auditor's report to many of the respondents – 43% of whom rated it as the least important section of the report as compared to other sections.

Not unexpectedly, some sections of the annual report were rated more highly by different types of responding shareholders. For instance, among those with a significant experience of accounting, the most important section of the annual report was considered by 46% of them to be the profit and loss account, and by 32% to be the chairman's report. Similarly, 29% of the same respondents rated the profit and loss account to be of maximum influence in their investment decision making, whilst slightly fewer (27%) held the same opinion about the chairman's report. 19% of those with no accounting experience, on the other hand, regarded both the profit and loss account and the chairman's report to be of maximum influence. The relative importance of the chairman's report to this group was, in fact, greater than that of the profit and loss account. 46% believed it to be the most important section of the annual report – a figure some 11 percentage points higher than that for the profit and loss account. (The balance sheet was rated third, both in importance and influence, by those with and those without accounting experience.)

Differences in ranking were also observed among respondents with different levels of understanding of accounting information (as measured by the index of comprehension). Those respondents who had a level of comprehension higher than average believed the profit and loss account to be the most influential and, relatively, the most important section of the annual report – slightly ahead of the chairman's report. The balance sheet was ranked third. Respondents whose understanding was lower than average ranked the chairman's report substantially ahead of the profit and loss account – 58% of this group stated that the chairman's report was of prime importance compared to 35% who felt that the profit and loss account was the most important section. (The corresponding figures for those with higher than average comprehension were 32% and 40%, respectively.)

The chairman's report, however, did not appear to have much influence on the investment decisions of respondents with lower than average comprehension. Only 17% stated that it was of maximum influence. The influence of the profit and loss account was lower still – only 12% believed it to be of maximum influence. (Of the respondents with a higher than average understanding of accounting information, 27% rated the profit and loss account, and 26% the chairman's report, as being of maximum influence.)

It was interesting to note that, while 41% of respondents making their own investment decisions believed the profit and loss account to be the most important section of the annual report (closely followed by the chairman's report (36%)), the chairman's report was considered to be slightly more influential in investment decision making than the profit and loss account. 22% felt that the chairman's report was of maximum influence, compared to 20% holding the same view about the profit and loss account. (The balance sheet was ranked third in both influence and importance.)

To summarise, it can be seen from the above evidence that, whereas the respondents in total appear to have rated the profit and loss account slightly more highly than the chairman's report, those without accounting experience, and those who did not have a good understanding of accounting information, tended to regard the chairman's report as the most important and influential of the two statements. It is possible that these shareholders were seeking a less technical explanation of the company's financial position and progress, and hoped to escape from the mass of detailed figures produced in the profit and loss account and balance sheet. A further possibility is that these respondents were looking for a different type of information useful to them for decision making which is not to be found in the two major quantitative statements in the annual report, and that they looked to the chairman's report to supply it. It was, therefore, decided to ask respondents which pieces of information contained in the annual report they found to be particularly useful to them.

Useful Information in Annual Reports

The findings for this section are to be found in Table 25. The information shown in Table 25 corresponds closely with the respondents' views on the type of financial information considered to be useful to them regardless of its source (see Table 22). It is interesting to note, however, that the proportion of respondents which declared that profit and dividend information found in the annual report is most relevant was much lower than the proportion declaring that profit or dividend information from whatever source was important (Table 22). Perhaps the delay in producing the annual report, compared to the timeliness and continuing basis of other sources of financial information (as in the financial press), may partly account for this, and will be investigated in Chapter 7.

A further interesting point is the correlation between data being provided already by the annual report and the needs of the equity investor group specified in *The Corporate Report*.[5] Even information on future prospects appears to be found in the annual report, although it is not yet a legal or professional requirement. Information on future prospects was obtained from the chairman's report by 84% of the respondents who found such data relevant to them – the remaining few stating that they found it in the directors' report or in the profit and loss account (presumably by extrapolation).

TABLE 25

*Information in Annual Reports Found to be of Particular Relevance by Survey Respondents**

	%
Income information (current profits; trend of profits)	35
Future prospects of the company	17
Dividend information (cover; amount; trend)	10
Directors' holdings, directors' remuneration, changes in board	7
Company capital (share capital; long term borrowings)	7
Solvency, liquidity	6
Sales (home and overseas) *excluding* future sales prospects	6
Company development and expansion (capital investment; mergers)	5
Investment guides (earnings per share; earnings yield; price earnings ratio; return on capital)	5

* 87 respondents (29% of 301) stated that they found no information to be relevant

Not surprisingly, profit information was found mainly in the profit and loss account. 68% of the respondents finding it to be of particular relevance declared that it was obtained from this source. The remaining shareholders in this category appeared to obtain such information from either statistical data or the chairman's report. Dividend information, too, was found mainly in the profit and loss account – that is by 55% of the respondents who classified it as of particular relevance. The other respondents in this category stated they used the chairman's or directors' reports to obtain such data.

The chairman's report, therefore, appears to be used primarily for information on future prospects, but also as a summary of the general financial information available about the company – for example, 69% of respondents seeking information about company development or expansion used this report to obtain the required information. (Information of this nature could also be considered to be in the nature of future forecasting. In all, 22% of respondents sought data concerning the company's future in the annual report.)

The analysis, by background factors, of respondents' views on the pieces of information which they considered to be useful for investment purposes revealed that those who made their own investment decisions, had significant experience in accounting or had an above average understanding rating, were more interested in almost all of the items listed in Table 25 than those who received help in making their investment decisions, had no experience of accounting, and had a lower than average understanding rating. Those with significant accounting experience were much more interested in profit and sales data than other groups, but, otherwise, the comparisons were similar.

Reading Pattern of the Individual Responding Shareholder

Having examined in depth respondents' overall use of individual sections of the annual report, it was interesting to discover the reading pattern of the individual respondent – that is, to ascertain which sections of the report were read in conjunction with others in order to give him the information he required.

First of all, it was decided to divide the respondents into groups based on the pattern of their reading of the annual report. Two groups were relatively easy to separate from the others; namely, respondents who read all sections of the annual report thoroughly, and respondents who read none of these sections at all (groups 1 and 6, respectively, in Table 26).

TABLE 26
Annual Report Reader Groups

	%
1. Thorough readers of both quantitative and qualitative data (all sections of the annual report read thoroughly)	5
2. Thorough readers of quantitative data (at least profit and loss account *and* balance sheet read thoroughly)	23
3. Thorough readers of qualitative data only (only chairman's report and/or directors' report read thoroughly)	14
4. Readers of quantitative and qualitative data not falling into groups 1, 2, 3 or 5	29
5. Brief readers of quantitative data not falling into group 3 (profit and loss account *and* balance sheet read briefly)	24
6. Non-readers of annual reports	5
	100

62

The next stage was slightly more complex. The information given in Table 23 had revealed that, on the whole, respondents read the chairman's report more thoroughly than any other section of the annual report. To ascertain whether certain respondents relied mainly on largely descriptive data, it was decided to create a group which concentrated on the more qualitative information presented in the report – that is, those who read the chairman's and/or directors' report thoroughly. In all, 14% of respondents concentrated upon these two sections of the report (group 3, Table 26). Most of these respondents read thoroughly the chairman's report alone – only one reading the directors' report thoroughly to the exclusion of all other sections of the annual report.

Having separated the readers of qualitative data from the remaining respondents, the next part of the analysis concerned the isolation of those who relied heavily on the basic accounting statements presented in the annual report – the profit and loss account and the balance sheet. The 23% proportion of respondents who read at least both these sections thoroughly, and who therefore could be considered to be thorough readers of the quantitative data, are shown as group 2 in Table 26. Certain other respondents were found to read both the balance sheet and profit and loss account briefly – this group, who paid less attention to the quantitative statements than reading group 2 above, were categorised as brief readers of quantitative data, and shown as group 5, provided they did not read thoroughly *only* the chairman's report and/or directors' report. The remaining respondents were designated as group 4 – the residual reading pattern group. The overall reading pattern achieved was similar to that discovered in the pilot study.[6]

The overall pattern of reading of the annual report became clearer from the above analysis. Few respondents either read the entire annual report thoroughly or ignored it altogether. Only 28% read *both* the profit and loss account and balance sheet thoroughly (groups 1 and 2) indicating, relatively speaking, how few either had the interest or the ability to read the two main accounting statements intensively. It should be noted, however, that a further 36% of respondents (in groups 3 and 5) read both statements briefly, and an additional 13% (in group 4) read one statement thoroughly (invariably the profit and loss account) and the other briefly. In all, therefore, 77% of respondents read both the profit and loss account and balance sheet.

For purposes of further analysis, it was decided to divide the respondents into two types of reader – the thorough reader of the annual report and what was termed the less interested reader. The original intention was to consider groups 1 and 2 as thorough readers, with the remaining groups

63

classed as less interested readers since the respondents concerned did not read the main accounting statements thoroughly. Analysis showed, however, that some of the readers in group 2, while reading the profit and loss account thoroughly, ignored many other vital sections of the annual report and could scarcely be termed thorough readers of the report. Consequently, a further criterion for a thorough reader was adopted. Each respondent was awarded two points for each of the eight sections of the annual report read thoroughly, and one point for each section read briefly. No points were given if a section was ignored. The new criterion demanded that to be a thorough reader the respondent should not only have read the profit and loss account thoroughly but should also have amassed at least ten points for the intensity of his reading of the annual report. This, in effect, meant that thorough readers should have read thoroughly the two main accounting statements and, *on average*, have read all the other sections of the report at least briefly. If one of the other sections had been ignored altogether then another section would have had to have been read thoroughly. The adoption of the new criterion divided reader group 2 into two groups – group 2a containing respondents who scored 10 points or more, and group 2b consisting of 11 respondents who scored less than ten.

It can be seen from Appendix 35 (which shows the annual report reading patterns of the defined reader groups with the exception of groups 1 and 6 whose reading pattern is obvious) that group 2b is quite different from group 2a. While none of group 2b read the auditor's report, and only one respondent read the sources and application of funds statement, few of group 2a omitted to read these sections of the annual report. Similarly, whereas a majority of group 2b failed to read the notes to the accounts or the statistical data, only one respondent in group 2a did not read the notes, and only five did not look at the statistical data. More respondents in group 2a were also inclined to read the sections of the annual report thoroughly – 72% reading the chairman's report thoroughly (compared to 55% in group 2b), and at least one third in every case reading the other sections of the annual report thoroughly (excluding the two main accounting statements). Few members of group 2b read any of the other sections thoroughly.

Little more than one third of the respondents in group 3 (thorough readers of qualitative data) read the directors' report thoroughly, but only 9% of the group failed to read it – a percentage lower than that of any other group except, of course, group 1 (the respondents who read everything thoroughly). No member of this group failed to read the chairman's report. Indeed, 98% read it thoroughly. A further clue to this group's preference for summarised and less technical data is given by the fact that only 31% did not read the statistical summary presented in the annual report. The other sections of the annual report were not read by well over two fifths of the group, with the exceptions of the profit and loss account and balance sheet which few of these particular respondents failed to read.

The residual group (group 4) appeared to have concentrated mainly on the chairman's report and the profit and loss account. Each of these statements was read thoroughly by 39% of the group. Only 1% failed to read the chairman's report but 33% ignored the profit and loss account. The balance sheet was not read by 53% of this group and most of the other statements, with the exception of the directors' report, was ignored by more than one half of the respondents concerned.

Most of the respondents who read the profit and loss account and balance sheet briefly (group 5) also appeared to be interested in the chairman's report. One quarter of the group read it thoroughly and only 5% did not read it at all. The other statements, with the exception of the directors' report, which was slightly more popular, were not read by about two fifths of the group in each case.

Appendix 35, therefore, clearly shows that reader group 2a read the annual report far more intensively than the other groups, with the exception of group 1. The differences between the reader groups are summarised by Table 27.

TABLE 27
Level of Intensity of Reading of Company Annual Financial Reports

LEVEL OF INTENSITY	READER GROUPS						
	Thorough Readers			Less Interested Readers			
	1	2a	2b	3	4	5	6
	%	%	%	%	%	%	%
Read thoroughly	100	57	36	17	19	11	—
Read briefly	—	35	22	57	39	66	—
Do not read	—	8	42	26	42	23	100
	100	100	100	100	100	100	100

Table 27 is derived from Appendix 35, and shows *on average* each group's pattern of reading for each section of the annual report. The table was constructed by averaging the intensity of reading of each defined reader group across the entire annual report – that is, by averaging the percentages shown in each line of Appendix 35.

From Table 27, it would appear that the reader groups fall into two distinct categories. Group 1 read everything thoroughly. For group 2a, it can be said that, on average, each section of the annual report was read thoroughly by almost three fifths of the group and was ignored by only 8 % of these respondents. These two groups, therefore, have been classified as thorough readers of annual reports. Respondents in the other groups, on the whole, appear to read the sections in the annual report briefly if at all, and have been classified as less interested readers. The analysis to determine which type of shareholders are thorough readers of the annual report is presented in Chapter 8.

Summary

The evidence in this chapter indicates that, in general, the annual report appears to provide the responding shareholders with a considerable amount of relevant information. Many of the needs of the equity shareholder identified in *The Corporate Report* also appear (at least on the surface) to have been met by the present annual report although often voluntarily than by legal or professional compulsion (for example the chairman's comments about future prospects). Further evidence showed that many respondents appear to skim through the annual report – only 28 % read both the profit and loss account and balance sheet thoroughly. Those who had no background of accounting, or whose understanding of accounting information was poor, tended to read the chairman's report rather than the profit and loss account. The latter statement, however, was considered by the more experienced and knowledgeable of the respondents to be the most important and influential part of the annual report.

Finally, respondents were divided into two distinct groups (thorough and less interested readers), this being based upon their stated pattern of reading of the annual report, and their intensity of study of its contents. Chapter 7 will use this variable of intensity of reading to determine whether or not the respondents, who appeared to be less interested than others in reading the annual report, deliberately ignored it and sought from other sources the financial information useful to their needs.

REFERENCES

[1] *The Corporate Report*, ASSC, 1975, p 15.

[2] *Op cit*, p 20.

[3] *Ibid*, pp 37-8.

[4] T. A. Lee and D. P. Tweedie, 'Accounting Information: An Investigation of Private Shareholder Usage', *Accounting and Business Research*, Autumn 1975, p 281.

[5] *Op cit*, p 20.

[6] See T. A. Lee and D. P. Tweedie, 'The Private Shareholder: His Sources of Financial Information and His Understanding of Reporting Practices', *Accounting and Business Research*, Autumn 1976, pp 305-8.

CHAPTER 7

Assessing Use of Other
Sources of Information

Interest in Other Sources of Financial Information

Table 28 shows clearly that the most frequently used source of financial information other than the annual report was financial press reports.

TABLE 28

Use Made by Survey Respondents of Other Sources of
Financial Information About Companies

SOURCE OF INFORMATION	Read Thoroughly %	Read Briefly For Interest %	Not Read At All* %	Total %
Financial press reports	54	39	7	100
Occasional merger reports	46	36	18	100
Half-yearly financial reports	32	48	20	100
Stockbrokers' reports	31	27	42	100
Moodies or Extel cards	7	8	85	100

* Included in this column are respondents who failed to answer the particular part of this question. The rank correlation between the 'do not read' answers and 'no answers' for the five sources of information was 0.95. The other two categories of response revealed a negative correlation with the 'no answer' rankings.

7% of respondents failed to read these reports while 54% read them thoroughly – slightly more than paid similar attention to the chairman's report. Confirming the findings of the pilot survey, occasional merger reports were the next most widely read source of information,[1] being read far more intensively than half-yearly company reports. Perhaps it is the topical interest and the expectancy of dramatic changes outlined in these reports, rather than the relatively more mundane nature of the profit and loss account, which has led to the former reports being read even more thoroughly than the latter.

Half-yearly financial statements (the content of which may be slightly out of date relative to other sources at the time of publication) were only read thoroughly by one third of the respondents, with a further one fifth ignoring them altogether. A substantial 31% examined stockbrokers' reports in great detail, although 42% did not read them at all. These reports were read mainly by those who received help with their investment decisions, 41% of whom read them thoroughly. In contrast, Moodies or Extel were used by few respondents – 85% did not use these sources of financial information at all.

Several differences were observed in the interest shown in these other sources of information by different types of responding shareholder. Those who made their own investment decisions read all sources (with the sole exception mentioned above of stockbroker reports) more thoroughly than those who received assistance with their investment decisions. Financial press reports were the most popular source of financial information among the former group – 60% read them thoroughly, the same proportion as paid equivalent attention to the chairman's report. Only 39% of the group read half-yearly financial statements thoroughly.

Respondents with significant experience of accounting paid most attention to occasional merger reports (read thoroughly by 71%) and financial press reports (read thoroughly by 67%). Only 50% devoted the same degree of attention to half-yearly financial statements, although this was far higher than the 29% of respondents with no experience of accounting who read these reports thoroughly. The latter respondents were mainly concerned with financial press reports and occasional merger reports (49% and 43%, respectively, read these reports thoroughly) but, on the whole, did not read any of the sources of information to the same extent as respondents who had experience of accounting.

The greatest differences, however, were found when respondents' reading of other sources of financial information was analysed by the comprehension index. Those whose understanding of accounting information was higher than average (that is, ratings of above average and much above average) read far more intensively than those who had a lower than average comprehension (that is, ratings of below average and much below average). Both groups concentrated mainly on financial press reports and occasional merger reports, but the differences in the proportion of each group reading these sources thoroughly were extremely large. Those with higher than average understanding read all sources more intensively. 70% of this group read financial press reports thoroughly and 62% read occasional merger reports with the same degree of attention. The corresponding figures for the lower than average group were 41% and 30%, respectively. An even larger difference of some 37 percentage points was noticed, however, between the proportions in each group reading half-yearly financial reports thoroughly. Only 15% of respondents with a poor understanding read them intensively, and 38% did not read them at all; a further sign, perhaps, that the more technical accounting reports cannot or will not be read by those without knowledge of accounting matters.

Perceived Importance of Other Sources of Financial Information

An analysis was made to ascertain whether reading of other sources of information was linked to their influence in the investment decision making of respondents. They were asked, therefore, to rate each of the five sources cited on the five point scale of influence which was used previously in Chapter 6 in relation to the annual report. The results are shown in Table 29.

TABLE 29
Survey Respondents' Views on the Degree of Influence of Other Sources of Information About Companies on Their Investment Decisions

RANKING	Source of Information	Mean*	Standard Deviation
Of considerable to moderate influence			
1	Financial press reports	2.44	1.30
Of moderate to slight influence			
2	Stockbrokers' reports	3.33	1.57
3	Half-yearly financial reports	3.38	1.34
4	Occasional merger reports	3.48	1.29
Of slight to no influence			
5	Moodies or Extel Cards	4.65	0.85

* The 6 respondents who did not read any of the above sources of information about companies were omitted from the analysis. Respondents who did not rank any source of information were deemed to have considered it to be of 'no influence'. The rank correlation between 'no answers' and 'no influence' was 0.90. The relationship of all other categories of response to 'no answers' ranged from 0.0 to −0.7.

The striking feature of this analysis is the prominence which was given to financial press reports – higher than for any section of the annual report. There may be three reasons for this. First, financial press reports are usually more topical than annual reports[2] and half-yearly reports which tend to be outdated at the time of their publication. Secondly, press reports may take a broader and more objective view than the company itself. Finally, press reports may be easier to read than the more technical accounting statements and may, consequently, be used by many respondents for the same reasons as they apparently use the chairman's report.

Far more respondents rated financial press reports as having at least considerable influence on their investment decisions (60%) than held the same opinion about the profit and loss account (50%). Similarly, 28% rated financial press reports as having maximum influence on their investment decisions compared to 19% with regard to the profit and loss account. Only 13% of respondents stated that financial press reports had no influence on their investment decisions. The corresponding proportion for the profit and loss account was 25%.

Another interesting observation from Table 29 is that stockbrokers' reports have moved into second place in influence despite not being read by many respondents. (This result was also observed in the pilot survey.[3]) Indeed, 39% of respondents felt that these reports were of no influence whatsoever on their investment decisions while a lower proportion of 18% considered them to be of maximum influence. 29% of the responding shareholders considered half-yearly financial reports to be, at best, of only considerable influence on their investment decisions, and only 9% believed them to have a maximum influence. The occasional merger reports which many respondents had stated they read thoroughly appeared to be read more out of topical interest than for long-term investment purposes. Few respondents stated that these reports had much influence on their investment decisions.

The latter finding was confirmed by respondents' views on the *relative* importance of these sources of financial information (see Appendix 36 where the same ranking methods have been used for other sources as had been used to rank sections of the annual report in relative importance in Chapter 6). Only 5% of respondents rated occasional merger reports as being the most important of the other sources of financial information cited in this tudy. Financial press reports, however, were considered by 52% to be the most important other source, with a further 31% rating them as second most important. Half-yearly financial reports were thought to be the next most important source – 21% of respondents stating that they were of primary importance compared to other sources. It is interesting to note that far more respondents thought that half-yearly reports were important relative to other sources than believed they were useful influences on investment decisions.

Analysis of respondents' views on the importance and influence of these sources of information revealed certain differences. Those who had no accounting experience, had a lower than average understanding of accounting information, or who did not make their own investment decisions, tended to rate all sources, with one notable exception, as being less important and of less influence on their investment decisions than those with accounting experience, a higher than average understanding of accounting information and investment decision making independence. The one exception was stockbrokers' reports. 41% of respondents who did not make their investment decisions unaided rated these reports as of maximum decision influence, compared to only 7% who made their own decisions. A mere 7%, both of those with a higher than average level of understanding and with significant accounting experience, rated stockbrokers' reports of maximum influence whereas one fifth, both of those with no accounting experience and of those with lower than average understanding, accorded them the same degree of influence. Financial press reports were, however, considered to be of most influence by all groups concerned.

Useful Information Found in Sources Other Than the Annual Report

To ascertain the reasons why responding shareholders read reports other than the annual report, a question was asked which sought to discover which information derived from these sources they found particularly useful. A great variety of answers were given to this question, and only the more typical responses are shown.

It can be seen that general information about the company (that is, pertaining to its activities, labour force and industrial relations record, and geographical location) were all of interest to many of the respondents. Certain of this information is occasionally given in the annual report and *The Corporate Report*, for example, has recommended that statistics relating to the employment record of companies should be given in annual reports in the future.[4] At present, however, it would seem that this sort of information is sought outwith the company itself – 56% of respondents seeking such data finding it in the financial press, with only 11% obtaining it from half-yearly financial reports.

TABLE 30
*Information Derived from Sources Other Than Annual Reports Found to be
of Particular Relevance by Survey Respondents*

	%
General information about the company (company activities; labour; geographical spread)	18
Income data (profit performance; trend)	15
Share price information	15
Future prospects (contracts; production plans; future demand)	13
General trend information (past record; growth; past trends – unspecified but excluding income and dividend trends)	8
Company development and expansion (mergers; capital investment)	8
Investment guides (return on capital; price earnings ratio, etc)	5
Dividend information (dividend cover; prospects)	5

The financial press was the main source of much of the other information for respondents. Not unexpectedly, share prices were almost entirely extracted from this source, and it was also the largest single source of data on future prospects – 33% of respondents seeking views on this topic used this source, the remainder obtaining such opinions from all of the other sources examined. It should be noted at this stage, however, that information on a company's future prospects, and its development and expansion, was one of the most relevant pieces of information to the respondents. 19% indicated that information included in one or other of these categories, both of which relate to a company's future, was relevant to them. 39% of those seeking information on company development and mergers used the financial press, and 48% used merger reports.

The half-yearly company financial report was, therefore, used to a limited degree to supply information required. In one aspect, however, it was preferred to all other sources – that is by 61% of respondents seeking news of profit levels. As profit had been considered by over half of the sample to be the most important single piece of financial information (see Chapter 6), the interim report would appear to fill a vital function in meeting the need for this information.

It is interesting to note the difference between the percentage of respondents stating that certain data were important to them and the percentage actually seeking it. For instance, 52% had stated that profit information was most important to them, yet only 43% actually sought such information – 28% from the annual report alone, 8% solely from other sources (mainly interim reports), and 7% using both the annual report and other sources. Similarly, dividend information was considered important by 36% of respondents, but only 14% obtained such information. Again, the annual report was the most common single source (9%). 4% obtained dividend information from sources other than the annual report, and 1% from both the latter and other sources. Opinions about a company's prospects, however, were more relevant to respondents than they had originally admitted. Only 18% had stated that such information was important, yet 28% found this information relevant to them – 15% obtaining relevant data in the annual report, 11% from other sources, and 2% from both the annual report and other sources. When data on company development and expansion is coupled with forecast information, it can be seen that 40% of respondents sought data on a company's future – a figure only slightly lower than the percentage of respondents who sought profit data. Clearly, information on a company's future was extremely important to a great many of the responding shareholders, and this evidence gives support to *The Corporate Report* suggestion that a statement of future prospects would be welcomed by equity investors.[5]

In general, respondents who had a significant experience of accounting, a higher than average comprehension of accounting information, or who made their own investment decisions, tended to find most of the information shown in Table 30 more relevant than their counterparts who had no accounting experience, lower than average understanding of accounting information, or who received assistance with their investment decisions. Only share price data and general company information were considered more relevant by the latter three groups of respondents in comparison to the views of the former groups. Those who had significant experience of accounting were far more interested in profit data than any other group but, otherwise, no major differences between groups were observed. It would seem that the types of respondents who were interested in data provided by the annual report were also more interested than other respondents in information supplied in other sources of financial information. The following section examines this point more specifically.

Use of All Sources of Financial Information

In Chapter 6, respondents were divided into two distinct reading groups –

thorough and less interested readers of annual reports. One reason for the respondents merely skimming through the annual report may have been their inability to understand it. (This is examined in detail in Chapter 8.) Other reasons may be that they found other sources of financial information easier to read or that these other sources may have contained information not available in the annual report. (It was shown in the last section that few respondents used both the annual report and other sources to obtain information on a company's profits, dividends or future prospects.)

This section examines whether or not less interested readers did in fact compensate for their failure to use the annual report thoroughly by using other sources of information. Specifically, the following hypothesis has been tested:

H_4 Those respondents who did not read annual reports at all, or read them only briefly, read other sources of financial information about companies more thoroughly than those who read the annual report thoroughly.

Table 31 describes the reading of these other sources of financial information analysed by the two annual report reading groups.

TABLE 31
Extent of Survey Respondents' Use of Other Sources of Information

READERS GROUPS	n	FPR t %	FPR b %	FPR n %	OMR t %	OMR b %	OMR n %	HFR t %	HFR b %	HFR n %	SR t %	SR b %	SR n %	MEC t %	MEC b %	MEC n %
Thorough readers of annual reports	72	69	31	—	67	21	12	61	29	10	42	22	36	14	15	71
Less interested readers of annual reports	229	49	42	9	39	41	20	22	54	24	27	29	44	5	6	89

* FPR = financial press reports; OMR = occasional merger reports; HFR = half-yearly financial reports; SR = stockbrokers' reports; MEC = Moodies or Extel cards; t = thorough reading; b = brief reading; n = no reading.
All percentages in each section equal 100 in aggregate.

The table shows clearly that the thorough readers of annual reports tended to read all other sources of financial information more intensively than less interested readers. The financial press was the source used most thoroughly by the latter group but the proportion reading press reports carefully was 20 percentage points below that of thorough readers who examined them with equal care. (In fact, no thorough reader ignored financial press reports.) The greatest reading difference between the two groups (39 percentage points) concerned the thorough reading of half-yearly reports. The evidence suggests that less interested readers of annual reports tended to ignore the more formal accounting information, and to rely mainly upon the financial press, stockbrokers' reports, and merger reports.

The differences in reading patterns were significant at the 1% level for all sources except stockbrokers' reports. (It will be shown in Chapter 8 that 90% of those who sought help with their investment decisions were less interested readers of annual reports.) It would seem, therefore, that hypothesis H_4 cannot be accepted. Indeed, it would seem that the reverse was true, and that less interested readers tended not to use more data from other sources than respondents who read thoroughly annual reports. Generally speaking, it would seem that responding shareholders tended either to be interested in (or able to understand) financial data from whatever source or disinterested in (or unable to understand) such information.[6]

Further evidence on this point was given by the fact that respondents who read three or more financial press reports also read *all* other sources of financial information more thoroughly than those who read fewer newspapers. For example, 42% of those who read three or more financial press reports regularly also read half-yearly financial reports thoroughly, whereas only 12% of those who read no financial newspapers paid the same degree of attention to these reports. The percentages of each of these two groups reading other sources of financial information thoroughly were as follows (readers of three or more financial newspapers being shown first) – occasional merger reports (54%, 12%); stockbrokers' reports (31%, 24%); and Moodies or Extel cards (15%, 0%).

Summary

The evidence of this chapter has indicated that financial press reports were considered to be the most important source of financial information about companies other than the annual financial report. Indeed, respondents rated the financial press as being of even more influence on their investment decisions than any individual section of the annual report. The interim financial reports issued by companies were not read by one fifth of respondents, and were considered to be of far less influence than financial press reports.

It transpired that respondents who read the annual report intensively also read other sources of financial information more thoroughly than those who paid less attention to the annual report. It appears, in general, that the same respondents were reading all sources of financial information carefully, the others being more inclined to glance at financial information regardless of its source. Perhaps this was due to their inability to understand such information. Chapter 8 considers this crucial question and discovers the type of shareholder who reads financial information thoroughly.

REFERENCES

[1] See T. A. Lee and D. P. Tweedie, 'Accounting Information: An Investigation of Private Shareholder Usage', *Accounting and Business Research*, Autumn 1975, pp 285-6, which shows that the shareholders investigated in the pilot study read sources of financial information other than the annual report with a similar degree of intensity to the present respondents.

[2] See, for example, R. Ball and P. Brown, 'An Empirical Evaluation of Accounting Income Numbers', *Journal of Accounting Research*, Autumn 1968, pp 159-77 and G. J. Benston, 'Published Corporate Accounting Data and Stock Prices', *Empirical Research in Accounting: Selected Studies*, 1967, pp 1-54.

[3] Lee and Tweedie, *op cit*, pp 286-7.

[4] *The Corporate Report*, ASSC, 1975, pp 51-3.

[5] *Ibid*, p 20 and pp 55-6.

[6] These results confirm those obtained in the pilot study. See T. A. Lee and D. P. Tweedie, 'The Private Shareholder: His Sources of Financial Information and His Understanding of Reporting Practices', *Accounting and Business Research*, Autumn 1976, pp 305-8.

CHAPTER 8

Understanding, Reading Behaviour and Respondents' Background

In Chapters 4 and 5 evidence from the interview survey was presented which revealed a relatively low level of understanding of financial reporting practice by the respondents as a whole. Indeed, only a small minority (24%), who were designated as having an understanding above the average of the group, could achieve a score of more than 62% of the maximum possible. In Chapters 6 and 7, the reading behaviour of respondents was examined in detail, and it was shown that only 24% could be reasonably regarded as thorough readers of annual reports. Indeed, only 5% read each section of the annual report thoroughly. It was also found that lack of reading of the annual report was not compensated; thorough readers of annual reports tending also to be thorough readers of other sources of financial information.

Thus, having divided the respondents into thorough and less interested readers of annual reports, and into those with above and below average understanding of reporting practice, it is now appropriate to establish precisely the groups to which individual repondents belonged. This has been done mainly by reference to their background characteristics reviewed in Chapter 2 – that is, size of shareholding in the survey company, XYZ; number of shareholdings held; occupation; accounting experience; type of investment decisions; and readership of the financial press. The following sections describe this analysis of data, the purpose of which is to test the validity of the undernoted hypotheses:

H_5 Those respondents who were thorough readers of annual reports had a substantially better understanding of reporting practice than less interested readers.

H_6 Those respondents with larger shareholdings in the survey company were more thorough readers of annual reports, and had a substantially better understanding of reporting practice, than those with smaller shareholdings.

H_7 Those respondents with larger portfolios of investments were more thorough readers of annual reports, and had a substantially better understanding of reporting practice, than those with smaller portfolios.

H_8 Those respondents in accountancy and related occupations were more thorough readers of annual reports, and had a substantially better understanding of reporting practice, than those in other occupations.

H_9 Those respondents with significant accounting experience were more thorough readers of annual reports, and had a substantially better understanding of reporting practice, than those with little or no experience.

H_{10} Those respondents making their own investment decisions without expert help were more thorough readers of annual reports, and had a substantially better understanding of reporting practice, than those who made decisions with help from an expert.

H_{11} Those respondents who read from several financial press sources were more thorough readers of annual reports, and had a substantially better understanding of reporting practice, than those who made little or no use of the financial press.

Summarising, therefore, it was hoped to provide evidence to support the following assertions – that respondents who are thorough readers of financial information have a reasonable understanding of it; and that the larger their investment interests in companies, the more relevant their occupation and experience to accounting, and the more they make investment decisions on a 'do-it-yourself' basis (relying on such information sources as the financial press), the more likely they are to be thorough readers of annual reports and to have a reasonable understanding of reporting practice.

Readership and Understanding

Hypothesis H_5 required a cross-analysis of reader groups with levels of actual understanding, and this is given in Table 32 supported by further detail in Appendix 37.

Without doubt, it can be seen that thorough readers of annual reports fell into the average and higher than average categories of understanding, and less interested readers into the average and lower than average categories

79

(results significant at a level of less than 1%). In fact, 49% of thorough readers had higher than average understanding compared with only 17% of less interested readers. Similarly, 21% of the thorough group had much above average understanding; only 8% of the less interested group came into this category. 32% of the less interested group had lower than average understanding, whereas only 7% of the thorough group could be similarly classified.

TABLE 32

Reading of Annual Report and Level of Understanding of Survey Respondents

READING OF ANNUAL REPORT		LEVEL OF UNDERSTANDING					
		Much above average	*Above average*	*Average*	*Below average*	*Much below average*	*Total*
	n	%	%	%	%	%	%
Thorough readers	72	21	28	44	6	1	100
Less interested readers	229	8	9	51	20	12	100

Chi square = 37.52; 4 degress of freedom; significance = 0.00

Again with results significant at a level of less than 1%, the data in Appendix 37 amplify the above comments, and reveal several additional points worthy of mention. First, thorough readers of quantitative data tended to have a much better understanding of financial reporting practice than thorough readers of non-quantitative data (36%, 51%, and 9%, respectively, of groups 1, 2a and 2b having a higher than average understanding compared with 15% of group 3). This is to be expected given that quantitative data demands a thorough reading because of its complexity. Secondly, complete lack of reading of annual reports did not prohibit some understanding of reporting practice – 21% of group 6 having an average understanding, though 79% had a lower than average understanding.

The next lowest level of understanding concerned less interested readers of quantitative data – 39% of group 4 having a lower than average comprehension of the matters tested. This is not surprising as quantitative data cannot and should not be read casually or briefly if it is to be properly understood.

As a final point on understanding and readership, it is interesting to note (in Appendix 38), that, in addition to actual understanding and thorough readership being positively related, perceived understanding and thorough

readership were similarly linked – that is, 92% of thorough readers perceived they understood reported information, compared with 69% of less
interested readers (results significant at a level of less than 1%). In other
words, most of the thorough readers (9 out of 10) believed they understood
reported information although in actual fact, only 5 out of 10 had an actual
understanding above the average of the responding group as a whole. This
reinforces the point that perceived and actual understanding in this survey
were somewhat dissimilar, and that thorough readership of annual reports did
not guarantee reasonable understanding.

Overall, therefore, the evidence presented in this section appears to support
hypothesis H_5 that thorough readers tend to have a better understanding of
reporting practice than less interested readers. However, thorough reading of
annual reports does not mean that all such respondents had a higher than
average or, indeed, average understanding of such matters.

Understanding, Readership and Shareholdings

Table 33 describes the relationship between respondents' shareholdings in the
survey company and levels of understanding.

TABLE 33
*Shareholdings in Survey Company and Level of Understanding of
Survey Respondents*

SIZE OF SHAREHOLDING IN SURVEY COMPANY*		LEVEL OF UNDERSTANDING					
		Much above average	Above average	Average	Below average	Much below average	Total
	n†	%	%	%	%	%	%
0 — 100	118	14	11	52	15	8	100
101 — 500	138	9	15	48	14	14	100
501 +	44	9	14	50	23	4	100

Chi square = 8.51; 8 degrees of freedom; significance = 0.39

* in £1 units
† one shareholding could not be traced in the share register due to a failure to
reference it at the sampling stage.

NOTE: For purposes of further testing of hypothesis H_6, the above figures were
suitably aggregated (horizontally), and the resultant data were found to be
significant at the 90% level. This further strengthens the comments made
in the text.

From this cross-analysis, it appears that, in each of the three shareholding groups, there was little difference in levels of understanding by respondents. For example, the higher than average understanding rates for the three shareholding groups were 25%, 24% and 23%, respectively, whereas the lower than average rates for the same groups were 23%, 28% and 27%, respectively. These data were significant at the 39% level indicating a strong possibility that size of shareholding provided little explanation of differences in the levels of understanding attributable to respondents.

A similar, and stronger, conclusion can be drawn from the data in Table 34.

TABLE 34

Shareholdings in Survey Company and Readership of Annual Reports

SIZE OF SHAREHOLDING IN SURVEY COMPANY*		*Thorough Readers of Annual Reports*	*Less Interested Readers of Annual Reports*	*Total*
	n†	%	%	%
0 — 100	118	22	78	100
101 — 500	138	25	75	100
501 +	44	27	73	100

Chi square = 0.54; 2 degrees of freedom; significance = 0.76

* in £1 units
† one shareholding could not be traced in the share register due to a failure to reference it at the sampling stage.

This tabulation establishes which respondents in each of the stated shareholding groups were thorough or less interested readers of annual reports. In fact, thorough readers were contained in each shareholding group in roughly the same proportion – that is, 22% in the smallest shareholding group, 25% in the middle group, and 27% in the largest one. These data were significant at the 76% level, suggesting little possibility in this case of any significant relationship between the size of respondents' shareholdings and the extent of their readership of annual reports.

The impression from the above analyses is that, at least for this particular group of private shareholders, understanding and readership do not necessarily vary with the size of shareholding owned. Thus, hypothesis H_6 (respondents with larger shareholdings were more thorough readers, and had substantially better understanding, than those with smaller shareholdings) appears to be invalid.

Understanding, Readership and Portfolios

One of the background variables sought in the shareholder interviews was the number of shareholdings owned by each respondent. Responses were divided into 4 groupings – 1 to 5, 6 to 10, 11 to 20, and 21 or more items. This variable has been used in a further cross-analysis against levels of understanding and extent of readership. Tables 35 and 36 contain the resultant data.

TABLE 35
Number of Shareholdings and Level of Understanding of Survey Respondents

NUMBER OF SHAREHOLDINGS HELD BY SURVEY RESPONDENTS		LEVEL OF UNDERSTANDING					
		Much above average	*Above average*	*Average*	*Below average*	*Much below average*	*Total*
	n	%	%	%	%	%	%
1 – 5	67	10	6	55	17	12	100
6 – 10	62	2	10	55	19	14	100
11 – 20	78	15	14	41	19	11	100
21 +	94	14	20	49	12	5	100

Chi square = 21.31; 12 degrees of freedom; significance = 0.05

NOTE: For purposes of further testing of hypothesis H_7, the above figures were suitably aggregated (both vertically and horizontally), and the resultant data were found to be significant at a level of less than 1 %. This further strengthens the comments made in the text.

The data in Table 35 would suggest that as the size of the respondent's portfolio increased so his level of understanding of reporting practice also increased. In other words, those respondents with the larger portfolios had a higher level of understanding (in aggregate) than those with smaller portfolios. For example, taking the portfolio groupings, and ranging them from the smallest to the largest, the proportion of each having a higher than average level of understanding was 16%, 12%, 29%, and 34%, respectively, and the lower than average response rates were 29%, 33%, 30%, and 17%, respectively. These data were significant at the 5% level, indicating understanding does appear to be highest amongst those respondents with the larger portfolios.

83

TABLE 36

Number of Shareholdings and Readership of Annual Reports

NUMBER OF SHAREHOLDINGS HELD BY SURVEY RESPONDENTS		Thorough Readers of Annual Reports	Less Interested Readers of Annual Reports	Total
	n	%	%	%
1 — 5	67	28	72	100
6 — 10	62	18	82	100
11 — 20	78	26	74	100
21 +	94	23	77	100

Chi square = 2.17; 3 degrees of freedom ; significance = 0.54

NOTE: For purposes of further testing of hypothesis H_7, the above figures were suitably aggregated (vertically), and the resultant data were found to be significant at the 92% level. This further strengthens the comments made in the text.

The strength of the relationship between portfolio size and readership of annual reports (as outlined in Table 36) is not as strong as that for size and understanding. In fact, the results were significant at the 54% level, indicating that portfolio size does not explain differences in the thoroughness of reading of the respondents concerned. This is reflected in the results of the cross-analysis; a relatively similar percentage of each portfolio group being classified as thorough readers – ranging from 18% of the 6-10 group to 28% for the 1-5 group.

Hypothesis H_7, relating size of portfolios to understanding and readership, does not appear to have been fully validated by the evidence from this study. Understanding of reporting practice was greater in the larger portfolio groups, but the extent of reading of the annual report did not vary in the same way. It therefore appears that, as with the size of respondents' shareholding in XYZ, portfolio size is not a particularly significant factor in determining which private shareholders are likely to be thorough readers of financial information. However, it does appear to have a much stronger influence on private shareholder comprehension.

Understanding, Readership and Occupations

In order to test hypothesis H_8 (above average understanding and thorough

84

reading were greatest amongst those respondents in accountancy and related occupations), Tables 37 and 38 were constructed, each containing data that were significant at a level of less than 1%, and providing strong evidence to suggest that occupation does have an influence on these matters. First, Table 37 deals with occupation and understanding.

TABLE 37
Occupations and Level of Understanding of Survey Respondents

RESPONDENTS' OCCUPATIONS		LEVEL OF UNDERSTANDING					
		Much above average	Above average	Average	Below average	Much below average	Total
	n	%	%	%	%	%	%
Accountancy, investment, etc	48	38	29	33	—	—	100
Non-financial management	65	12	17	57	12	2	100
Housewives	34	—	—	35	21	44	100
Others	154	4	10	55	22	9	100

Chi square = 122.95; 12 degrees of freedom; significance = 0.00

NOTE: For purposes of further testing of hypothesis H_8, the above figures were suitably aggregated (both vertically and horizontally), and the resultant data were found to be significant at the 0% level. This further strengthens the comments made in the text.

From the data in Table 37, it is reasonably clear that those respondents in an accountancy or related occupation had a level of understanding of the reporting matters tested well in excess of those respondents in other occupations. 67% of the accountancy group had a higher than average understanding, compared with 29% of non-financial managers, and 14% of sundry occupations (no housewives had such comprehension). Indeed, 38% of the accountancy group had a much above average understanding, and none had a lower than average understanding. The worst group was housewives, with 65% thereof with a lower than average understanding. It would therefore appear that the respondents in accountancy and related occupations had by far the best understanding of all the respondents concerned. A similar distinction can be made in relation to readership of the annual report.

TABLE 38
Occupation and Readership of Annual Reports

RESPONDENTS' OCCUPATION		Thorough Readers of Annual Reports	Less Interested Readers of Annual Reports	Total
	n	%	%	%
Accountancy, investment, etc.	48	52	48	100
Non-financial management	65	31	69	100
Housewives	34	3	97	100
Others	154	17	83	100

Chi square $= 35.01$; 3 degrees of freedom; significance $= 0.00$

NOTE: For purposes of further testing of hypothesis H_8, the above figures were suitably aggregated (vertically), and the resultant data were found to be significant at the 0% level. This further strengthens the comments made in the text.

52% of respondents in the accountancy group were thorough readers, whereas only 31% of non-financial managers, 3% of housewives, and 17% of sundry occupations could·be similarly classified. It is surprising that only one half of those in relevant occupations make thorough use of the annual report, particularly as it was evidenced in Chapter 7 that the less interested readers of annual reports tend not to compensate for this by a thorough reading of other sources of financial information. However, as in the above analysis of understanding, it is the accountants (and related professionals), followed by the non-financial managers, who can be regarded as the thorough readers of annual reports. Thus, from this evidence, hypothesis H_8 appears to be valid.

Understanding, Readership and Accounting Experience

One way of cross-checking the results in the previous section is to examine the alternative background variable, accounting experience, in relation to understanding and readership. The analyses, contained in Tables 39 and 40, were both significant at a level of less than 1%, and largely confirm the conclusions reached in the previous section.

TABLE 39
Accounting Experience and Level of Understanding of Survey Respondents

ACCOUNTING EXPERIENCE		LEVEL OF UNDERSTANDING					
		Much above average	Above average	Average	Below average	Much below average	Total
	n*	%	%	%	%	%	%
Significant	42	43	24	33	—	—	100
Little	72	10	15	57	11	7	100
None	178	4	11	51	21	13	100

Chi square = 69.28; 8 degrees of freedom; significance = 0.00

* 9 respondents (3% of 301) did not indicate their accounting experience and have been omitted from this analysis.

NOTE: For purposes of further testing of hypothesis H_9, the above figures were suitably aggregated (both vertically and horizontally), and the resultant data were found to be significant at the 0% level. This further strengthens the comments made in the text.

Those respondents with significant accounting experience had a far better overall understanding of reporting practice than those with little or no experience; 67% of the former having a higher than average understanding, compared with only 25% and 15%, respectively, of the latter groups. Further, no respondent with significant accounting experience had a lower than average understanding.

TABLE 40
Accounting Experience and Readership of Annual Reports

ACCOUNTING EXPERIENCE*		Thorough Readers of Annual Reports	Less Interested Readers of Annual Reports	Total
	n	%	%	%
Significant	42	45	55	100
Little	72	32	68	100
None	178	17	83	100

Chi square = 17.47; 2 degrees of freedom; significance = 0.00

* 9 respondents (3% of 301) gave no indication of their accounting experience.

NOTE: For purposes of further testing of hypothesis H_9, the above figures were suitably aggregated (vertically), and the resultant data were found to be significant at a level of less than 1%. This further strengthens the comments made in the text.

Readership followed a similar pattern (see Table 40). 45% of those respondents with significant experience were thorough readers of the annual report, with the corresponding figures for those with little or no experience being 32% and 17%, respectively.

The above comments therefore reinforce the overall picture which is emerging from this study – that those respondents with a reasonable understanding of reporting matters tend to be the thorough readers of annual reports, and also tend to be those in accounting or related occupations, thus having a significant accounting experience. Nevertheless, as the above analysis of experience shows, not all respondents in relevant occupations or with significant experience, can be regarded as having a reasonable understanding or as being thorough readers. Hypothesis H_9, on the other hand, dealing with experience, appears to be valid – that is, those respondents with the greatest experience tend to be the thorough readers and have the better understanding of reporting practice.

Understanding, Readership and Investment Decisions

One of the more surprising results of this study has been the number of respondents (69%) who made their own investment decisions without any help or advice from experts. It was therefore necessary to see whether or not these persons had a better understanding of reporting matters, and were more thorough readers of annual reports, than the remaining respondents who relied in some way on help from experts. Hypothesis H_{10} was formulated for this purpose, and Tables 41 and 42 describe the relevant cross-analyses.

TABLE 41
Investment Decision Making and Level of Understanding of Survey Respondents

INVESTMENT DECISION MAKING		LEVEL OF UNDERSTANDING					
		Much above average	*Above average*	*Average*	*Below average*	*Much below average*	*Total*
	n	%	%	%	%	%	%
Decisions made entirely on own	209	15	15	50	15	5	100
Decisions made with help from an expert	92	2	10	49	20	19	100

Chi square = 23.70; 4 degrees of freedom; significance = 0.00

NOTE: For purposes of further testing of hypothesis H_{10}, the above figures were suitably aggregated (horizontally), and the resultant data were found to be significant at a level of less than 1%. This further strengthens the comments made in the text.

88

With data significant at a level of less than 1 %, Table 41 provides evidence to validate that part of hypothesis H_{10} dealing with understanding – that is, those respondents making their own decisions tended to have a better understanding than those who relied on experts. 30 % of the former had a higher than average understanding compared with only 12 % of the latter; with 15 % of the former also having a much above average understanding compared with only 2 % of the latter. The lower than average understanding data confirm the same point – 20 % of the group making its own decisions coming into this category, whereas 39 % of the other group also came into it.

In Table 42, similar differences appear with regard to reading of the annual report – the results again being significant at a level of less than 1 %.

TABLE 42
Investment Decision Making and Readership of Annual Reports

INVESTMENT DECISION MAKING		Thorough Readers of Annual Reports	Less Interested Readers of Annual Reports	Total
	n	%	%	%
Decisions made entirely on own	209	30	70	100
Decisions made with help from expert	92	10	90	100

Chi square = 13.45; 1 degree of freedom; significance = 0.00

30 % of respondents making their own decisions were thorough readers of the annual report, whereas only 10 % of the other group fell into this category. Thus, there does appear to be evidence to support the contention that those relying on advice and help from experts had more reason to do so than did those who made their own decisions – the latter making more thorough use of annual reports and having a better understanding of reporting practice. The second part of hypothesis H_{10} therefore appears to be valid – those making their own investment decisions tend to be more thorough readers of annual reports than those relying on experts.

However, as the previous analysis in Table 9 in Chapter 2 revealed, most of those respondents in accountancy or related occupations, or with significant accounting experience, tended to make their own investment decisions.

Thus, given such respondents also had by far the better understanding of reporting matters, and tended to be the thorough readers of annual reports, it appears likely that it is much the same group which is being looked at in this analysis – that is, those who made their own investment decisions, who had higher than average understanding and were thorough readers, would appear also to be (in the main) those in accountancy or related occupations, and with significant accounting experience.

Understanding, Readership and the Financial Press

The final cross-analysis in this section concerns the use made by respondents of the financial press, and is made to test the validity of hypothesis H_{11}, that respondents making most use of financial press sources tend to be those with a better understanding of reporting practice, and more thorough readers of annual reports, than those making little use of such sources.

The data contained in Tables 43 and 44, significant at the 1 % level, appear to confirm this hypothesis, and largely confirm data already analysed in Table 31 of Chapter 7 that thorough readers of annual reports are also thorough readers of financial press reports (69 % of the former group coming into this category).

TABLE 43
Reading of Financial Press and Level of Understanding of Survey Respondents

NUMBER OF FINANCIAL PRESS SOURCES READ		LEVEL OF UNDERSTANDING					
		Much above average	Above average	Average	Below average	Much below average	Total
	n	%	%	%	%	%	%
3 +	48	21	27	46	4	2	100
2	94	15	11	50	20	4	100
1	118	8	12	52	15	13	100
0	41	—	7	44	24	25	100

Chi square = 43.02; 12 degrees of freedom; significance = 0.00

NOTE: For purposes of further testing of hypothesis H_{11}, the above figures were suitably aggregated (horizontally), and the resultant data were found to be significant at the 0 % level. This further strengthens the comments made in the text.

48% of respondents reading three or more financial press sources had a higher than average understanding, compared with (in descending order of reading) 26%, 20%, and 7%, respectively, of the other groups. Looking at lower than average understanding, the corresponding figures (again for descending order of reading) were 6%, 24%, 28% and 49%. Very clearly, the more the financial press was read, the more likely its readers were to have higher than average understanding as defined in this study.

TABLE 44

Reading of Financial Press and Readership of Annual Reports

NUMBER OF FINANCIAL PRESS SOURCES READ		Thorough Readers of Annual Reports	Less Interested Readers of Annual Reports	Total
	n	%	%	%
3 +	48	35	65	100
2	94	25	75	100
1	118	25	75	100
0	41	5	95	100

Chi square = 11.82; 3 degrees of freedom; significance = 0.01

Similar differences are to be seen in Table 44 in connection with readership – 35% of respondents reading three or more sources being thorough readers of annual reports, compared with only 5% of those who did not read the financial press. As stated above this confirms results previously described in Chapter 7.

Summary

All of the evidence presented in the above sections enables a relatively clear picture of the typical responding shareholder to emerge. It would be wrong to generalise completely on the basis of the sample covered but, given the strength of the survey results analysed above, together with comparable and similar results achieved in the earlier pilot study, it is not unreasonable to suggest that the following conclusions may be more widely applicable to more than just the private shareholders who participated in this survey.

First, it was thorough readers of annual reports who had the most reasonable understanding of reporting practice of all the respondents concerned. This is to be expected but, given that thorough readers were a minority group in this study, it is worrying to see so many respondents who had so little understanding and who paid so little attention to reported information.

Secondly, variations in the size of shareholding in the survey company, produced little variation in levels of understanding and extent of readership of financial information. Indeed, there appeared to be a strong case for suggesting that a respondent with a small shareholding was likely to be as knowledgeable (or as ignorant) and to read as thoroughly (or as briefly) as a respondent with a large shareholding. In other words, a respondent's interest in or knowledge of financial reporting did not appear to be dependent on the size of his shareholding.

Thirdly, relatively similar results were achieved in relation to the size of respondents' portfolios – particularly with regard to thorough reading of the annual report. The size of a respondent's portfolio did not appear to affect the extent to which he read (or did not read) financial information, although it did appear to affect the extent to which he understood reporting practice – respondents with larger portfolios did appear to have a better understanding than those with smaller portfolios. All in all, however, when coupled with the previous findings, the overall impression is that the small private shareholder is likely to be as knowledgeable and as thorough in his reading as the large private shareholder – size of investment appears to play little part in these matters.

Fourthly, it is most evident that those respondents in accountancy and related occupations or, alternatively, those with significant accounting experience were those with the best understanding of reporting practice. They were also found to be predominantly the thorough readers of annual reports. Thus, accountancy experience and qualifications appear to be essential ingredients in the comprehension and reading of financial information by this group of respondents.

Fifthly, it was also determined that those respondents who made their own investment decisions had a better understanding, and were more thorough readers, of financial data than those who rely in some way or another on an expert. Given that many of the former group were those with accountancy occupations or experience, it appears that the comments in the previous paragraph largely apply to this group as well.

Finally, from the evidence of this study, there are grounds for suggesting that respondents who were thorough readers and had a reasonable understanding tended to read the financial press more extensively than those who had less knowledge and were less interested readers. This supports an earlier finding that thorough readers of annual reports also were thorough readers of financial press sources.

Overall, the picture which emerges from the above analyses and conclusions is that those respondents who had a reasonable understanding of reporting practice were those who thoroughly read the annual report (and, from a previous finding, other sources of financial information). They tended to be accountants or related professionals, and had a significant experience of accounting matters. They also tended to be those who made their own investment decisions and read widely and regularly in the financial press. They appeared to do this irrespective either of the size of their shareholdings in the survey company or, to a far lesser extent, of the size of their portfolios. It would not appear to be wrong to say, on the basis of this evidence, that, for this group of private shareholders, financial reports (which are mainly written by accountants) are most read and understood by accountants and those in related occupations. This is a serious conclusion, which will be discussed later in the text, for the majority of private shareholders are presumably non-accountants who, again from the evidence of this survey, tend not to understand or thoroughly read available financial information.

Before continuing with this theme, and thereby attempting to produce reasonable solutions to the problem, it is also necessary to ascertain the particular areas of financial reporting which are best and least understood by the respondents, and this is done in the following Chapter 9.

CHAPTER 9

Areas of Misunderstanding of Reporting Practice

The previous chapter provided evidence of the responding shareholders who, typically, had a poor understanding of reporting practice. If, however, boards of directors and the accountancy profession wish to improve communication with private shareholders then the identification of which shareholders have the greatest difficulty in understanding financial reports is only the first stage in the process. This chapter therefore considers survey evidence concerning the next stage – that is, the discovery of which particular aspects of reporting practice are misunderstood by private shareholders.

The analysis is presented in five sections, each of which considers one of the five areas of understanding identified earlier in Chapter 5 – the general nature of financial reporting; the nature of financial statements; accounting terminology; accounting valuation bases; and financial ratios. Chapter 8 revealed that the important factors related to understanding of reporting practice appeared to be two variables measuring a respondent's contact with accounting (occupation and experience of accounting); and two variables which measured his interest in accounting information (thorough reading of the annual report and independence of investment decision making). (Reading of the financial press has not been included in this analysis due to its close relationship with the thorough reading variable.) This evidence has therefore been utilised in this chapter to refine the previous results, and to pinpoint the precise areas of misunderstanding.

Readers wishing to avoid the detailed analysis given in this chapter should read the summary at the end of the chapter which highlights the main findings.

Understanding of the General Nature of Reporting

The respondents' understanding of the general nature of financial reporting

94

practice was tested by the three questions which considered the legal responsibility for financial statements, the objectives of financial statements, and the accuracy of reported data. It will be remembered that, in Chapter 5, respondents were awarded two points for answers which were deemed to be reasonably accurate, one point for vague answers, and no points for questions which were answered incorrectly or not at all. Therefore, a respondent's understanding score for the general nature of reporting could range from 0 to 6 points. To simplify the analysis, however, respondents' scores were divided into three groups, the top group scoring two thirds or more of the available points, the middle group scoring between one third and two thirds, and the bottom group scoring one third or less.

Table 45 contains the first analysis of respondents' understanding of the general nature of reporting, expressing its relationship to occupation, accounting experience, reading of the annual report and investment decision making.

TABLE 45
Understanding of General Nature of Financial Reporting

BACKGROUND VARIABLE		UNDERSTANDING SCORE				
	n	6, 5 %	4, 3 %	2, 1, 0 %	Total %	Significance
Occupation						
Accounting, investment, etc.	48	27	35	38	100	
Non-financial management	65	8	41	51	100	
Housewives	34	15	26	59	100	
Others	154	12	27	61	100	0.02
*Accounting Experience**						
Significant	42	26	36	38	100	
Little	72	17	30	53	100	
None	178	10	33	57	100	0.05
Reading of Annual Report						
Thorough readers	72	18	38	44	100	
Less interested readers	229	13	30	57	100	0.14
Investment Decision Making						
Decisions made entirely on own	209	15	35	50	100	
Decisions made with help from an expert	92	11	25	64	100	0.08

* 9 respondents failed to disclose their experience of accounting and have been omitted from this analysis

It is evident that all four variables revealed differences in understanding but in only two cases (occupation and accounting experience) were the results significant at the 5% level. Even a significant accounting experience or an occupation involving contact with accounting did not appear to lead to an unduly high level of comprehension of the general nature of financial reporting. Approximately one quarter of each of these groups obtained a score in the top range, and 38% of both groups could only, at best, score two points in answer to the three questions. It appears, therefore, that an occupation related to accountancy (or a significant experience of the subject) did not provide these respondents with a particularly good knowledge of the general background to financial reports – knowledge which is useful if the financial information presented is to be interpreted in its correct context. The following sections provide evidence of a more detailed nature to support this general conclusion.

1. **Responsibility for the Annual Report**

    Those respondents with some contact with accountancy did show that they had a far better understanding of where the responsibility for financial reports lay, as compared with those with no such background. 69% of those with significant experience, as opposed to 39% of those with no experience of accounting, gave a reasonably accurate answer to this question. This result was confirmed by the finding that 77% of those employed in accountancy, investment, financial management or banking had a similar level of comprehension, compared to only 42% of those in 'other' occupations.

    Those who made their own investment decisions (50%) and those who read the annual report thoroughly (61%) also provided more answers showing a reasonable understanding of legal responsibility than those who relied on assistance with their investment decisions (37%) or who were less interested readers of the annual report (42%). The level of comprehension of these two groups was, however, somewhat lower than that of those who were involved with accountancy.

2. **Objectives of Accounting Statements**

    Analysis revealed that few respondents (even accountants) understood the objectives of annual financial statements. Indeed, those with some form of experience in accountancy revealed no greater understanding than those with none. 26% of those with a significant experience of accountancy, and 21% of those whose occupation involved accountancy, had a reasonable understanding of reporting objectives. But 29%

of those with no accounting experience and 24% of those in 'other' occupations revealed a similar level of comprehension. In addition, while just half of the two latter groups failed to show even a vague understanding of the objectives, 45% of both former groups revealed a similar lack of understanding. (The annual report reading and investment decision making groups had similarly low levels of comprehension.)

3.   **Nature of Reported Information**
      Understanding of the accuracy of reported accounting information was spread evenly among the groups of respondents. In most cases about one half of each group realised that accounting data can be only an approximation of the underlying reality. The only notable exception to this pattern was found among the investment decision making groups. In this case, 53% of those making their own decisions were aware of the approximation of accounting information, compared to only 41% of those who sought help in making their decisions.

In summary, it can be seen that few respondents appear to have understood the general background to financial reports. Even some form of understanding of or contact with accountancy only helped the respondents to identify those legally responsible for the information presented in the annual report. In fact, these respondents' comprehension of the accuracy and objectives of the accounting information presented in the annual report proved to be no better than that of those without the advantages of some form of training in accountancy. The results therefore suggest, as they did in the pilot survey,[1] that ignorance of the true nature of reported information and the purposes for which it is prepared is common both to accountants and to non-accountants.

Understanding of the Nature of Financial Statements

Most groups revealed a better understanding of the contents of the sections of the annual report than of financial reporting concepts. Respondents had been asked questions relating to the contents of five main sections of the annual report – the chairman's report, the directors' report, the profit and loss account, the balance sheet, and the auditor's report. After answers to each question had been marked according to the scoring system mentioned in the previous section, the respondents were divided into three groups based on their understanding score as shown in Table 46. (All differences were significant at the 1% level.)

TABLE 46
Understanding of Nature of Financial Statements

BACKGROUND VARIABLE		UNDERSTANDING SCORE				
	n	10,9,8 %	7,6,5,4 %	3,2,1,0 %	Total %	Significance
Occupation						
Accounting, investment, etc.	48	44	48	8	100	
Non-financial management	65	25	64	11	100	
Housewives	34	3	44	53	100	
Others	154	16	63	21	100	0.00
*Accounting Experience**						
Significant	42	45	48	7	100	
Little	72	29	58	13	100	
None	178	13	62	25	100	0.00
Reading of Annual Report						
Thorough readers	72	30	60	10	100	
Less interested readers	229	17	59	24	100	0.00
Investment Decision Making						
Decisions made entirely on own	209	25	60	15	100	
Decisions made with help from an expert	92	11	58	31	100	0.00

* 9 respondents failed to disclose their experience of accounting and have been omitted from this analysis

Once again, there is evidence to show the importance of a respondent's association with accounting matters. First, considering those scoring between 10 and 8 points in answer to the five questions, it can be seen that respondents with an occupation involving accountancy, or those with significant experience of accounting, had a far higher level of understanding than any other group. Indeed, the differences between those in 'accountancy' and 'other' occupations (28 percentage points) and between those with a significant experience of accounting and those with no such experience (32 percentage points) are striking.

One surprising feature of the analysis in Table 46 is the fact that thorough readers of annual reports do not appear to have had an exceptionally high knowledge of the contents of the various sections of the report. This may well be due to a difficulty in constructing such a variable – that is, due to its reliance on the respondents' own interpretation of what amounts to a thorough reading of any particular section of the report.

Not unexpectedly, those who made their own investment decisions were more familiar with the contents of the annual report than those who obtained assistance with these decisions. Obviously in the latter case, the need to know the location and type of information offered was not so essential.

A more detailed analysis of the respondents' understanding of the contents of particular sections of the annual report gave insights into where the problems lay.

1. **The Chairman's Report**

   The chairman's report was the most widely understood section of the annual report. Over 85% of the thorough readers of annual reports and of those whose occupation or experience involved a considerable degree of accountancy, and 79% of those who made their own investment decisions, could give a reasonable description of the contents of the chairman's report. Approximately two-thirds of those who received help with their investment decisions, or who were less interested readers of the annual report or had no contact with accountancy, gave answers of equal quality. This understanding of the contents of the chairman's report reflects the respondents' obvious familiarity with this statement and re-emphasises its importance to most users of the annual financial report.

2. **The Directors' Report**

   By way of contrast, the contents of the directors' report was not well understood by all groups. Even among those whose occupation was accountancy and related areas, only 19% could give a reasonable description of its content. An identical percentage of those who had a significant experience of accounting gave answers of equal quality. Fewer of those involved in 'other' occupations, and of those who had no experience of accounting, could match these answers (16% and 12% respectively) but the differences were small. Those who made their own investment decisions had a marginally better understanding of the reports than those who had assistance in making their decisions but, again, the percentage of those who could give a reasonable description of the contents of the report (16%) was very low. There was no difference in the level of comprehension of thorough readers and less interested readers of annual reports, but few were able to demonstrate that they were familiar with the directors' report (14% of each group).

3. **The Profit and Loss Account**

There was a marked difference in comprehension (15 percentage points) between thorough and less interested readers in their understanding of the profit and loss account. 38% of thorough readers gave a reasonable description of the statement's content. (This was not particularly high when it is remembered that one of the criteria for selecting thorough readers was their intensive level of reading of the profit and loss account. On the other hand, however, only 14% of thorough readers failed to describe the content of the profit and loss account, compared to 30% of less interested readers.)

Those respondents who made their own investment decisions indicated a slightly better understanding of the profit and loss account than those who required assistance with these decisions. Their comprehension was not, however, particularly high, and only 29% gave a reasonable description of the statement. Much higher levels of understanding were noted among those whose occupation or experience involved a significant degree of accounting. 50% and 55%, respectively, of these groups provided reasonable descriptions of the contents of the profit and loss account. Far fewer of those in 'other' occupations (21%), and those with no experience of accounting (17%), described the statement equally well. Indeed, only 10% of the two former groups failed to give even a vague description, compared with 30% of the two latter groups.

4. **The Balance Sheet**

The balance sheet was best understood by the 'accounting' respondents. 67% of those with significant experience of accounting (compared to 26% of those with none) and 65% of those with an accounting-based occupation (compared to 33% of those in 'other' occupations) gave a reasonable description of balance sheet content. Many of the 'non-accountants' were totally ignorant about the balance sheet. No fewer than 53% of those with no experience of accounting, and 49% of those in 'other' occupations, failed to give even the most elementary description of such a statement. It would appear, therefore, that the 'non-accounting' respondents experienced major difficulties in interpreting the annual financial report concerning the construction and presentation of the balance sheet and, to a slightly lesser extent, the profit and loss account. (This will be investigated further in the next section.)

Other groupings also produced a similar lack of understanding of the contents of the balance sheet. Only about one third of both the less interested reader group and that containing respondents who received assistance with their investment decisions gave reasonable descriptions. More of the thorough readers of annual reports (50%) and those making their own investment decisions (40%) indicated similar answers although, again, their level of understanding was considerably below that of those with an accountancy background. (24% of thorough readers failed to give even an elementary account of the balance sheet despite claiming that they read it thoroughly.)

5.   **The Auditor's Report**

'Accounting' respondents also revealed slightly more knowledge about the auditor's report than other respondents. 55% of those with significant accounting experience, and 48% of those in an occupation connected with accountancy, had a reasonable understanding of it – percentages which were, respectively, 19 and 8 percentage points higher than those with no accounting experience or those in 'other' occupations. 41% of those with no accounting experience had no knowledge whatsoever of the contents of the audit report and, even 29% of those with significant experience of accounting revealed the same lack of understanding. Their level of ignorance was high enough to confirm the suspicion mentioned earlier in Chapter 6 that even those with such experience tend to ignore the auditor's report.

45% of respondents making their own investment decisions were able to specify the type of information found in the auditor's report – (compared with only 32% of those who received assistance with their own investment decisions) and, while this figure is lower than those for either of the groups with a considerable background in accounting, it is reassuring to discover that a considerable proportion of this group was aware of the nature of the report, and presumably was able to take account of the information therein. It should, however, be noted that 37% of this group had no understanding of the auditor's report whatsoever.

6.   **Summary**

The evidence suggests that, in general, those respondents with a considerable accountancy content in their training or occupation, and those with a substantial interest in the annual report (that is, those who made their own investment decisions and those who read the report thoroughly) had a greater knowledge of the contents of various sections of the annual report than their counterparts who either had no knowledge of accounting, were less interested in reading the annual report, or received assistance in making their investment decisions.

All groups analysed had a better understanding of the chairman's report than any other section of the annual report – the most poorly understood section being the directors' report. The profit and loss account, balance sheet and auditor's report were all understood better by those respondents with experience of accounting and related matters than those who had no knowledge of the subject. Indeed, the differences in understanding of the profit and loss account and balance sheet between these respondents were of such a magnitude as to suggest that these vital quantitative sections of the annual report may only be properly understood by private shareholders with some form of training in accountancy. This may be due, in part, to the terminology used by the reporting accountant in the profit and loss account and balance sheet. The next section therefore examines some of the accounting terms commonly found in the profit and loss account and balance sheet, and gives a clue to the difficulties faced by non-accountants in understanding the quantitative sections of financial reports.

Understanding of Accounting Terminology

The questions testing respondents' understanding of accounting terminology examined a vital part of the communication process. For communication to take place between boards of directors and owners of companies, it is essential that the terms used in financial reports are understandable to their recipients. Each of the six terms which were used to test respondents' comprehension of accounting terminology (profit; depreciation; current assets; equity capital; reserves; and accrued charges) were drawn from the financial statements of XYZ and, consequently, should not have been unfamiliar to those who read the company's annual report.

It was noted earlier (in Chapters 4 and 5) that respondents' understanding of accounting terminology was not particularly good. The present analysis, which again divides respondents' scores into three groups, and which is shown in Table 47, reveals a more serious problem than the general lack of understanding shown earlier. (With one marginal exception, the results presented in Table 47 were significant at the 1% level.)

TABLE 47
Understanding of Accounting Terminology

BACKGROUND VARIABLE		UNDERSTANDING SCORE				
		12,11,10,9	8,7,6,5	4,3,2,1,0	Total	Significance
	n	%	%	%	%	
Occupation						
Accounting, investment, etc.	48	52	44	4	100	
Non-financial management	65	11	48	41	100	
Housewives	34	—	21	79	100	
Others	154	5	41	54	100	0.00
*Accounting Experience**						
Significant	42	53	33	14	100	
Little	72	17	50	33	100	
None	178	4	38	58	100	0.00
Reading of Annual Report						
Thorough readers	72	25	51	24	100	
Less interested readers	229	10	37	53	100	0.00
Investment Decision Making						
Decisions made entirely on own	209	16	43	41	100	
Decisions made with help from an expert	92	8	35	57	100	0.02

* 9 respondents failed to disclose their experience of accounting and have been omitted from this analysis

The outstanding feature of the analysis is the contrast between the high level of understanding revealed by respondents with an association with accounting matters and the extremely low level of comprehension shown by those without any training in the subject.

Considering, first, those respondents whose understanding score ranged from 9 to 12 points, it can be seen that no fewer than 52% of those whose occupation involved an association with accounting were in the top scoring group, compared to an almost insignificant 5% of 'other' occupations – a material difference of 47 percentage points. A similar result was obtained by analysing the scores by accounting experience. 53% of respondents with a significant experience of accounting were in the top group, whereas only 4% of those with no experience achieved a similar score – a substantial difference of 49 percentage points.

At the other end of the comprehension scale (0 to 4 points), only 4% of those whose occupation concerned accounting and 14% of those with a significant experience of the subject were to be found. In contrast to this, no fewer than 54% of those in 'other' occupations, and 58% of those with no experience of accounting, achieved comparably low understanding scores.

When considering the so-called 'interest' variables, it was found that respondents who read the annual report thoroughly, and respondents who made investment decisions without help, had a better comprehension of accounting terminology than less interested readers or those who were assisted by experts in making their investment decisions, respectively. The understanding of the two former groups, however, was much lower than the accounting occupation and experience groups. Indeed, even among those who made their own investment decisions, no fewer than 41% were in the lowest scoring group. This indicates the possibility that many of these respondents may be making decisions based on incorrect assumptions about the meaning of some of the accounting information reported to them.

To understand where respondents had particular difficulty in this area, it was essential to consider each term tested. This is discussed below, beginning with two terms used primarily in the profit and loss account, the other four being found in the balance sheet.

1. **Profit**

   Profit was the term which made most sense to the 'non-accounting' respondents. Being a word in everyday use, this was not unexpected. It could also be an explanation for so many respondents with some form of training in accountancy failing to give a reasonably precise definition of the term. 43% of those with a significant experience in accounting, and 58% of those whose occupation involved the subject, gave reasonable explanations; these figures being 14 and 25 percentage points higher than those achieved by respondents with no experience of accountancy or in 'other' occupations, respectively.

The differences in understanding among the annual report reading and investment decision making groups were minimal. About one third of each group gave a reasonable definition of profit.

2. **Depreciation**

Depreciation is also a word in common usage and, once again, this would appear to have led to a narrowing of the understanding gap between the various groups – possibly also due in part to those respondents with some contact with accounting being rather casual in their defining of the term.

Only 29% of respondents with significant experience of accounting gave a reasonable definition of depreciation, compared with 28% of those with no experience. At the other end of the understanding continuum, however, only 7% of the former group failed to give even a vague description of the term, in contrast to 20% of the latter group. These results were confirmed by considering the occupation variable. 33% of those in accountancy-based occupations gave reasonable definitions compared to 25% of those in 'other' employments. As before, the main difference between the groups lay with respondents who could give no definition or explanation. 4% of those in accountancy-based occupations failed to give such an explanation, compared to 22% of those in 'other' occupations. Little difference was noted in the comprehension of the annual report reading and investment decision making groups. Approximately one quarter of each group gave a reasonable definition of depreciation.

3. **Equity Capital**

Thorough readers of annual reports revealed a greater knowledge of the meaning of equity capital than less interested readers. Even so, their understanding of the term was not particularly high – 31%, as opposed to 20% of the latter group, gave a reasonable definition or explanation. Respondents who made their own investment decisions also gave more reasonable answers than those receiving assistance. 25% of the former group gave a reasonable response compared to 15% of the latter.

The biggest differences, however, lay between respondents with an accounting background and those without such training. Reasonable definitions of equity capital were given by 48% of those with accounting experience and 46% of those employed in accounting, investment, banking or financial management. On the other hand, only 16% of respondents with no accounting experience, and 18% of those in 'other' employment, gave answers of equal quality. Indeed, 54% and 49%,

105

respectively, of these two latter groups failed to reveal any comprehension of the term.

4. **Current Assets**

Non-accounting respondents also revealed a significant lack of understanding of the term, current assets. Only 16% of those with no experience of the subject, and 18% of those in 'other' occupations, could give reasonable descriptions of it – figures which were 32 and 28 percentage points, respectively, lower than for respondents who had a significant experience of accounting and for those who held accounting-based jobs. Indeed, as many as 67% of those with no experience of accounting failed to give any indication of understanding the meaning of the term. 62% of those in 'other' employments revealed a similar lack of comprehension.

The differences in respondents' comprehension were not so obvious when analysed in terms of the 'interest' variables. 32% of those who read annual reports thoroughly revealed a reasonable level of understanding of current assets compared to 14% of less interested readers. An even smaller difference (8 percentage points) existed between the two investment decision making groups. In this case, the most knowledgeable respondents were, again, those who made their own decisions (21% giving reasonable definitions of the term).

5. **Reserves**

The differences among all groups widened when respondents were asked to define the term, reserves. 38% of those making their own investment decisions could give a reasonable definition, compared with 23% of those receiving assistance with their decisions. More than half (51%) of thorough readers of annual reports provided an equally good definition, compared with 28% of less interested readers. The greatest differences, however, were once again detected by the 'accounting' variables.

69% of respondents with a significant experience of accounting gave reasonable definitions of reserves, whereas only 26% of those with no experience could give an equally good answer – a major difference of some 43 percentage points. An even greater difference of 54 percentage points lay between those employed in accountancy, investment, banking or financial management (75% of whom gave reasonable definitions) and those in 'other' occupations.

As with profit and depreciation, reserve is a term in common usage but in the balance sheet it is used in a rather specialised way. The fact

106

that so many non-accounting respondents gave a completely erroneous description of it (54% both of those who had no experience of accountancy and of those employed in 'other' occupations) was due mainly to its every-day use to denote a sort of 'piggy-bank'. This answer was the most common response of the 'non-accounting' respondents – 38% appeared to hold the view that reserves measured actual cash. A misunderstanding of this nature indicates that the essential structure of the balance sheet identity (assets = net worth + liabilities) is almost certainly unknown to these respondents.

6. **Accrued Charges**

Accrued charges is essentially an accounting term without a common usage outwith the financial world. If terms such as these are to be used in communications to the layman then it would seem imperative that they should be explicitly and simply defined. That this is not usually the case is revealed in the finding that 79% of respondents with a significant degree of accountancy experience, and 77% of those in accounting-related employment, adequately defined the term, whereas this was achieved by only 20% of those with no experience of accounting, and by 23% of those in 'other' employments. The differences of 59 percentage points in the experience variable, and 54 percentage points in the occupation variable, are so large as to underline the present rather casual attitude on the part of reporting accountants towards defining terms in financial reports. Further evidence of this point is given by the finding that 73% of respondents with no experience of accounting, and 71% of those in 'other' occupations, gave either no answer or an incorrect answer. 51% of thorough readers of annual reports defined accrued charges reasonably, as opposed to 28% of less interested readers. Another indication that interest as well as training may be related to the communication problem is given in the evidence that 40% of respondents making their own investment decisions understood· the meaning of accrued charges, compared with only 19% of those who received some assistance in this respect. Even among the former group, however, many of the respondents appear to have guessed at the meaning of the term – 53% failed to give even a vague definition of it.

7. **Summary**

Overall, the dominant feature of this section has been the marked difference between the ability of those with and without an accounting background in understanding the terminology of accounting. The differences were less noticeable in respondents' understanding of the (mainly) profit and loss account terms of profit and depreciation (especially with regard to the latter). Balance sheet terminology, however, revealed wide differences in comprehension between the groups with differing levels of accounting experience. Indeed, the reason for approximately one half of the non-accounting respondents' failure to give even an elementary account of the balance sheet (described in the previous section) may now be clearer. It would therefore seem that reporting accountants, if they wish to communicate to *all* sections of the investing public, must be prepared to define the terminology they use, and perhaps even explain the nature of the financial statements in the annual report.

One factor, however, which mitigates against the accusation that reporting accountants have been lax in considering the needs of the investor lacking training in accounting is the interest of such respondents in the annual report. The evidence here suggests that those who made their own investment decisions were more knowledgeable than those who rely on others. Similarly, those who read the annual report thoroughly revealed greater comprehension than those who paid less attention to the report. It should be noted, however, that the comprehension levels, both of respondents who read the annual report and of those who made their own investment decisions, were always lower than that shown by those with experience of accounting. It would seem that interest in the annual report is not enough.

The next section considers a related problem to terminology – that of valuation, an understanding of which is equally vital for the private shareholder if he is to assess properly the meaning of financial statements.

Understanding of Accounting Valuation Bases

The three questions on the valuation in financial statements of plant and machinery, stock and work-in-progress, and quoted investments were attempts to assess how respondents regarded the information presented to them in the balance sheet. Did they, for example, assume that the balance sheet contained current values or were they aware of the accounting principle of historic cost valuation?

Chapter 4 showed that, while almost three quarters of the respondents appeared to understand that plant and machinery was valued at historic cost, only a minority knew the correct valuation method employed by reporting accountants for inventory and quoted investments.

TABLE 48

Understanding of Accounting Valuation Bases

BACKGROUND VARIABLE		UNDERSTANDING SCORE				
	n	6,5 %	4,3 %	2,1,0 %	Total %	Significance
Occupation						
Accounting, investment, etc.	48	35	44	21	100	
Non-financial management	65	18	37	45	100	
Housewives	34	—	—	100	100	
Others	154	8	29	63	100	0.00
*Accounting Experience**						
Significant	42	33	48	19	100	
Little	72	12	42	46	100	
None	178	10	21	69	100	0.00
Reading of Annual Report						
Thorough readers	72	25	44	31	100	
Less interested readers	229	10	25	65	100	0.00
Investment Decision Making						
Decisions made entirely on own	209	17	32	51	100	
Decisions made with help from an expert	92	6	24	70	100	0.01

* 9 respondents failed to disclose their experience of accounting and have been omitted from this analysis.

Using the same scoring procedure as before, and dividing respondents' scores into three groups as shown in Table 48, it can be seen that again those with an association with accounting revealed the highest level of understanding. 35% of those whose occupation involved accountancy, and 33% of those who had a significant experience of accounting, had a reasonable understanding of the method of valuation of two of the assets concerned and, at least, a vague understanding of the third. Only 8% of those in 'other' occupations, and 10% of those with no experience of accounting, had the same degree of comprehension. Indeed, Table 48 reveals that 63% and 69%, respectively, of the two latter groups obtained scores in the lowest of the three understanding categories, whereas approximately one fifth of those whose occupation or experience involved a considerable degree of accounting had an equally low score. While this analysis provides evidence that accounting experience and understanding of valuation methods are related, it also reveals that a not inconsiderable minority of those who had an accounting background did not understand the valuation methods in use at the present time. (All analyses presented in Table 48 were significant at the 1% level.)

Thorough readers of annual reports and those who made their own investment decisions yet again revealed more understanding than those who did not read the annual report thoroughly and those who relied on others to make their investment decisions. Despite this, however, no fewer than 51% of those who made their investment decisions independently could only achieve an understanding score in the lowest of the three comprehension grades. The fact that 70% of those who sought help from experts achieved a similar score merely confirms their need for advice. Those whose understanding was weakest were obviously correct in seeking assistance but half of those who made their own investment decisions may well have been drawing erroneous conclusions from the data presented to them.

An examination of the respondents' understanding of the valuation of each of the three assets gives an insight into areas where further explanation of the valuation basis in financial statements may be required.

1. **Plant and Machinery**

   Well over one half of almost all groups of respondents used for analytical purposes gave a reasonable description of the method of valuation of plant and machinery. Even 64% of those with no experience in accounting, and 69% of those in 'other' occupations, gave an accurate description. Their understanding, however, was, not unexpectedly, rather overshadowed by that of respondents with a significant experience of accounting (91%), and respondents employed in accountancy-related occupations (88%). While those with no experience of accounting appeared to have had a relatively high degree of comprehension of the valuation method used, it must be noted that no fewer than 34% of this group gave either an incorrect answer or no answer.

   Those respondents making their own investment decisions revealed a higher level of understanding than those who relied on assistance – 74%

as opposed to 62%. Thorough readers of annual reports also exhibited a greater degree of knowledge than less interested readers. In the case of the former group, 85% gave a reasonable description of plant valuation – a figure some 19 percentage points higher than that of the latter group.

The valuation of plant and machinery, therefore, posed problems for some 'non-accounting' respondents but, on the whole, their knowledge of this part of the valuation process was reasonably good.

2. **Stock and Work-in-Progress**
    A majority of respondents with some form of accounting background understood that stock and work-in-progress are usually valued (fundamentally) at historic cost or (more precisely) at the lower of cost or net realisable value. 67% of those with significant accounting experience, and 58% of those in an occupation which involved a knowledge of accountancy, gave the correct answer. Only 27% of those with no experience, and 29% of those in 'other' occupations, could do likewise. Indeed, 70% of those with no experience and 68% of those in 'other' occupations revealed that they had no understanding of the valuation method.

    Looking at the 'interest' variables, it can be seen that thorough readers of annual reports (56%), and respondents who made their own investment decisions (41%), tended to have a reasonable knowledge of stock values compared with respondents who relied on others to assist them with their investment decisions (24%) and less interested readers of annual reports (29%). None of these groups, however, revealed a level of understanding to compare with that of respondents with accounting experience. Indeed, even among those who made their own investment decisions, 55% had no idea of the valuation basis.

3. **Quoted Investments**
    71% of respondents who made their own investment decisions gave an incorrect answer, or no answer, to the question of quoted investment values. Even the finding that slightly more of this group than those who received assistance could give a correct answer (24% as opposed to 13%) cannot disguise the possibility that those who make their own investment decisions are likely to have little knowledge of the true meaning of the figure given in the balance sheet for quoted securities.

    Few respondents who were less interested readers of annual reports gave the correct valuation method (18%). Thorough readers as a group were slightly better but, nevertheless, only 31% understood how quoted

111

investments were valued. Even respondents with a significant experience of accounting, and those with an accountancy-related occupation, did not reveal a great deal of understanding of the valuation method. Only 33% of the former and 40% of the latter groups could give the correct answer. Indeed, no fewer than 55% of the significant accounting experience group, and 50% of those in jobs in accounting, investment, banking or financial management, gave a completely incorrect answer or no answer at all. While these results were better than those achieved by those with no accounting experience (80% of whom were unable to give even a vaguely accurate description) and by those in other occupations (79% of whom had an equally poor understanding), the fact that so few of those with a great deal of accounting experience knew the correct present basis of valuation of quoted investments leads to the conclusion that more should be done to inform investors of the valuation methods used. (Only 16% of those with no experience of accounting and 17% of those in other occupations knew the correct valuation method.)

It should, however, be noted that the survey company, XYZ used the term 'investments at cost' (including unquoted investments) on the face of its balance sheet, and quoted investments were shown in the notes to the accounts as being valued at cost. The valuation of plant and machinery was also clearly shown in the notes and that of stocks in the statement of accounting policies.

4. **Summary**

This analysis reveals once again that respondents with some form of experience of accountancy tended to have an advantage over others in understanding reported accounting information. Even so, those with such experience did not reveal an unduly high level of understanding of the valuation of stocks or quoted investments. Only the valuation of plant and machinery was well understood by most respondents. This asset is one of the few whose valuation basis is frequently shown on detailed balance sheets. The modern practice (used by XYZ) of confining details of cost and depreciation to the notes to the accounts, which evidence has shown (in Chapter 6) are often ignored by many of the responding shareholders, does not appear to have led to any great difficulty in this case. Difficulties did arise, however, with the valuation of inventory and quoted investments. As mentioned earlier, in the annual report of XYZ details of the valuation of these items are given partly in the financial statements and partly in the notes to the accounts or statement of accounting policies. This practice must involve the interested shareholder in a search through the detailed technical statements of the annual report. Therefore, in view of the poor understanding of the valuation of these items, and the misconceptions which could arise concerning the solvency and liquidity of the company, it may well be advisable to state the valuation method clearly and concisely on the face of the balance sheet. If the proposals of the Sandilands Committee on Inflation Accounting[2] are implemented (some of which appeared to be erroneously anticipated by the respondents), there may well remain a case for *emphasising* the valuation method to ensure that readers of the annual report have an accurate comprehension of the meaning of the figures given in the financial statements.

Understanding of Financial Ratios

The final test of respondents' understanding concerned financial ratios, three of which were examined. Each is used frequently in the financial press as well as in certain annual reports. The results of the analysis of interviewees' responses are summarised in Table 49.

Table 49, which shows the respondents' scores divided into three groups, reveals that few of the 'non-accounting' respondents understood the meaning of the three ratios. (The analyses were all significant at the 1% level). Only 8% of those with no accounting experience, and 7% of those in 'other' occupations, gave reasonable explanations of two of the ratios and, at least, a vague interpretation of the third. On the other hand, 36% of those with significant experience of accounting, and 33% of those in an occupation related to accounting, gave answers of this quality.

Turning to the 'interest' variables shown in Table 49, a significant difference was observed between the understanding of thorough and less interested readers of annual reports. Respondents who made their own investment decisions also knew more about the financial ratios than those who needed help in making these decisions. Indeed, 81% of this latter group scored, at best, only 2 out of a possible 6 points, although it should be noted that one half of those making their own decisions also achieved this score.

1. **Price-earnings Ratio**

   The price-earnings ratio question did not seek to ascertain whether respondents knew the detailed implications of the ratio, or the differing

TABLE 49
Understanding of Financial Ratios

BACKGROUND VARIABLE		UNDERSTANDING SCORE				
	n	6,5 %	4,3 %	2,1,0 %	Total %	Significance
Occupation						
Accounting, investment, etc.	48	33	38	29	100	
Non-financial management	65	12	36	52	100	
Housewives	34	—	12	88	100	
Others	154	7	26	67	100	0.00
*Accounting Experience**						
Significant	42	36	36	28	100	
Little	72	6	26	68	100	
None	178	8	28	64	100	0.00
Reading of Annual Report						
Thorough readers	72	18	46	36	100	
Less interested readers	229	9	23	68	100	0.00
Investment Decision Making						
Decisions made entirely on own	209	15	34	51	100	
Decisions made with help from an expert	92	4	15	81	100	0.00

* 9 respondents failed to disclose their experience of accounting and have been omitted from this analysis.

methods of calculating earnings per share, but was a guide as to whether they knew what the ratio was intended to measure. Not unexpectedly, respondents with some background of accounting answered better than others. 40% of those involved in accountancy, investment, banking or financial management knew the meaning of the ratio, compared with only 10% in 'other' occupations. Similarly, 33% of those with significant accounting experience, as opposed to 12% of those with no experience, also had a good comprehension of it. No fewer than 74% of those with no experience of accounting, and 76% of those in 'other' occupations, did not even have a vague idea of the ratio.

65% of respondents making their own investment decisions were similarly ignorant. Only 20% of this group accurately defined the ratio, yet this was significantly higher than the mere 3% of respondents who relied on assistance with their investment decisions. Thorough readers of annual reports were slightly better in their understanding – 26% had a good knowledge of the ratio – a figure some 15 percentage points higher than that for less interested readers.

2. **Dividend Yield**

More respondents had at least a vague idea of how to define the dividend yield ratio than was the case with the price-earnings ratio. But, few respondents showed that they really understood its true meaning. Those with some background of accounting revealed the highest degree of knowledge but this was not particularly high. Only 29% of those with a significant accounting experience, and 23% of those employed in accountancy-related occupations, gave the correct calculation method. Those without such a background had an even poorer understanding of the ratio. 11% of those with no accounting experience, and 12% of those in 'other' occupations appeared to be able to calculate a dividend yield.

Approximately one fifth of both the thorough readers of annual reports and those who made their own investment decisions appeared to understand the meaning of the ratio. While this was considerably higher than the comprehension of less interested readers, and of those who relied on assistance in making their decisions, it does confirm that this ratio, which is so often quoted, was really only properly understood by relatively few of the responding shareholders.

3. **Dividend Cover**

The final ratio, dividend cover, was the most widely understood of the three covered in this study with, once again, respondents with an accounting background revealing the highest level of comprehension of all those interviewed. 67% of those with significant experience of accounting, and 58% of those with an accountancy-related occupation, knew the meaning of the ratio. In comparison with this, only 33% of those with no accounting experience, and 31% of those in 'other' occupations, also revealed a similar degree of understanding.

A majority (54%) of the thorough readers of annual reports, and 42% of respondents who made their own investment decisions, gave a correct interpretation of dividend cover but, while these levels of comprehension were much higher than those of respondents who were less interested readers of annual reports or for those who received assist-

115

ance in choosing their investments, they were lower than that of the group with significant accounting experience.

4. **Summary**

Once again, accounting experience proved to be more important than the 'interest' variables in understanding accounting information. While respondents with such experience were not outstanding in their understanding of the three ratios tested, they had a much higher degree of comprehension than other groups. The lack of knowledge of the 'non-accounting' respondents leads to the conclusion that, while many of these respondents may read the financial press, few of them would apparently understand the subtleties of references to these key ratios, nor would many of them be able to use the ratios tested for their own benefit.

Overall Summary and Conclusions

The most important finding in this chapter is the discovery that a great many private shareholders who did not have any experience of accounting appeared to be at an extreme disadvantage in the interpretation of accounting information compared to others who had such a background. This difficulty was recognised in the report of the Trueblood Committee:

'Accounting information should be presented so that it can be understood by reasonably well-informed, as well as by sophisticated, users. In effect, presenting information understandable only to sophisticated users establishes a bias. Investors with means to do their own research already have an advantage over others. The form and content of the annual report should not add to this advantage'.[3]

And in *The Corporate Report:*

'Understandability calls for the provision, in the clearest possible form, of all the information which the reasonably instructed reader can made use of and the parallel presentation of the main features for the less sophisticated'.[4]

Despite these sentiments, however, the evidence here has shown that private shareholders with a non-accounting background had difficulty in describing the nature of the profit and loss account and balance sheet. Striking differences in understanding these two statements (especially the balance sheet) emerged between those respondents who had training in accounting and those who had none. Evidence was also presented in the chapter that this may be due to two major reasons:

(1) Poor communication between the reporting accountant and the private shareholder; and

(2) lack of interest on the part of the latter person.

Considering, first, the problem of communication, the evidence revealed that terminology used in the balance sheet appeared to be generally too difficult for the 'non-accounting' respondent to comprehend. Some of the terms used are now in everyday usage (for example, reserve) but are used in a specialised and, therefore, abnormal way by the reporting accountant. Other terms such as current assets, equity capital and accrued charges are technical terms which are seldom explained to the layman. If a non-accountant considers reserves to be equivalent to cash balances, it is obvious that he cannot understand the basic nature of the balance sheet, and is likely to be confused by *his* notion of assets appearing on both sides of the balance sheet. It would therefore seem that there is a strong case for technical terms, and terms in common usage which the accountant employs in a specialised way, to be explained to the user of accounting information, either by means of a glossary or on the face of the financial statements. A simple explanation of the balance sheet identity may also be necessary.

Contributing to the layman's confusion is the problem of his determining the nature of accounting valuation practices. Many of the 'non-accounting' respondents (and an unduly large proportion of those with training in accounting) failed to realise that stock and work-in-progress, and quoted investments are traditionally shown at cost (though, of course, net realisable value will be used if it is less than cost). Many appeared to believe that a current value was placed on these assets. For example, 40% and 50% of those with no experience of accounting believed that stocks and quoted investments, respectively, were valued at current cost. The corresponding figures for those with significant experience of accounting were 21% and 52%, showing clearly the general confusion over the valuation of quoted investments.

While many companies do give information on valuation in the annual report, it would seem that a case should be made for valuation practices to be made explicit on the face of the balance sheet rather than be hidden in the notes to accounts (which were not so widely read), as often happens at present. If current value proposals are adopted by the accountancy profession, clarification of the basis of valuation will still be required.

The solution does not, of course, lie entirely with the providers of accounting information. The private shareholder, too, must accept part of the blame for this apparent breakdown in communication. In the evidence presented in this chapter, it is relatively obvious that respondents who took the trouble to read annual reports thoroughly, and those who made their own investment decisions and were presumably more interested in financial reports, tended to have a better understanding of accounting information and practices than

117

those who were less interested readers of the annual report or who relied upon assistance to make their investment decisions. In virtually every test of comprehension given to the respondents, however, the investor with accounting training revealed a greater degree of understanding than either the thorough reader or the independent investment decision maker, indicating that interest alone is insufficient to ensure reasonable comprehension.

A further point is that in Table 9 it was shown that most of the 'accounting' respondents made their own investment decisions and, in Table 40, it was also shown that a higher proportion of respondents with a significant degree of training in accountancy than any other group in the accountancy experience variable were thorough readers of annual reports. It would seem, therefore, that the ability to make investment decisions independently and to read the annual report thoroughly may, to a certain extent, be *dependent* on a good understanding of accounting.

Obviously a major problem faces the accountancy profession if it intends to fulfil its objective of stewardship more completely by closing the communication gap between reporting accountants and private shareholders whose knowledge of accountancy is almost non-existent and who are likely to receive approximately 90% of the reports issued by the typical quoted company. The respondents' own solutions to this problem are presented in the next chapter, together with the researchers' own ideas on the matter.

REFERENCES

[1] T. A. Lee and D. P. Tweedie, 'Accounting Information: An Investigation of Private Shareholder Understanding', *Accounting and Business Research*, Winter 1975, pp 8-10.
[2] *Inflation Accounting*, HMSO, 1975.
[3] *Objectives of Financial Statements*, AICPA, 1973, p 60.
[4] *The Corporate Report*, ASSC, 1975, p 29.

CHAPTER 10

Improving the Annual Report

Perceived Interpretive Ability

Before making suggestions for improving the annual report, it is imperative that its uses are fully understood. The Scope and Aims Working Party of the Accounting Standards Committee has stated its views on the information needs of various financial report users[1] and, so far as the equity investor was concerned, many of these needs have been confirmed in this study by respondents who considered data relating to profit, future prospects and dividends to be important to them (see Chapters 6 and 7).

Evidence from the previous pilot study, however, gave an indication that the respondents concerned may have been unable to obtain information which would be useful to them – in particular data of an interpretive nature which, without some knowledge of the meaning of financial statements, cannot be read directly from the annual report. It was therefore decided in the main study to obtain respondents' perceptions of their ability to judge a company's performance and financial stability. In this way, it was hoped that an assessment could be made of their ability to cope with interpretive data from the annual report.

Respondents were asked initially to state whether they believed they could assess five financial aspects of a company's operations, all of which were included in *The Corporate Report's* list of equity investor needs. These related to profitability, potential bankruptcy, capacity to survive, managerial efficiency, and investment policy. The responses to the questions concerned are shown in Table 50.

While few respondents were prepared to state that they could not assess any aspect of a company's performance and financial stability, many appeared to be unsure of their ability to do so. The table shows that profitability was felt by the group as a whole to be the easiest feature to assess – possibly because most of those concerned may have been interpreting profitability simply in terms of profit or sales figures taken directly from the profit and loss account. Only 6% mentioned the possibility of measuring profit in relation to capital employed.

TABLE 50

Survey Respondents' Opinions on Their Ability to Assess a Company's
Performance and Financial Stability

LEVEL OF ASSESSMENT	ASSESSABLE CHARACTERISTICS				
	Profit-ability	Potential bankpruptcy	Capacity to survive	Managerial efficiency	Invest-ment policy
	%	%	%	%	%
Able to assess the factor	42	32	33	25	28
Unable to assess the factor	11	13	14	14	16
Uncertain whether or not able to assess the factor	47	55	53	61	56
	100	100	100	100	100

One third of the respondents believed that they could assess potential bankruptcy or capacity to survive, but only about half of these shareholders appeared to look at the balance sheet (mainly for data about creditors and borrowings) for information on these subjects. Others tended to rely on the profit and loss account and information from company chairmen or the financial press to guide them in this respect. The respondents who stated that they were able to judge investment policy also tended to rely on others to assess this feature of corporate behaviour for them – usually in the form of company chairmen. The profit and loss account, however, appeared to be used by respondents for assessing managerial efficiency. Indeed, three fifths of those who stated that they could judge managerial efficiency (15% of the total respondents), simply equated managerial efficiency with profit.

Not surprisingly, respondents with an accounting background, and those who had a higher than average understanding of reporting practice, were more confident of their ability to judge a company's performance and financial stability than those with no accounting experience and those whose understanding of the reporting process was lower than average. Additionally, the two latter groups were more definite than the former in their view that they could not assess the five company features on which they were questioned.

Respondents' Views on Improving the Annual Report

Given that a majority of respondents appeared to be either uncertain of their ability to assess a company's performance or financial stability or were convinced that they did not have sufficient skill to do so, it could be argued that they felt the existing form of annual report was not suitable to their needs or did not take sufficient cognizance of their relatively low level of financial knowledge. Consequently, the respondents were asked a series of questions designed to discover their views on means by which the annual report could be made more meaningful to them.

The first question asked whether the financial information given in the present type of annual report was sufficient for the needs of shareholders. From this it appears that a majority (72%) opposed *The Corporate Report's* suggestions for additional financial statements, and stated that the information given at present was sufficient (only 22% held the opposing viewpoint). This was confirmed by replies to the second question which sought to discover opinions on any further information which respondents felt should be disclosed. 53% either indicated that no additional information was necessary or gave no answer to the question (see Table 51).

TABLE 51
*Survey Respondents' Views on Additional Information Which Should be Shown in Annual Reports**

	%
Increased disclosure of existing information	15
Price level adjusted accounts	5
Current cost/value accounts	4
Trading account items – more details of costs and revenues	4
Summaries of accounts, simpler language in accounts	3
More detailed information on company's divisions/subsidiaries	3
Other answers	22

* 160 respondents (53% of 301) either indicated no additional information was necessary or gave no answer; 14 respondents (5% of 401) gave multiple answers.

121

The remaining respondents gave a variety of answers, the most common being that more details should be given about items already mentioned in the annual report. For example, only 8 % explicitly stated that financial statements adjusted for the effects of inflation should be shown in the annual report.

This lack of enthusiasm for additional data could well have been caused by the respondents' apparent lack of understanding of the annual report. Certainly, their replies to a question asking whether there was anything in particular in the annual report which they did not fully understand seemed to confirm this supposition. These are summarised in Table 52.

TABLE 52

Aspects of the Annual Report Which Survey Respondents' Considered They Did Not Fully Understand*

	%
Nothing, the annual report is perfectly understandable	28
No answer/don't know	24
Terminology; technicalities	14
Everything; most of the annual report is incomprehensible	13
Balance sheet	10
Profit and loss account	3
Other answers	16

* 12 respondents (4 % of 301) gave multiple answers.

28 % of respondents felt that the annual report was perfectly understandable. A further 24 % could not or did not answer the question, but the remainder tended to support earlier conclusions concerning their lack of knowledge of accounting information. 13 % declared that most if not all of the annual report was incomprehensible to them, while others were more specific and mentioned the balance sheet (10 %) or the terminology used in the report (14 %).

The terminology and complexity of the financial statements clearly appeared to worry respondents for, on being asked what measures they felt were necessary to improve their use and understanding of annual reports, a majority (53 %) opted for a simplified version of the present report (see Table 53).

TABLE 53
Improvements in Financial Reporting*

	%
Simpler Reports	
Respondents' suggestions that reports should be less technical; in layman's language; summarised; or augmented by a simple version	53
Improvement of Shareholder Knowledge	
Respondents' suggestions that self education or courses in accounting were required	13
Changes to Existing System	
Need for some form of inflation accounting	3
Other Views	

* 45 respondents (15% of 301) either stated that they did not know what changes were received or gave no answer to the question. 3 respondents (1% of 301) gave multiple answers.

Appendix 39, which shows the full range of respondents' answers in this connection, reveals that one third believed that the language used at present in financial statements was too technical in nature, and felt that they should be presented in terms comprehensible to the layman.

Further evidence of respondents' views that the present form of annual report may not be suitable for their needs was given by the answers of 20% of them who stated that summarised versions or simple explanations of the key features of the annual report would help to increase their understanding and use of financial information supplied by companies. A few other respondents believed that the answer lay in education in accounting (and suggested that courses should be given to increase shareholder understanding) or in the individual shareholder making his own efforts to increase his knowledge of the subject.

It was interesting to note that the non-accounting respondents were the most enthusiastic about simplified reports. 58% of those with no accounting experience believed that this would be of assistance to them, compared with only 33% of those with significant accounting experience (findings which were significant at the 2% level). Evidence that those who did not understand accounting terminology would prefer a simplified report was also given by the finding that 65% of those with a lower than average understanding of accounting information, compared with 38% of those with a higher than

123

average level of understanding, believed that some form of simplification would be beneficial to their use and understanding of the annual report (findings which were significant at the 2% level).

Respondents who received assistance with their investment decisions were, however, those who were most enthusiastic about simplified reports. No fewer than 69% of this group, in comparison with 46% of those who made their own investment decisions (the differences between these groups were significant at the 1% level), were in favour of simplification. This evidence provides a clue that a reason for many of the responding shareholders using expert advice may have been their inability to comprehend the annual report. In this connection, it is interesting to observe that the annual report reading group which appeared to support the idea of simplification most strongly was that containing those respondents who did not read any section of the annual report – 71% of this group said that such a change would improve their use and understanding of the report. Further evidence that some respondents may have felt excluded from the dissemination of financial information about companies was given in the finding that the group most in favour of accounting education for shareholders was that containing those respondents who sought assistance with their investment decisions.

Summary

The evidence of this chapter seems to indicate that few respondents were confident of their ability to use the present form of annual report to interpret corporate performance and financial stability. While *The Corporate Report* may list needs which are truly vital to shareholder understanding of a company's financial state, at present very few of the private shareholders surveyed would appear to be able to extract relevant information from the report, mainly because of the terminology used in the report and the complexity of the financial statements.

Respondents did not appear to favour the presentation of further information in the annual report, and were more concerned with the provision of existing information in a simplified form which was comprehensible to them. This approach was especially popular with the non-accountants and those whose understanding of accounting information was lower than the average for the group as a whole. It would seem from this evidence that, so far as the private shareholder in general is concerned, *The Corporate Report's* proposals for the inclusion of additional information in the annual financial report should be made secondary to the need to ensure that data given at present are understandable to the non-accountant.

The Corporate Report recognises this problem when it calls for:

'the parallel presentation of the main features for the use of the less sophisticated'.[2]

It would seem, however, that this point should be emphasised and attention paid to the type of simplified report which would be suitable for these shareholders.[3]

The Corporate Report is a stimulating attempt to find a more balanced package of financial information to present to those interested in a company's activities. Nevertheless, as one writer has stated:

'. . . while we contemplate the possible revolution in the company's accountability, it is imperative that the accountant's method of communicating quantitative and qualitative information should evolve, so that the full benefits of change may be enjoyed by the wider audience the proposed corporate report is intended to reach'.[4]

REFERENCES

[1] *The Corporate Report*, ASSC, 1975, p 20.
[2] *Ibid*, p 29.
[3] Research on this topic is at present being conducted by the authors at the Universities of Edinburgh and Liverpool.
[4] D. P. Tweedie, 'The Corporate Report: Evolution or Revolution?', *The Accountant's Magazine*, October 1975, p 346.

CHAPTER 11

Summary, Conclusions and Recommendations

Summary

Until comparatively recently, the objectives of financial reports have received scant attention from accountants. Lately, however, there has been agreement on the need to specify such objectives prior to formulating particular measurement and valuation procedures for reporting purposes.[1] *The Corporate Report*[2] is an outstanding example of this change in emphasis, identifying several report user groups with specific information needs. Nevertheless, it is no more than a first step in a long process towards financial reporting improvements. It contains recommendations which, in effect, are no more than hypotheses which will require thorough testing.[3]

The testing stage is now under way. For example, at the University of Manchester, research is being undertaken into the framework of financial reporting practice. Part of this work has been concerned with a determination of reporting objectives, and evidence has been forthcoming that stewardship and investment decisions are the primary matters with which financial reports should be concerned.[4] It confirms part of *The Corporate Report's* general conclusions that each identifiable user group may have several needs for accounting information. This has been reinforced by other studies which have cast doubts on the ability of general purpose financial statements to meet the needs of diverse user groups.[5]

The research on which this monograph is based was designed to investigate these particular reporting problems in greater depth than hitherto. In particular, it examined the information needs of one major user group (equity investors) and, more specifically, a sub-section of this group (private shareholders). The intention was to study certain substantial problems facing a user group which, typically, holds the largest number of individual share-holdings in any company without necessarily owning a majority of its shares.

Due to the existing corporate legal provisions, private shareholders are presumably expected to cope with the highly technical and complex financial reports which they receive from companies. It also appears reasonable to assume that many of these shareholders are interested in making investment decisions and are concerned with the 'safety' of their investments once the decisions have been made. The small size of their individual holdings, relative to those of the institutional shareholder, should not be taken as indicative of lack of interest or concern in these matters. The problem is one of ensuring that they are provided with financial information which is adequate to their particular needs. This study was therefore concerned with examining private shareholders' problems in using and understanding the existing form of financial information which, at present, appears to be directed more to the needs of the sophisticated user (such as the financial analyst) rather than to those of the unsophisticated layman. It was also concerned with ascertaining whether or not the private shareholder was capable of reasonably assessing corporate financial progress and position, as well as managerial stewardship. For, if he cannot understand the financial reports he receives, the private shareholder is not only prevented from making rational investment decisions, but also has little idea of whether or not his investment is being soundly managed.

Clearly, the needs of the private shareholder, as recognised in *The Corporate Report*[6], are not being met if he is in the position of being unable to understand the information presented to him. It was felt to be necessary, therefore, first, to attempt to support many of the *Report*'s conclusions with reliable research-based evidence and, secondly, to identify areas where the communication process between a company and its private shareholder was inadequate. In this way, it was hoped to be able to discover possible means of bridging any identifiable communications gap in order to aid the reporting accountant in fulfilling his role of provider of information.

The private shareholders interviewed in the study were predominantly male, held relatively few shares in the survey company, and had little or no experience of accounting and related matters. Most of them made their own investment decisions without assistance from experts. Evidence from the previous pilot study, and from non-respondents to this study, indicates that this profile may well be typical of the private shareholder in the U.K.

Approximately three out of every four respondents believed that they understood the accounting information contained in the annual report.

Therefore, the initial impression was of the reporting accountant largely succeeding in communicating to these particular private shareholders. Further investigation, however, revealed that perception and reality were far removed from one another. Tests of actual understanding in five key reporting areas provided evidence that respondents' comprehension of financial reporting practice was consistently low, with the nature of financial statements being best understood and financial ratios being least understood by the group as a whole.

A general index of understanding was constructed from respondents' responses, and this revealed that those who believed they did not understand accounting information had a low level of comprehension relative to the interview group as a whole; while those who claimed they did understand tended to have a higher level of comprehension (again relative to the group as a whole). The latter finding was especially true of respondents who stated they understood accounting information and found it relevant to their investment decisions. This last point emphasises the almost self-evident observation that the annual report, if it is to succeed as a communications link between company management and shareholders, must be relevant to the needs of the latter group. It must not only be understood but also be read thoroughly by all concerned. Unfortunately, the interview findings indicate that most of the responding shareholders tended to skim through the annual report, with thorough attention usually being given mainly to the chairman's report. Only a small minority, for example, read thoroughly both the profit and loss account and balance sheet.

On the basis of their reading of the annual report and, in particular, their attention to its financial statements, respondents were divided into two reading groups – thorough readers and less interested readers. It was felt that those respondents who did not read the annual report thoroughly might well look elsewhere for financial information relevant to their needs. This, however, was not the case. Those who read the annual report thoroughly were more inclined than less interested readers to use other sources of financial information thoroughly. In other words, thorough readers of annual reports tended to be the thorough readers of other information sources; and less interested readers of annual reports tended to be the less interested readers of other information sources. There therefore appeared to be two distinct types of private shareholders in this study – those who made maximum possible use of all available sources of information, and those who made little or no use of the same.

Financial press reports were considered by respondents to be the most important source of information other than the annual report. Indeed, they indicated that the former were of more influence on their investment decisions than any individual section of the latter. Some respondents used financial press reports to obtain information which is not legally required to be disclosed in the annual report – for example, general information relating to a company's activities, its labour problems, and the geographical spread of its operations. (It is interesting to note that *The Corporate Report* recommendations, if implemented, would supply some of this information.[7]) Generally, however, the data considered most important by respondents are to be obtained from the annual report (that is, profits, chairmen's views on future prospects, and dividends).

One question came to light in the analysis, and required some explanation. If the annual report appeared to be capable of meeting some of the information needs of the respondents, why did relatively few of them read it thoroughly? The evidence pointed conclusively to the fact that those who did not read it thoroughly were unable to do so because of a lack of understanding of reporting matters. Additionally, it transpired that respondents with accounting experience had a much higher understanding than those who lacked such a background. Consequently, the former group were found to read the annual report more thoroughly than the latter group. It therefore appeared that a knowledge of accounting may well be essential if the annual report is to be read thoroughly and understood properly.

The main comprehension difficulties faced by the 'non-accounting' respondents appeared to concern the valuation procedures and accounting terminology used in the annual report, and financial ratios. While they had a reasonable impression of plant valuations, those applied to quoted investments and stocks and work in progress were virtually unknown to them. Accounting terms used mainly within the profit and loss account context were reasonably well understood, but balance sheet terminology remained a mystery to many of these shareholders. As a result, it is extremely unlikely that they could possibly come to any reasoned conclusions regarding the financial progress or position of a company and, indeed, those respondents without an accounting experience were obviously lacking in confidence as to their ability to make judgments of these matters. It is therefore doubtful whether changes to the measurement and valuation procedures now used in financial statements would improve their comprehensibility *vis-à-vis* many of these private shareholders – particularly those lacking knowledge of accounting and related matters.

Respondents who had reason to be more interested in financial information (those who made their own investment decisions without help) had a higher level of understanding of reporting practice when compared with those who received assistance with their decisions and who could be presumed to have less interest in such matters. However, the comprehension of the former group was well below that of respondents with considerable accounting experience. In other words, interest in financial reports appeared to be insufficient – some form of training in accounting and related matters would also appear to be necessary (at least from the evidence of this study).

Conclusions

The overall impression gained from this study (and from the previous pilot study) is that a considerable communications gap exists between companies and their private shareholders. Indeed, not all 'accounting' respondents indicated a reasonable understanding of such matters as valuation bases and financial ratios. This leads to two possible conclusions which are not exclusive:

(1)   Much needed education in accounting and related matters must be considered for the benefit of private shareholders lacking such knowledge; and

(2)   the entire basis of the presentation and disclosure of financial information must be thoroughly examined with a view to meeting the needs of private shareholders.

The evidence presented in this monograph strongly suggests that the main cause of the breakdown in communication relates to the form and content of the annual report. While attention must be paid to the important needs of the financially literate, it is essential that recognition be given to evidence that many private shareholders must be assumed to be guessing at company financial progress and position. In other words, many investment decisions may be based on inaccurate interpretations (or no interpretation) of the facts as disclosed in financial reports. Additionally, companies may not be effective enough in reporting their stewardship function to shareholders.

Unfortunately, at least within the context of this study, the trend at present is to consider the provision of annual reports which are more complex than those in current use. The complexities of the Sandilands' recommendations,[8] and the additional reports suggested in *The Corporate Report*[9] will almost certainly make the annual report even more formidable to the 'non-accounting' private shareholder. Admittedly, many of *The Corporate Report* proposals should provide the private shareholder with information which evidence in this study suggests he is seeking at the present time (for example, employee data and future prospects). Yet the possible introduction of additional statements, coupled with the changes brought about through the use of current cost data, do not appear to be compatible with the major problems of the private shareholder, again as evidenced in this study.

The greatest problems facing the private shareholder appear to be the complexity of the reporting system and the terminology used in financial statements. These are perhaps not unexpected conclusions but, prior to the pilot study and this main survey, little was known of the exact dimensions of the problems associated with private shareholder use and understanding of financial reports. It is not surprising to find that the chairman's report was rated the most popular section of the annual report – particularly by the 'non-accounting' respondents. It is usually more comprehensible than other parts of the report,[10] and appears to have been used by many respondents as a surrogate for the main financial statements. Indeed, these respondents tended, typically, to steer clear of major statements containing large quantities of quantitative data. Accountants could therefore be criticised for not fulfilling one of their main roles[11] (one which, incidentally, led to the growth of the accountancy profession[12]) – that is, reporting to shareholders on their company's profit or loss and state of affairs, each in a form which is reasonably comprehensible to all recipients.

The evidence of this study suggests that accountants have, however unintentionally, produced a financial reporting system which is capable of being used thoroughly and reasonably understood only by accountants or equivalent professionals. The widespread use of chairmens' reports by respondents also suggests that company chairmen may be usurping the traditional role of the reporting accountant – again, albeit unintentionally. In addition, the auditor's report does not cover the comments of chairmen and, therefore, the latter are not subject to the same degree of scrutiny as the main financial statements.

It is the balance sheet which appears to have caused most problems for private shareholders in this study. In particular, the terminology employed in it is a mixture of technical terms and everyday words, frequently used in a specialised context, and often removed from their normal meaning[13] – for example, reserves, current in 'current assets' and equity in 'equity capital'. It is therefore not surprising to have found so many respondents appearing not to understand the nature of the balance sheet and other financial statements.

131

Recommendations

In an attempt to improve communications between companies and their private shareholders, it is most strongly recommended that attention be paid to either or both of the following suggestions:

(1)   *Seek means of simplifying the present system of financial reporting which is based on measures of profitability and financial position.* (This should be done irrespective of the valuation bases adopted and should also incorporate, wherever possible, interpretive statements outlining the main features of the financial results being reported.)

(2)   *Seek alternative systems of financial reporting which lend themselves to providing private shareholders with comprehensible data which are relevant both for investment decisions and stewardship.* (This may mean an examination of systems which do not rely on the concepts of profit and financial position to the same extent as at present.)

Of these two suggestions, the most immediately practicable appears to be the first as it incorporates changes to the existing system of financial reporting. Little is known of alternative systems, although one of the writers has been developing such a system for some years and is presently undertaking research into its feasibility.[14] In the long-term interests of the accountancy profession it is felt that the second suggestion must not be ignored but, due to the immediacy of the problems evidenced in this study, it is the first suggestion which is developed as follows:

(1a)   *Present the private shareholder with a general outline of both the profit and loss account and balance sheet*
       Simplified versions of both financial statements could be produced in addition to but separate from those presently disclosed in the annual report. This has already been recommended in *The Corporate Report*,[15] and was also a suggestion of a majority of respondents.

(1b)   *Provide the private shareholder with a reasonable understanding of the main financial statements*
       This could be done in a variety of ways. For example, by presenting a glossary of technical terms, produced by the Accounting Standards Committee, and reproduced in all annual reports of quoted companies in the first instance. Alternatively, by giving explanations of the terms actually used in the financial statements within the statements them-

132

selves. In addition, it is further recommended that everyday words used in a technical sense (for example, reserves), or technical terms used in an everyday context (for example, balance sheets) should either be replaced in financial reporting or the attention of the report user should be drawn to their specific meaning within a financial statement context.

(1c) *Provide the private shareholder with a reasonable understanding of the balance sheet in particular*

Private shareholders should be more aware of the articulation of the balance sheet and profit and loss account and, particularly, the present use by the reporting accountant of the balance sheet as a statement of balances appearing in the accounting records. Consequently, the effects of the matching principle would require explanation, and this would apply whether the basic data were accounted for on a historic cost or current cost basis. Finally, it would be beneficial to private shareholders for reporting accountants to provide a simple and general explanation of the balance sheet identity (that is, assets being equated with liabilities and shareholders' equity).

(1d) *Assist the private shareholder in interpreting the main features of financial statements*

Boards of directors could be made responsible for explaining the main features of their financial statements, and for discussing their companies' financial stability, liquidity[16] and profitability. This could be done with the aid of prescribed and clearly explained financial ratios. Prescription of such matters could be left to the Accounting Standards Committee. It would also be desirable if such interpretive material was verified and reported on by company auditors. Alternatively, such statements could be made the responsibility of the latter persons. Due to the subjectivity involved, boards of directors could then be allowed to state any objections they had to the expressed views of auditors.

Finally, if either of the above suggestions was felt to impair the independence of auditors, an independent firm of accountants, stockbrokers or merchant bankers could comment in the way already indicated. Again, boards of directors could be given the right of reply.

(1e) *Provide the private shareholder with financial information desired by him which at present is not legally required to be disclosed*

As recommended in *The Corporate Report*,[17] statements of future prospects could usefully be introduced in annual reports.[18] These could then be subject to verification in the same way as required in the City Code on Take-overs and Mergers.[19] Employment reports are

133

another matter which respondents indicated would be of use to them, and which *The Corporate Report* has recommended.

These suggestions are tentative ones. They are, however, very seriously recommended in light of the research findings obtained.[20]

Similar work in relation to institutional shareholders is currently being undertaken at the Universities of Liverpool and Edinburgh in order to obtain a complete picture of shareholder use and understanding of financial reports. In addition, research into the feasibility of the above suggestions is now underway at the same institutions.

The above specific recommendations would obviously involve boards of directors, reporting accountants, and company auditors in a great deal of additional effort and responsibility in the preparation of the annual report. *The Corporate Report*, however, has already made the position quite clear:

'In our view *the fundamental objective of corporate reports is to communicate economic measurements of and information about the resources and performance of the reporting entity useful to those having reasonable rights to such information.* To fulfill this objective we conclude that corporate reports should be relevant, *understandable*, reliable complete, objective, timely and comparable.'[21] (italics added)

It is doubtful whether it will be possible to satisfy each of these criterion to such an extent as to have an absolutely relevant, understandable, reliable, complete, objective, timely and comparable annual report. Some reasonable compromise must be achieved by trading part of one against another in order to arrive at an acceptable balance. In doing so, the criterion of user comprehension must not be ignored to the extent to which it has been throughout the history of corporate reporting. The needs of all individuals and bodies with a reasonable right to financial information must be acknowledged and respected. Financial reports must not be conceived solely in terms of the so-called sophisticated user. To do so would be to ignore the needs of the majority of shareholders in most companies. It could also result in the ignoring of the particular needs of other financially unsophisticated groups which, undoubtedly, are likely to be major recipients of company financial reports – for example, company employees. There is already evidence that public companies are producing simplified and explanatory versions of their annual reports for the benefit of their employees. It would appear only equitable for the same progress to take place *vis-à-vis* private shareholders. It would also appear to be appropriate for the Accounting Standards Committee to examine requirements in this area with a view to achieving acceptable and useful standards by which boards of directors, reporting accountants and company auditors could be guided. Otherwise, to adapt the familiar Orwellian statement:

'All shareholders are equal. But some shareholders are more equal than others.'

Such appears to be the unintentional reality in financial reporting. It needs to be remedied. The remedy lies in the hands of members of the accountancy profession.

REFERENCES

[1] See, for example, D. E. Stone, 'The Objectives of Financial Reporting in the Annual Report', *The Accounting Review*, April 1967, pp 331-7.

[2] *The Corporate Report*, ASSC, 1975.

[3] D. P. Tweedie, 'The Corporate Report: Evolution or Revolution?', *The Accountant's Magazine*, October 1975, p 344.

[4] B. Carsberg, A. Hope and R. W. Scapens, 'The Objectives of Published Accounting Reports', *Accounting and Business Research*, Summer 1974, pp 162-73.

[5] See, for example, H. K. Baker and J. A. Haslem, 'Information Needs of Individual Investors', *Journal of Accountancy*, November 1973, pp 66-9; and G. Chandra, 'Information Needs of Security Analysts', *Journal of Accountancy*, December 1975, p 70.

[6] *The Corporate Report*, p 20.

[7] *Op cit*, pp 51-3.

[8] *Inflation Accounting*, HMSO, 1975.

[9] *The Corporate Report*, pp 47-60.

[10] One researcher, however, has evidenced that even the chairman's report may be difficult to understand – see M. D. Still, 'The Readability of Chairmen's Statements', *Accounting and Business Research*, Winter 1972, pp 36-9.

[11] T. A. Lee, *Company Auditing: Concepts and Practices*, Gee and Co., 1972, pp 11-12.

[12] T. A. Lee, *Company Financial Reporting: Issues and Analysis*, Nelson, 1976, pp 23-34; and P. Bird, *Accountability: Standards in Financial Reporting*, Haymarket Press, 1973, pp 1-13.

[13] See R. J. Chambers, *Accounting, Evaluation and Economic Behaviour*, Prentice Hall, 1966, p 171.

[14] See, for example, T. A. Lee, 'Goodwill – an Example of Will-O'-the-Wisp Accounting', *Accounting and Business Research*, Autumn 1971, pp 318-28; T. A. Lee, 'A Case for Cash Flow Reporting', *Journal of Business Finance*, Summer 1972, pp 27-36; and T. A. Lee, 'Enterprise Income: Survival or Decline and Fall?', *Accounting and Business Research*, Summer 1974, pp 178-92.

[15] *The Corporate Report*, p 45.

[16] See *Inflation Accounting, op cit*, p 46 for support of this point – particularly cash flow data.

[17] *The Corporate Report, op cit*, pp 55-6.

[18] This has been advocated on several occasions over the years – for example, R. Schattke, 'Expected Income – A Reporting Challenge', *The Accounting Review*, October 1962, pp 670-76; W. W. Cooper, N. Dopuch and T. F. Keller, 'Budgeting Disclosure and Other Suggestions for Improving Accounting Reports', *The Accounting Review*, October 1968, pp 640-47; C. R. Tomkins, 'The Development of Relevant Published Accounting Reports', *Accountancy*, November 1969, pp 815-20; K. F. Skousen, R. A. Sharp and R. K. Tolman, 'Corporate Disclosure of Budgetary Data', *Journal of Accountancy*, May 1972, pp 50-7; and

T. A. Lee, 'A Case for Cash Flow Reporting', *Journal of Business Finance*, Summer 1972, pp 27-36.

[19] *The City Code on Take-overs and Mergers*, Issuing Houses Association, 1972. A further check could be obtained by the reporting of actual financial results and previous periods' forecast results with an explanation of any material differences – see Lee (A Case for Cash Flow Reporting), *op cit*, p 31.

[20] They have also been largely supported in a recent paper issued by the Accounting Standards Review Committee of The Institute of Chartered Accountants of Scotland – 'The Corporate Report: a Scottish Viewpoint', *The Accountant's Magazine*, April 1976, pp 123-5, especially p 124.

[21] *The Corporate Report*, p 78.

Appendices

APPENDIX 1

Interview Questionnaire for Private Shareholders

Note

Most of the questions were pre-coded for purposes of analysis. However, for 7 of the items, the interviewees were given a card specifying the question. This was done because of the complexity of the questions concerned. These are identifiable below. For all other items, the questions *only* were read out to the interviewees.

1. What pieces of financial information about companies do you consider to be important to you as a shareholder?

2. (*Show Card 1 when seeking their response*)
   What parts of company annual financial reports do you read, and to what degree do you read each part?

	Do not read at all	*Read briefly for interest*	*Read thoroughly*
Chairman's report			
Report of directors			
Profit and loss account			
Balance sheets			
Auditors report			
Sources and application of funds statement			
Notes to accounts			
Statistical data			

(*If answer is 'do not read at all', for all items, ask why not. Skip to Question 5 and then to Question 8*)

3. (*For those who read thoroughly all or part of company financial reports*)
    Do you undertake any form of analysis of the data contained in company financial reports?
    Yes/no

4. *If answer is 'yes' to Question 3*, what form of analysis do you undertake?

	Figures taken without further analysis	Financial ratios prepared		Funds flow prepared		Any other (specify)
		Historic	Pre-dicted	Historic	Pre-dicted	
No comparison made						
Comparison of current and previous year's data						
Comparison of several years' data						
Comparison of current year's data with that for other companies						
Any other (specify)						

5. What is (or are) the main purpose(s) of the financial statements contained in the company annual financial report? Which is the most important one? (*Indicate by * the most important if more than one*)

To make company directors accountable
to shareholders

To provide information for the
Inland Revenue

To give shareholders an indication of
the value of the company

To give shareholders an indication of
the market value of their shares

To give shareholders data of use for
investment decisions

To justify the dividend payments
proposed by the company

Any other (specify) ....

Do not know

6. (*Show respondents Card 2 when seeking their response*)
    What ranking of importance would you give to the following parts of company annual financial reports? 1 = most important, 2 = next important, and so on.
    What degree of influence does each source have in relation to your investment decisions? 1 = maximum, 2 = considerable, 3 = moderate, 4 = slight, 5 = none.

	Importance	*Influence*
Chairman's report		
Report of directors		
Profit and loss account		
Balance sheets		
Auditors report		
Source and application of funds statement		
Notes to accounts		
Statistical data		

7. What particular data contained in any of the previously-indicated parts of the company annual financial report do you find particularly relevant to you? (*Specify part of report as well*)

    Data specified   *Part of report specified*

8. Who is (are) legally responsible for providing company annual financial reports to shareholders?

    Company chairmen

    Boards of directors

    Financial directors

    Company accountants

    Auditors

    Any other persons (specify)

    Do not know

9. (*Show Card 3 to respondents when seeking their response*)
    Which of the following sources of information about companies do you read, and to what degree do you read each?

	Do not read at all	Read briefly for interest	Read thoroughly
Six monthly financial reports			
Financial press reports			
Occasional merger reports			
Moodie's or Extel cards			
Stockbrokers reports			
Any other (specify)			

(*If answer is 'do not read at all', for all items, ask why not. Skip to Question 12*)

142

10. What particular data contained in any of the previously-indicated sources of information do you find particularly relevant to you? (*Specify source as well*)

Data specified   *Source specified*

11. (*Show Card 4 to respondents when seeking their response*)
What ranking of importance would you give to the following sources of financial information? 1 = most important, 2 = next important, and so on.
What degree of influence does each source have in relation to your investment decisions? 1 = maximum, 2 = considerable, 3 = moderate, 4 = slight, 5 = none.

	Importance	Influence
Six monthly financial reports	☐	☐
Financial press reports	☐	☐
Occasional merger reports	☐	☐
Moodie's or Extel cards	☐	☐
Stockbrokers reports	☐	☐
Any other (specify)	☐	☐

12. What do the following terms mean to you? (*Answers to be as brief as is possible*)
Profit
Price earnings ratio
Dividend yield
Dividend cover

13. Can you describe the kind of information you would expect to find in the following parts of a company annual financial report? (*Brief answers*)
Chairman's report
Report of the directors
Profit and loss account
Balance sheet
Auditor's report

143

14. Can you describe briefly what you would understand by the following terms commonly used in company financial reports?
Depreciation
Equity capital or interest
Current assets
Reserves
Accrued charges

15. (*Show respondents Card 5 when seeking their response*)
What basis of valuation is normally used to determine the following items often included in company annual financial reports?

	Original cost	Original cost less depreciation	Replacement cost	Realisable value	Other (Specify)	Do not know
Plant and machinery						
Stocks and work in progress						
Quoted investments						

16. Do you believe the financial information given in the present type of company annual financial report is sufficient for shareholders?

Yes/no/do not know

17. Is there any additional financial information which you think share-holders should be given in company annual financial reports?

Budgets

Profit forecasts

Price-level adjusted accounts

Current value accounts

Funds flow statements

Cash flow statements

Human resource statements

Increased disclosure of existing information (specify) ....

Other (specify) ....

18. Which of the following financial aspects of a company are you able to realistically assess annually from the present type of company annual financial report?

Profitability

Potential bankruptcy

Capacity to survive

Managerial efficiency

Investment policy

19. What financial data do you use to assess the above factors?

Data specified

Profitability

Potential bankruptcy

Capacity to survive

Managerial efficiency

Investment policy

20. (*Show respondent Card 6 when seeking their response*)
Do you consider the financial results which are annually reported to you by companies to be

An accurate reflection of their
financial progress and position

An approximation of their financial
progress and position

An inaccurate reflection of their
financial progress and position

Other (specify) ....

21. (*Show respondents Card 7 when seeking their response*)
Which of the following statements correspond most closely to your impression of company annual financial reports?

You are able to understand the information
contained in such reports and it is of
considerable relevance and use to you with
regard to investment decisions.

You are able to understand the information
contained in such reports but find it
irrelevant or of little use to you with
regard to investment decisions. (*State
reason for its irrelevance*)

You are unable to understand the
information contained in such reports
sufficiently for it to be of use to you
with regard to investment decisions.
(*State reason for non-understanding*)

Any other reason (specify)

22. Is there anything in particular in the present type of company annual financial report which you do not fully understand? (*Specify briefly*)

24.   What financial newspapers do you read?

Accounting Experience
Accounting qualification   (state which) ....
Financial management
Courses in accounting   (state which) ....
Bookkeeping experience
None

Sex

Occupation (If retired, specify)

(a)   Do you make your own investment decisions?
yes/no
(If 'no', specify who does.)

(b)   Do you buy and sell shares regularly?
yes/no

(c)   How many companies do you hold shares in?

```
 1 —  5    ┌────────┐
 6 — 10    ├────────┤
11 — 20    ├────────┤
20 +       ├────────┤
           └────────┘
```

APPENDIX 2

Questionnaire for Non-Respondents

1. *Accounting Experience* (Please tick appropriate box)

    Accounting Qualification (State which)

    ....

    Financial Management

    Courses in Accounting (State which)

    ....

    Bookkeeping Experience

    None

2. *Occupation* (If retired, please specify former occupation)

3. Do you make your own investment decisions? (Please tick appropriate box)

    Yes

    No

    If your answer to Q.3 is 'No' could'you please specify below the occupation of the person who makes your investment decisions. (If this person is your husband or wife, could you please state that fact in addition to the occupation).

4. Do you buy and sell shares regularly? (Please tick appropriate box)

    Yes

    No

5. In how many companies do you hold shares? (Please tick appropriate box)

    1 — 5

    6 — 10

    11 — 20

    20 +

148

APPENDIX 3

Shareholdings in Survey Company Held by Respondents

Share Units Held (expressed in £1 units)	%
0 — 20	7
21 — 50	12
51 — 100	20
101 — 200	30
201 — 500	16
501 — 1000	9
1001 — 2000	4
2001 +	2
Unidentified shareholding	—
	100

APPENDIX 4

Occupations of Survey Respondents

	%	%
In Accountancy and Related Employment		
Accountancy	7	
Investment, banking, and broking	8	
Financial management	1	16
	—	
In Non-financial Management		
Managers and directors	17	
Engineers in industry	5	22
	—	
Housewives		11
Other Occupations		
Architects	1	
Medical and dental practitioners	7	
Teachers and lecturers	8	
Lawyers	6	
Others	29	51
	—	
		100

149

APPENDIX 5

Accounting and Related Experience or Knowledge of Survey Respondents

	%	%
Significant Experience etc.		
Possession of an accounting qualification	9	
Financial management experience	5	14
	—	
Little Experience etc.		
Studied accounting	13	
Bookkeeping experience	11	24
	—	
No experience etc.		59
Experience unknown		3
		100

APPENDIX 6

Financial Press Read Regularly by Survey Respondents

	%	%
National Dailies		
Financial Times	36	
Times, Telegraph, Guardian	32	
Other dailies	7	75
	—	
Regional Dailies		
Scotland	37	
Newcastle	2	
Liverpool	—	
London	2	41
	—	
Sunday Newspapers		
Sunday Times, Telegraph, etc.		21
Financial and Investment Journals		
Investors' Chronicle	8	
Economist and others	6	14
	—	
		151*

* See Table 10 for explanation of multiple reading

APPENDIX 7

Shareholdings in Survey Company and Perceived
Understanding of Survey Respondents

SIZE OF SHAREHOLDING IN SURVEY COMPANY*		PERCEIVED UNDERSTANDING			
		Understand and find relevant	Understand and find irrelevant	Do not under-stand	Total
	n†	%	%	%	%
0 — 100	118	37	39	24	100
101 — 500	137	41	35	24	100
501 +	44	34	30	36	100

Chi square = 3.56; 4 degrees of freedom; significance = 0.47

* Expressed in £1 units.

† 1 shareholding could not be traced in the share register due to a failure to reference it at the sampling stage; and 1 respondent failed to indicate his perceived understanding.

APPENDIX 8

Number of Shareholdings and Perceived Understanding of
Survey Respondents

NUMBER OF SHAREHOLDINGS HELD BY SURVEY RESPONDENTS		PERCEIVED UNDERSTANDING			
		Understand and find relevant	Understand and find irrelevant	Do not under-stand	Total
	n*	%	%	%	%
1 — 5	66	27	44	29	100
6 — 10	62	29	31	40	100
11 — 20	78	44	40	16	100
21 +	94	49	30	21	100

Chi square = 18.34; 6 degrees of freedom; significance = 0.01

* 1 respondent failed to indicate his perceived understanding.

APPENDIX 9

Occupations and Perceived Understanding of Survey Respondents

RESPONDENTS' OCCUPATION		PERCEIVED UNDERSTANDING			
		Understand and find relevant	Understand and find irrelevant	Do not under- stand	Total
	n*	%	%	%	%
Accountancy, investment, etc,	48	67	31	2	100
Non-financial management	65	42	41	17	100
Housewives	34	24	41	35	100
Others	153	32	33	35	100

Chi square = 33.41; 6 degrees of freedom; significance = 0.00

* 1 respondent failed to indicate his perceived understanding.

APPENDIX 10

Accounting Experience and Perceived Understanding of Survey Respondents

ACCOUNTING EXPERIENCE		PERCEIVED UNDERSTANDING			
		Understand and find relevant	Understand and find irrelevant	Do not under- stand	Total
	n*	%	%	%	%
Significant	42	60	40	—	100
Little	72	44	40	16	100
None	177	32	33	35	100

Chi square = 27.85; 4 degrees of freedom; significance = 0.00

* 9 respondents (3% of 301) did not indicate their accounting experience and have been omitted from this analysis; 1 respondent failed to indicate his perceived understanding.

APPENDIX 11

Investment Decision Making and Perceived Understanding

INVESTMENT DECISION MAKING		PERCEIVED UNDERSTANDING			
		Understand and find relevant	*Understand and find irrelevant*	*Do not under-stand*	*Total*
	n*	%	%	%	%
Decisions made entirely on own	208	45	34	21	100
Decisions made with help from an expert	92	25	38	37	100

Chi square = 13.21; 2 degrees of freedom; significance = 0.00

* 1 respondent failed to indicate his perceived understanding of reported accounting information and has been omitted from this analysis.

APPENDIX 12

Reading of Financial Press and Perceived Understanding of Survey Respondents

NUMBER OF FINANCIAL PRESS SOURCES READ		PERCEIVED UNDERSTANDING			
		Understand and find relevant	*Understand and find irrelevant*	*Do not under-stand*	*Total*
	n*	%	%	%	%
3 +	48	58	23	19	100
2	94	39	43	18	100
1	117	39	37	24	100
0	41	12	32	56	100

Chi square = 33.84; 6 degrees of freedom; significance = 0.00

* 1 respondent failed to indicate his perceived understanding.

APPENDIX 13

Actual Understanding of Legal Responsibility for
Annual Financial Statements

	%	%
Reasonable Understanding		
Board of directors		52†
No Understanding		
Company chairmen	12	
Finance directors	—	
Company accountants	4	
Company secretaries	18	
Auditors	9	
Other answers (including 'do not knows' and 'no answers')	12	55†
	—	
		107*

† 17 of the respondents (6% of 301) indicated an incorrect category in addition to the 'board of directors' category and were re-designated for purposes of Table 13 as having a vague understanding.

* 21 respondents (7% of 301) indicated two responsibility categories.

154

APPENDIX 14

Actual Understanding of the Objectives of Annual Financial Statements

	%	%
Reasonable Understanding		
Accountability to shareholders	27	
Data for investment decisions	15	42†
	—	
Vague Understanding		
Justification for dividends	3	
Vague answers indicating accountability	4	7
	—	
No Understanding		
Data for Inland Revenue	3	
Indicate value of company	30	
Indicate market value of shares	6	
Fulfilling a legal obligation	12	
Keeping people informed	19	
Other answers (including 'do not knows' and 'no answers')	14	84
	—	
		133*

† 46 of these respondents (15% of 301) gave a reasonable answer coupled with an incorrect one, and were re-designated for purposes of Table 13 as having a vague understanding.

* 76 respondents (25% of 301) indicated two objectives, and 12 respondents (4% of 301) indicated three objectives.

APPENDIX 15

Actual Understanding of the Accuracy of Reported Accounting Information

	%	%
Reasonable Understanding Annual accounting information gives an approximation of financial progress and position		49
Vague Understanding Annual accounting information is partly an approximation and partly an accurate reflection of financial progress and position		1
No Understanding Annual accounting information gives: an accurate reflection of financial progress and position	47	
an inaccurate reflection of financial progress and position	1	
Other answers (including 'do not knows' and 'no answers')	2	50
	—	
		100

APPENDIX 16

Actual Understanding of Contents of Chairman's Report

	%
Contents of chairman's report stated to include:	
a review of past year's financial results and a statement of future prospects	61
a review of past year's financial results	19
a statement of future prospects	9
a statement of future policy	7
a review of major events and developments during past year	9
comments relating to the economic, political and/or taxation environment	9
comments on labour relations	4
Other answers	9
'Do not knows' and 'no answers'	3
	130*

* 66 respondents (22% of 301) gave two content items; 10 respondents (3% of 301) gave three items; and 1 respondent (0% of 301) gave four items.

Note

For purposes of Table 14, all of the above-mentioned specific items were classified as correct answers, and certain of the 'other answers' were also classified as correct. *Reasonable understanding* was attributed to those respondents who either gave the first-mentioned item or who gave two or more of the other correct items, in both cases with no incorrect answer given. *Vague understanding* was attributed to those respondents who either gave only one correct item or who gave two correct and one incorrect items. The remaining respondents were classified as having *no understanding*.

APPENDIX 17

Actual Understanding of Contents of Directors' Report

	%
Contents of directors' report stated to include:	
a review of past year's financial results	49
a statement of future prospects	13
information regarding:	
directors	14
issues of new capital	2
changes in assets	1
dividends and retentions	3
turnover and profit of different classes of business	10
principal activities of company and subsidiaries	4
employees	3
Other answers	12
'Do not knows' and 'no answers'	25
	136*

* 83 respondents (28% of 301) indicated two content items, and 13 respondents (4% of 301) indicated three items.

Note

For purposes of Table 14, each of the above-mentioned specific items (with the exception of 'future prospects') were classified as correct answers, and certain of the 'other answers' were also classified as correct. *Reasonable understanding* was attributed to those respondents who gave two or more correct items and no incorrect ones. *Vague understanding* was attributed to those respondents who either gave one correct item only or two correct and one incorrect items. The remaining respondents were classified as having *no understanding*.

APPENDIX 18

Actual Understanding of Contents of Profit and Loss Account

	%
Contents of profit and loss account stated to include:	
sales or turnover	15
revenues and expenses	18
trading expenses	4
expenses required legally to be disclosed	4
profit or trading results	38
trading profit and expenses required legally to be disclosed (†)	7
profit, sales and trading expenses(†)	5
dividends and/or profit retentions	6
Other answers	17
'Do not knows' and 'no answers'	10
	124*

* 73 respondents (24% of 301) gave two content items.

Note

For purposes of Table 14, all of the above-mentioned specific items were classified as correct answers, and certain of the 'other answers' were also classified as correct. *Reasonable understanding* was attributed to those respondents who either gave item (†) or who gave two of the other correct items, in both cases with no incorrect answer given. *Vague understanding* was attributed to those respondents who either gave only one correct item or who gave two correct and one incorrect items. The remaining respondents were classified as having *no understanding*.

159

APPENDIX 19

Actual Understanding of Contents of Balance Sheet

	%
Contents of balance sheet stated to include:	
assets only	9
liabilities and/or share capital only	3
details of liquidity or working capital	3
assets and liabilities	27
assets, liabilities, and net worth	11
financial state of company at a point in time	4
Other answers	2
Obviously incorrect answers	19
'Do not knows' and 'no answers'	23
	101*

* 4 respondents (1% of 301) gave two content items.

Note

For purposes of Table 14, all of the above-mentioned specific items were classified as correct answers, and certain of the 'other answers' were also classified as correct. *Reasonable understanding* was attributed to those respondents who either gave the fourth or fifth-mentioned specific item, provided no incorrect item was also given. *Vague understanding* was attributed to those respondents who gave either one of the other specific items (with no incorrect answer given) or who gave two correct and one incorrect items. The remaining respondents were classified as having *no understanding*.

APPENDIX 20

Actual Understanding of Contents of Auditor's Report

	%
Auditor's report stated to be a reporting that:	
the financial statements have been verified and are satisfactory	27
the financial statements show a true and fair view	14
the financial statements are in accordance with accounting principles	1
proper books and records have been kept	7
the financial statements are correct	12
Other answers	6
Obviously incorrect answers	14
'Do not knows' and 'no answers'	22
	103*

* 10 respondents (3 % of 301) gave two content items.

Note

For purposes of Table 14, all of the above-mentioned specific items were classified as correct answers. *Reasonable understanding* was attributed to those respondents who gave either the first, second or third-mentioned specific item, provided no incorrect item was also given. *Vague understanding* was attributed to those respondents who gave either one of the other specific items (with no incorrect answer given) or who gave two correct and one incorrect items. The remaining respondents were classified as having *no understanding*.

APPENDIX 21

Actual Understanding of Term 'Profit' in Financial Statements

	%	%
Reasonable Understanding		
Surplus from trading revenue after deduction of various expenses	27	
Surplus available for distribution and retention	7	34
	—	
Vague Understanding		
Sum or surplus remaining after deducting expenses	18	
Cash produced from trading	19	
Other vague answers	2	39
	—	
No Understanding		
Answers merely mentioning profit and generally not defining the term	14	
Incorrect answers	11	
'Do not knows' and 'no answers'	2	27
	—	
		100

APPENDIX 22

Actual Understanding of Term 'Depreciation' in Financial Statements

	%	%
Reasonable Understanding		
Amount written off fixed assets over time or life of assets concerned	13	
Loss in value of fixed assets; wear and tear on fixed assets	13	26
	—	
Vague Understanding		
Amount written off assets	18	
Loss in value of assets; wear and tear on assets	27	
Answers suggesting depreciation is a means of replacing fixed assets	7	
Other vague answers	4	56
	—	
No Understanding		
Answers suggesting fixed and current assets are depreciated	4	
Answers suggesting current assets are depreciated	3	
Other incorrect answers	9	
'Do not knows' and 'no answers'	2	18
	—	
		100

163

APPENDIX 23

Actual Understanding of Term 'Current Assets' in Financial Statements

	%	%
Reasonable Understanding		
Stock, debtors, cash, etc. (any two or more of these items)		18
Vague Understanding		
Stock, debtors, cash, etc. (any one of these items)	7	
Liquid or readily realizable assets	16	
Assets used in course of trading	2	25
	—	
No Understanding		
Assets held at date of reporting	15	
Current and fixed assets mentioned	21	
Present worth of assets	6	
Other incorrect answers	10	
'Do not knows' and 'no answers'	5	57
	—	
		100

APPENDIX 24

Actual Understanding of Term 'Equity Capital' in Financial Statements

	%	%
Reasonable Understanding		
Ordinary shareholders' capital, interest or funds		22
Vague Understanding		
Shareholders' (unspecified) capital, interest or funds		33
No Understanding		
Answers involving loan stock and other borrowings	1	
Other incorrect answers	16	
'Do not knows' and 'no answers'	28	45
	—	
		100

APPENDIX 25

Actual Understanding of Term 'Reserves' in Financial Statements

	%	%
Reasonable Understanding		
Past profits not distributed but available for distribution	28	
Capital and revenue reserves mentioned	5	33
	—	
Vague Understanding		
Funds set aside for contingencies and/or specific purposes	18	
Other vague answers	3	21
	—	
No Understanding		
Money set aside for contingencies and/or specific purposes	31	
Other incorrect answers	7	
'Do not knows' and 'no answers'	8	46
	—	
		100

APPENDIX 26

Actual Understanding of Term 'Accrued Charges' in Financial Statements

	%	%
Reasonable Understanding		
Expenses or charges due but not yet paid	32	
Apportionment of costs to appropriate periods	2	34
	—	
Vague Understanding		
Specific accrued charges mentioned	6	
Other vague answers	1	7
	—	
No Understanding		
Incorrect answers	9	
'Do not knows' and 'no answers'	50	59
	—	
		100

APPENDIX 27

Actual Understanding of Traditional Plant Valuation Bases

	%	%
Reasonable Understanding		
Original cost less depreciation		70
Vague Understanding		
Original cost		3
No Understanding		
Replacement cost	7	
Realizable value	3	
Original cost and replacement cost or realizable value	1	
Other incorrect answers	1	
'Do not knows' and 'no answers'	15	27
	—	
		100

APPENDIX 28

Actual Understanding of Traditional Stock Valuation Bases

	%	%
Reasonable Understanding		
Original cost	23	
Lower of cost and net realizable value	12	35
	—	
Vague Understanding		
Sundry answers mentioning original cost		4
No Understanding		
Replacement cost	7	
Realizable value	30	
Other incorrect answers	3	
'Do not knows' and 'no answers'	21	61
	—	
		100

APPENDIX 29

Actual Understanding of Traditional Quoted Investments Valuation Bases

	%	%
Reasonable Understanding		
Original cost	13	
Original cost with market value given as a note	8	21
Vague Understanding	—	
Sundry answers indicating original cost and realizable value		5
No Understanding		
Realizable value	52	
Other incorrect answers	1	
'Do not knows' and 'no answers'	21	74
	—	
		100

APPENDIX 30

Actual Understanding of Term 'Price-Earnings Ratio'

	%	%
Reasonable Understanding		
Definitions relating share price to earnings per share		15
Vague Understanding		
Answers indicating the ratio involved earnings and share prices		15
No Understanding		
Incorrect answers	13	
'Do not knows' and 'no answers'	57	70
	—	
		100

APPENDIX 31

Actual Understanding of Term 'Dividend Yield'

	%	%
Reasonable Understanding		
Dividend as a return on current share price		14
Vague Understanding		
Dividend as a return on the price paid for shares	16	
Other vague answers	27	43
	—	
No Understanding		
Incorrect answers	24	
'Do not knows' and 'no answers'	19	43
	—	
		100

APPENDIX 32

Actual Understanding of Term 'Dividend Cover'

	%	%
Reasonable Understanding		
Number of times dividend is covered by available profit	28	
Number of times dividend is covered by net profit	8	36
	—	
Vague Understanding		
Amount of profit available to pay dividends	3	
Other vague answers	6	9
	—	
No Understanding		
Incorrect answers	19	
'Do not knows' and 'no answers'	36	55
	—	
		100

APPENDIX 33

Understanding Scores for Individual Financial Reporting Matters

UNDERSTANDING SCORE	General Nature of Reporting [a]	Nature of Financial Statements [b]	Accounting Terminology [c]	Accounting Valuation Bases [d]	Financial Ratios [e]
	%	%	%	%	%
0	9	2	1	19	30
1	9	2	6	2	20
2	36	5	12	36	10
3	11	11	13	5	17
4	21	15	14	24	11
5	7	18	11	4	8
6	7	13	12	10	4
7		13	12		
8		13	6		
9		6	6		
10		2	3		
11			3		
12			1		
	100	100	100	100	100
Mean	2.74	5.41	5.14	2.65	1.97
Standard deviation	1.61	2.23	2.74	1.81	1.82
Skewness coefficient	0.27	—0.17	0.39	0.19	0.54

Maximum possible scores:
  a = 6; b = 10; c = 12; d = 6; e = 6; total = 40

APPENDIX 34

Survey Respondents' Views of the Relative Importance of Sections of the Company Annual Financial Report

PART OF ANNUAL REPORT	DEGREE OF IMPORTANCE RELATIVE TO OTHER SECTIONS OF THE ANNUAL REPORT*									
	1	*2*	*3*	*4*	*5*	*6*	*7*	*8*	*Total*	*Mean*
	%	%	%	%	%	%	%	%	%	
Profit and loss account	39	29	15	7	3	1	1	5	100	2.38
Chairman's report	41	17	13	7	8	4	3	7	100	2.80
Balance sheet	18	19	21	13	9	6	2	12	100	3.60
Directors' report	5	14	15	17	13	11	8	17	100	4.67
Sources and application of funds statement	4	5	14	17	15	15	9	21	100	5.21
Notes to accounts	5	5	8	13	15	12	16	26	100	5.60
Auditor's report	5	4	9	8	11	8	12	43	100	6.02
Statistical data	2	3	5	9	15	13	15	38	100	6.22

* n = 287; the 14 respondents who did not read any section of the annual report were not asked the question. Respondents who did not rank any section of the report were deemed to have considered it to be of the least importance (rank 8). The rank correlation between 'no answers' and 'rank 8' was 0.90. The relationships of all other categories of response to 'no answers' were, with one minor exception (rank 7), much lower.

APPENDIX 35

Annual Report Reading Patterns of Defined Reader Groups

READER GROUP*	PART OF ANNUAL REPORT							
	CR	DR	PL	BS	AR	SAF	NA	SD
n	%	%	%	%	%	%	%	%
Reader Group 2(a)								
Read thoroughly	72	38	100	100	36	38	40	33
Read briefly	28	52	—	—	43	41	58	59
Not read	—	10	—	—	21	21	2	8
58	100	100	100	100	100	100	100	100
Reader Group 2(b)								
Read thoroughly	55	9	100	100	—	—	18	9
Read briefly	36	64	—	—	—	9	27	36
Not read	9	27	—	—	100	91	55	55
11	100	100	100	100	100	100	100	100
Reader Group 3								
Read thoroughly	98	36	—	—	—	—	—	—
Read briefly	2	55	95	83	43	52	57	69
Not read	—	9	5	17	57	48	43	31
42	100	100	100	100	100	100	100	100
Reader Group 4								
Read thoroughly	39	20	39	5	8	10	14	17
Read briefly	60	49	28	42	32	38	35	31
Not read	1	31	33	53	60	52	51	52
88	100	100	100	100	100	100	100	100
Reader Group 5								
Read thoroughly	26	16	—	—	8	13	15	12
Read briefly	69	54	100	100	51	49	47	53
Not read	5	30	—	—	41	38	38	35
74	100	100	100	100	100	100	100	100

* CR = chairman's report; DR = directors' report; PL = profit and loss account; BS = balance sheet; AR = auditor's report; SAF = sources and application of funds statement; NA = notes to accounts; and SD = statistical data.

APPENDIX 36

Survey Respondents' Views of the Relative Importance of Sources of Financial Information other than the Annual Report

SOURCE OF INFORMATION	DEGREE OF IMPORTANCE RELATIVE TO OTHER SOURCES OF INFORMATION							
	1	*2*	*3*	*4*	*5*	*6*	*Total*	*Mean**
	%	%	%	%	%	%	%	
Financial press reports	52	31	12	2	1	2	100	1.76
Half yearly financial reports	21	30	23	13	3	10	100	2.79
Occasional merger reports	5	20	32	25	6	12	100	3.43
Stockbrokers' reports	20	13	14	24	11	18	100	3.47
Moodies' or Extel Cards	2	4	5	13	36	40	100	4.99
Other	4	3	2	2	1	88	100	5.59

* n = 295; the 6 respondents who did not read any of the above sources of information about companies were omitted from the analysis. Respondents who did not rank any source of information were deemed to have considered it to be of least importance (i.e. rank 6). The rank correlation between 'no answers' and 'rank 6' was 0.56. The relationship of all other categories of response to 'no answers' were all lower and, with one exception, revealed an inverse relationship.

APPENDIX 37

Reading of Annual Report and Level of Understanding of Survey Respondents

READING OF ANNUAL REPORT	LEVEL OF UNDERSTANDING					
	Much above aver-age	Above aver-age	Aver-age	Below aver-age	Much below aver-age	Total
n	%	%	%	%	%	%
1. Thorough readers of both quantitative and non-quantitative data	14	14	22	57	—	7	100
2a. Thorough readers of mainly quantitative data: with relatively extensive coverage of non-quantitative data	58	22	29	42	7	—	100
2b. with less extensive coverage of non-quantitative data	11	9	—	64	18	9	100
3. Thorough readers of non-quantitative data only	42	5	10	64	14	7	100
4. Less interested readers of quantitative and non-quantitative data	88	8	8	45	25	14	100
5. Less interested readers of quantitative data	74	11	12	54	18	5	100
6. Non-readers of annual report	14	—	—	21	14	65	100

Chi square = 94.72; 24 degrees of freedom; significance = 0.00

APPENDIX 38

Reading of Annual Report and Perceived Understanding

READING OF ANNUAL REPORT		PERCEIVED UNDERSTANDING			
		Understand and find relevant	Understand and find irrelevant	Do not under-stand	Total
	n*	%	%	%	%
Thorough readers	72	64	28	8	100
Less interested readers	228	31	38	31	100

Chi square = 28.33; 2 degrees of freedom; significance = 0.00

* 1 respondent did not indicate his perceived understanding and has been omitted from this analysis.

174

APPENDIX 39

Survey Respondents' Views on Measures Necessary to Improve Their Use and Understanding of Annual Reports*

	%	%
Simpler Reports		
Less technical and in layman's language	33	
Summarised or condensed reports	16	
Reports augmented by a simple explanation of main points, key ratios, etc.	4	
Simple version of report supplied with full version available if required	3	56
	—	
Improvement of Shareholder Knowledge		
Courses in accountancy, etc. required	7	
Self education by shareholders required	6	13
	—	
Changes to Existing Systems		
Need for some form of inflation accounting		3
Other Views		
Existing system is satisfactory	12	
Reports should be less ornate/less expensive	5	
	—	17

* 45 respondents (15% of 301) either stated they did not know what changes were required or gave no answer to the question. 6 respondents (2% of 301) gave multiple answers.

175

Selected Bibliography

Surprisingly, despite its obvious importance, little has been written on the subject of financial report usage and understanding. The following are therefore given as a selection of those items which appear to be relevant to this study. There could be others which we have failed to include because they have not come to our attention. For this error of omission, we apologise to the writers concerned.

H. K. Baker and J. A. Haslem, 'Information Needs of Individual Investors', *Journal of Accountancy*, November 1973, pp 64-9.

N. M. Bedford, *Extensions in Accounting Disclosure*, Prentice Hall, 1973, particularly pp 3-83.

J. N. Birnberg and N. Dopuch, 'A Conceptual Approach to a Framework for Disclosure', *Journal of Accountancy*, February 1963, pp 59-63.

S. L. Buzby, 'The Nature of Adequate Disclosure', *Journal of Accountancy*, April 1974, pp 38-47.

B. Carsberg, A. Hope and R. W. Scapens, 'The Objectives of Published Accounting Reports', *Accounting and Business Research*, Summer 1974, pp 162-73.

R. C. Clift, 'Accounting Information and the Capital Market', in *Australian Company Financial Reporting*, Australian Society of Accountants, 1975, pp 83-98.

The Corporate Report, ASSC, 1975.

E. S. Hendriksen, 'Disclosure in Financial Reporting', in *Accounting Theory*, Irwin, revised edition, 1970, pp 559-81.

Inflation Accounting, HMSO, 1975, pp 42-66.

J. R. Jordan, 'Financial Accounting and Communications', in *Accounting: a Book of Readings* (G. G. Mueller and C. H. Smith, eds.), Holt Rinehart and Winston, 1970, pp 127-44.

T. A. Lee, 'A Case for Cash Flow Reporting', *Journal of Business Finance*, Summer 1972, pp 27-36.

T. A. Lee, *Company Financial Reporting: Issues and Analysis*, Nelson, 1976, pp 77-80 and 113-16.

T. A. Lee, 'Sandilands and User Comprehension', *Journal of Business Finance and Accounting*, Spring 1976, pp 85-95.

T. A. Lee and D. P. Tweedie, 'Accounting Information: An Investigation of Shareholder Usage', *Accounting and Business Research*, Autumn 1975, pp 280-91.

T. A. Lee and D. P. Tweedie, 'Accounting Information: An Investigation of Shareholder Understanding', *Accounting and Business Research*, Winter 1975, pp 3-17.

T. A. Lee and D. P. Tweedie, 'The Private Shareholder: His Sources of Financial Information and His Understanding of Reporting Practices', *Accounting and Business Research*, Autumn 1976, pp 304-14.

Objectives of Financial Statements, AICPA, 1973.

J. E. Smith and N. P. Smith, 'Readability: A Measure of the Performance of the Communication Function of Financial Reporting', *The Accounting Review*, July 1971, pp 552-61.

F. J. Soper and R. Dolphin, 'Readability and Corporate Annual Reports', *The Accounting Review*, April 1964, pp 358-62.

M. D. Still, 'The Readability of Chairmen's Statements', *Accounting and Business Research*, Winter 1972, pp 36-9.

C. R. Tomkins, 'The Development of Relevant Published Accounting Reports', *Accountancy*, November 1969, pp 815-20.

D. P. Tweedie, 'The Corporate Report: Evolution or Revolution', *The Accountant's Magazine*, October 1975, pp 343-6.

The Institutional Investor
and Financial Information

THE INSTITUTIONAL INVESTOR
AND
FINANCIAL INFORMATION

A report sponsored by the Research Committee of
The Institute of Chartered Accountants
in England and Wales

T. A. Lee

*(Professor of Accountancy and Finance,
University of Edinburgh)*

D. P. Tweedie

*(Technical Director, The Institute of Chartered Accountants of Scotland, and
Visiting Professor in the International Centre for Research in Accounting,
University of Lancaster)*

THE INSTITUTE OF CHARTERED ACCOUNTANTS
IN ENGLAND AND WALES
CHARTERED ACCOUNTANTS' HALL, MOORGATE PLACE,
LONDON EC2P 2BJ
1981

Alsace Print-Production Ltd., London, SW1

Contents

Preface and Acknowledgements

In 1974, we embarked on the task of obtaining evidence of the use and understanding of financial information by shareholders of limited companies. It appeared then to us that it was important to establish whether or not shareholders used available information (and, if so, to what extent); and also whether or not they had a reasonable understanding of such information. Seven years later, we are now in a position to report on the last major part of this project — that is, a study of the financial experts in the shareholder community; namely, institutional investors and stockbrokers.

The earlier parts of the project had concerned the individual private shareholder, and his use and understanding of available financial information (see the bibliography for a list of the relevant publications). In this respect, we believed it was desirable to separate the private shareholder from his professional counterpart and, consequently, this study examines in some depth the latter person. The main objectives are the same as in the previous studies — to evidence the degree to which corporate financial reports and other sources of financial information about companies are used and understood by investors — in this case, by 'sophisticated' investors. We have gathered together what we believe to be unique evidence in this respect, telling us much about the way in which the professional investment community processes financial information prior to making its investment decisions.

The areas covered in this study are similar to those examined in relation to the private shareholder — that is, shareholder understanding of various aspects of traditional financial reporting practice (including, inter alia, financial statements, accounting terminology and asset valuation); and use of corporate annual reports and other sources of financial information (including, inter alia, interim financial statements and press reports). However, the opportunity has also been taken to expand the coverage to include such matters as the role of company visits by institutional investors and stockbrokers; the nature of the financial analysis process utilised by them; and their use and understanding of inflation accounting statements. It was felt that such extensions to the

ix

previously tested areas of information use and analysis provided us with a reasonable coverage of the major matters of concern in the general area of financial information use and understanding.

As in the main private shareholder study, the research method was by means of an interview questionnaire which enabled suitable data to be gathered for further analysis. The latter activity contained a mixture of straightforward reporting of response aggregates, together with suitable cross-analyses of processed data with various background characteristics of the respondents. These cross-analyses were also aided by the use of composite data which distinguished different types of readers of corporate annual reports, and different levels of reader comprehension.

All the respondents in this study could be classified as financial experts as they were employed by organisations forming part of the established financial community in the UK. Insurance companies, pension funds, investment and unit trusts, merchant banks and stockbroking firms were each represented in this study and, consequently, in terms of expertise and experience, were very different from the private shareholders examined in our earlier studies.

We believe the results of this study (which are summarised in the concluding chapter) are important giving, as they do, an almost unique observation of the financial expert using accounting information. Given the apparent importance of these experts to the accounting and investment communities, it is hoped our results will be of considerable interest not only to accounting policy makers but also to those producing or using corporate financial information.

Finally, the help of the following persons is gratefully acknowledged in interviewing respondents: Ann Black, Rosemary Blair, Keith Brown, Jonathan Cliff, Martin Dunkerton, Pat Groves, Chris Joy, Gerard Lafferty, Falconer Mitchell, Howard Moss, Simon Strauss and Rosemary Sutherland; for organising certain of the interviews, Jim Eckford and Chris Nash; and for typing and secretarial assistance, Jeannette Heggie, Murielle Hill, June Kerr and Jean Reilly. Without their help this project would have extended well into the 1980's. And, grateful thanks are extended to the Research Committee of The Institute of Chartered Accountants in England and Wales for its financial and other support for this project and to Professor Geoffrey Whittington for advice on an earlier draft.

Edinburgh   T. A. LEE
March 1981   D. P. TWEEDIE

CHAPTER 1

Introduction

A decade has passed since the publication by the Institute of Chartered Accountants in England and Wales of its *Statement of Intent on Accounting Standards in the 1970s*, and the subsequent formation of the Accounting Standards (Steering) Committee. Numerous *Exposure Drafts* and *Statements of Standard Accounting Practice* later, it must be concluded that the decade of the 1970s has not witnessed a significant improvement in the communication aspect of accounting and financial reporting. The latter function is a process of communication if it is nothing else, yet the work of the Accounting Standards Committee has been concerned almost exclusively with matters of accounting measurement.[1] The result of this approach has been a growing complexity in accounting statements which were probably already incomprehensible to many of their recipients. In our recent study into the use and understanding of financial reports by private shareholders we felt obliged to make the following statement:[2]

'The overall conclusion from this study is that available financial information about companies is generally little used or understood by private shareholders. This is probably an expected conclusion but it does mean that reporting accountants are failing to communicate adequately with a very large number of individuals, and that existing financial reports have become documents which are prepared by accountants for accountants'.

We would suggest that this should be a matter of major concern to members of the accountancy profession, and to boards of directors which are legally responsible for the communication of accounting data to shareholders. That it has been identified as a major problem by some finance directors recently is at least a small step forward in the right direction:[3]

'The whole tenor of that Green Paper appears to us to be based on the

1

assumption that, if anything is held to be useful to a third party, then it should be included in the Annual Report.

We believe that this attitude should be stopped in its tracks as it will be harmful to the concept of an intelligible Annual Report.

We recommend that the Annual Report should, where feasible, be simplified and made more intelligible to the shareholder and to the general reader (amongst whom we would place special emphasis on the employee)'.

Indeed, the Group of Scottish Finance Directors went further by suggesting that much of the information in the annual report, together with a wide range of extra information, should be put on file and that the 'sophisticated' shareholder should have access to it on request.[4] Thus it recognised that there are two distinct types of shareholder — those who understand little of the complexities of accounting, and who therefore have little use for available financial information, and those who do have such an understanding and use.[5]

This distinction in accounting and financial reporting is not new. For example, Mautz and Sharaf [6] and Rappaport,[7] inter alia, have advocated that financial reports should be aimed at the 'sophisticated' investor. So too has Buzby when exploring the nature of adequate disclosure in financial reports. Indeed, he advocated the identification of professional financial analysts as the primary user group, justifying his approach as follows:[8]

'The best service that accounting can render the average investor is to provide more and better information to the professional analyst'.

Baker and Haslem have presented a somewhat more moderate approach, advocating that financial reports should be consistent with the needs of the various classes of investors but that, in recognising the different requirements and levels of understanding associated with these classes, the content level of financial reports should not be brought down to the level of the lowest common denominator:[9]

'The modern corporation is too complex for this, and to do so would constitute a disservice to the information needs of certain classes of relatively sophisticated investors'.

We would suggest that such an orientation to the needs of the so-called 'sophisticated' shareholder makes certain interesting assumptions about these investors, all of which have relevance to the overall study of shareholder use and understanding of financial information. For example:

(1)   That there is a definable group of shareholders with a significantly different accounting experience compared with the typical private

2

shareholder already identified in our previous writings[10] — that is, that 'sophisticated' shareholders do exist.

(2) That 'sophisticated' shareholders are a sufficiently important and influential group of investors to be regarded as the main user group to which reported financial information should be directed — that is, that their needs should be satisfied before those of private shareholders.[11]

(3) That 'sophisticated' shareholders use available financial information more intensively, and have a greater understanding of it than private shareholders.

If these assumptions do not hold then, at least in our opinion, there can be no significant difference between private and 'sophisticated' shareholders to justify the place of eminence so often given to the latter group in the accounting and finance literature. Equally, the usual assumption in existing company legislation of there being no such difference would hold.

Each of these assumptions is in itself an extremely complex matter, and this study cannot be expected to present full evidence of their validity (although it may give indications of this). What we hope we can do in this study is to present detailed evidence in relation to the use and understanding of available financial information by a group of shareholders and their advisers, who appear at first sight to be:

(1) Separable from private shareholders in terms of its accounting experience — that is, enough to justify the term 'sophisticated' investors.

(2) Sufficiently important and influential to be regarded as a major user group to which reportable financial information could be primarily directed.

(3) Significantly different from private shareholders in terms of its use and understanding of available financial information.

This study will concentrate on the presentation of evidence on the 'sophisticated' shareholders' use and understanding of financial information with which to support point 3 above. (This report, however, does not seek to compare directly the results obtained in this research project with those resulting from the private shareholder survey.) However, before this can be done, we believe some comment should be made in support of points 1 and 2. In this way, the justification for this study will hopefully become evident.

3

Identifying the 'sophisticated' investor

In our previous study, the typical private shareholder in the company concerned (XYZ) could be described as follows:[12]

'Such a respondent is more likely to be male rather than female; have a holding of less than 500 £1 ordinary share units in XYZ; have a total portfolio of 10 or more items; be in a non-accounting, non-financial occupation and therefore have little or no experience of accounting or related matters; make his own investment decisions without expert help; and read regularly at least one financial press source'.

Excluding such holdings, and ignoring nominee holdings, overseas shareholders, and company holdings, this leaves institutional investors as the remaining major shareholding group — that is, the holdings of organisations such as unit trusts, insurance companies, pension funds, investment companies, and merchant banks. These investors can be said to be uniquely different from private shareholders in the following matters:

(1)   They are concerned with what can be described as non-personal investment on behalf of identifiable individuals — for example, for unit-holders in unit trusts, life policy-holders in life assurance companies, and employees in pension funds. As evidenced in the next section, these investments are of considerable size, well in excess of the portfolios of the typical private shareholder.

(2)   As defined by Briston and Dobbins:[13]

'Institutional investors are organisations which raise funds from individuals and corporations and invest as principals in the stock market, using professional management and operating within the constraints provided by their own articles and trust deeds, and tax and legal considerations'.

They therefore employ expert accounting and investment experience and expertise in order to manage their investment portfolios. Such experience is either employed directly (in the form of investment analysts and managers) or indirectly (in the form of stockbrokers). This is distinctly different from the picture of private shareholders described above.

How important is the 'sophisticated' investor.

Institutional investors of the type outlined in 1 above are concerned with large-scale corporate investment. This has been clearly evidenced in the recent research of Briston and Dobbins.[14] The following data have been derived from their work:

(1) J Moyle, *The Pattern of Ordinary Share Ownership 1957-1970*, Cambridge University Press, 1971. (Briston and Dobbins, p.139)

	1957 %	1963 %	1970 %
Institutional investors*	18	25	32
Individual investors	66	54	47
Other investors**	16	21	21
	100	100	100

* excluding banks
**including charities, other companies, public sector bodies, and overseas investors

(2) Royal Commission on the Distribution of Income and Wealth, *Report No.2*, Cmnd 6171, HMSO, 1975. (Briston and Dobbins, p.141)

	1963 %	1969 %	1970 %	1971 %	1972 %	1973 %
Institutional investors*	26	33	35	36	37	38
Individual investors	59	47	45	44	43	42
Other investors**	15	20	20	20	20	20
	100	100	100	100	100	100

* excluding banks
**including charities, other companies, public sector bodies, and overseas investors

(3) Estimated ownership of UK registered companies 1966-75. (Briston and Dobbins, p.146)

	1966 %	1967 %	1968 %	1969 %	1970 %	1971 %	1972 %	1973 %	1974 %	1975 %
Institutional investors*	26	27	29	30	31	33	36	38	41	42
Other investors**	74	73	71	70	69	67	64	62	59	58
	100	100	100	100	100	100	100	100	100	100

* excluding banks
**including individual investors

(4)   Future pattern of UK share ownership. (Briston and Dobbins, p.179)

	1976 %	1977 %	1978 %	1979 %	1980 %
Institutional investors*	44	46	47	49	51
Other investors**	56	54	53	51	49
	100	100	100	100	100

* excluding banks
**including individual investors
(extrapolation by linear regression with 95% confidence intervals)

Thus the size of institutional investment has risen from less than 20% in 1957 (using the Moyle data) to just over 40% in 1975 (Briston and Dobbins data), and with the likelihood of exceeding 50% in 1980 (Briston and Dobbins data). This quite clearly evidences the importance and the influence of the institutional investor — relatively few investors hold by far the largest slice of company shareholdings, and would, therefore, appear to have a considerable potential to influence stock market behaviour. Mere size, however, does not provide sufficient evidence of the importance of this group in terms of its behaviour in relation to the use of available financial information. In this respect, some writers would argue that the importance of institutional investors is substantial in relation to the effective operation of the stock market. For example, Briston has recently argued as follows:[15]

'There is a growing body of evidence to suggest that accounting information is already very quickly absorbed into share prices and that share prices at any time tend to reflect all available information regarding the company concerned. *This process is able to take place because of the existence of investment analysts and financial journalists who analyse both available and predicted accounting data and through their influence upon investors produce a reasonably efficient stock market in which shares are correctly priced at any specific instance of time.* It can thus be argued that it does not matter either to shareholders or to the stock market whether or not shareholders are able to interpret annual reports so long as they respond to the financial press and to stockholders' reports, and the evidence of all the surveys is that they do this'.

This view, that the stock market is efficient in terms of its use of available financial information because of the existence of expert users of such information, implies much about the role of institutional investors and stockbrokers who employ such expertise. Indeed, Briston has gone so far as to minimise the need to recognise the rights of the private shareholder in this respect:[16]

6

INTRODUCTION

. . . . . the level of private shareholder comprehension is of relatively minor importance given the existence of efficient stock markets'.

In other words, his approach expresses the opinion that all that really matters with respect to the use and understanding of available financial information is the availability of accounting and financial expertise which can impound all such data into share prices. As most of this expertise exists within financial institutions and stockbroking firms,[17] it is our opinion that the extent of their use and understanding of financial information is worthy of evidencing — even if it confirms what is already assumed in the so-called efficient markets approach.

The question of the validity of the efficient markets school of thought is yet another reason for testing for institutional expertise. As the above statements of Briston indicate, there is a considerable support for the so-called efficient markets hypothesis — that is (in its semi-strong version), that the market equilibrium prices of securities fully reflect *all* publicly available information (including accounting information), and that these equilibrium prices react simultaneously and in an unbiased fashion to new information. The validity of this approach places an onerous burden on professional analysts who appear to be the group which, potentially, has the expertise to use all publicly available information — for example, it assumes that:

(1) Professional analysts make full use of (according to the model used by the market) of all publicly available financial information contained in interim, final and other financial reports; and

(2) professional analysts in making full use of such information are equally able to cope with and understand the underlying accounting data and procedures.

These appear to be important assumptions to make, particularly when there is growing comment about the flaws in the efficient markets approach. Some writers such as Fama[18] would argue that there is sufficient evidence from empirical studies which is consistent with the hypothesis — for example, the Ball and Brown study of the aggregate effect on share prices of the publication of accounting income figures.[19] Others would take alternative stances which can roughly be divided into two main schools of thought:

(1) That which is basically sympathetic to the efficient markets case but which warns either: (a) of the research problems in testing it — for example, the assumptions to be made about the market and pricing models used, the difficulty of obtaining suitable data with

7

which to test, and the problem of measuring the costs and benefits associated with improving the quality of available information;[20] or (b) of using it as if it were a scientific theory with predictive as well as explanatory powers.[21]

(2) That there is little or no case for the efficient markets viewpoint, despite the evidence supposedly in support of it.[22] Chambers, for example, makes the following points in criticism of the hypothesis:[23]

(a) Neither the stock market nor financial information are homogeneous; the efficient markets research examines only aggregate effects, and ignores individual differences.

(b) The existing research results concentrate almost exclusively on the impact of accounting information on share prices, and ignore the equally pertinent impact of other types of information.

(c) The efficient markets approach says nothing about the problem of optimal allocation of scarce resources:[24]

'The efficient market hypothesis has little to do with efficiency, in the sense of securing the distribution of available funds in favour of firms that are demonstrably more competent than others in using them, while even the information on financial and commercial competence is of dubious quality'.

(d) The hypothesis has little to say regarding the quality of available information. If the quality is poor, then the market has been ingesting poor quality information in determining share prices:[25]

'The efficient market hypothesis entails that stock prices adjust rapidly to new information as it becomes available. But it says nothing about the quality of that information. It is conceivable that reported income figures can vary in the same direction (and even by the same percentage) as the substantive increments in net wealth without any close correspondence with these increments; traditional accounting has been shown to tolerate very great differences in the amounts of income reported after applying different permissible rules to the same objects and events'.

Chambers is not alone in this criticism. Anderson and Meyers, for example, felt that the efficiency of the market has not really been proved or even tested (in terms of the immediate impounding of information into share prices, and of the optimal allocation of scarce resources).[26] They suggested that the available evidence shows the market does react to information but does not explain whether or not that reaction reflects efficiency — in other words, there is no real answer available as to what is or causes efficiency.[27]

Findlay, too, has been critical of the efficient markets research — particularly the research which uses circular reasoning to conclude that, because the market reacts to accounting numbers, numbers have an information content.[28] In other words, far from seeing a market full of efficient users of information, Findlay views it as a situation of functional fixation — users reacting to accounting information because they believe everyone else is using it.[29]

None of the above points can be said to be encouraging in terms of credible support for an efficient stock market which relies on efficient and effective use of financial information. Indeed, there appear to be strong arguments which cause us to suspect the wisdom of the traditional assumptions concerning stock market behaviour in relation to available financial information. Certainly, it does not seem to merit the confident statements of writers over the years with regard to institutional users. For example, in 1950:[30]

'The institutions — government, banks and labour union experts — however, constitute a sector of the public which is educated to a full understanding of the science and art of accounting. *They can be depended upon to know the language of accounting, its conventions and the significance of the auditor's report*'.

And more recently in 1975:[31]

'. . . . .the trend toward increased financial disclosure apparently has not resulted in overcomplicated financial statements . . . . . it appears that most readers of financial statements have relatively little difficulty understanding these statements, and that the investing public generally is not very critical of the complexity of these statements'.

We would suggest that these are matters which almost demand investigation, particularly in relation to the financial institutions which are traditionally classed as 'sophisticated' users of available information. We believe it is wrong to assume that all such information is used and understood by these users. Proof must be provided of this in order to establish the validity of the assumed 'sophistication'. The remaining chapters of this book attempt to do just that.

REFERENCES AND FOOTNOTES

1 Readers in doubt about this are invited to examine the work of the Committee as it is presented in *Accounting Standards 1979*, The Institute of Chartered Accountants in England and Wales, 1979. 6 *Exposure Drafts* and 16 *Statements of Standard Accounting Practice*, all of which are relevant at the time of writing, cover such measurement matters as accounting for acquisitions and mergers, extra-ordinary items, current costs, deferred tax, groups of companies, foreign currency transactions, post balance sheet events, taxation under the imputation system, stocks and work in progress, depreciation, and research and development. Only in the cases of disclosure of accounting policies and funds statements are there any attempts to direct the attention of accountants to the problem of communication.

2 T. A. Lee and D. P. Tweedie, *The Private Shareholder and the Corporate Report*, The Institute of Chartered Accountants in England and Wales, 1977, p xv.

3 Group of Scottish Finance Directors, *The Future of Company Reports — Green Paper*, privately published, 19 December 1977, p2.

4 *Ibid*, p3.

5 This appears to have been recognised recently by the Accounting Standards Committee. At the time of writing it is considering the publication of an accounting guideline following the submission of a background research paper on this subject. See A. E. Hammill, *Simplified Financial Statements*, Institute of Chartered Accountants in England and Wales, 1979.

6 R. K. Mautz and H. A. Sharaf, *The Philosophy of Auditing*, American Accounting Association, 1961, p191.

7 D. Rappaport, 'Materiality', *Journal of Accountancy*, April 1964, p42.

8 S. L. Buzby, 'The Nature of Adequate Disclosure', *Journal of Accountancy*, April 1974, pp28-47, at p46.

9 H. K. Baker and J. A. Haslem, 'Information Needs of Individual Investors', *Journal of Accountancy*, November 1973, pp64-69, at p68.

10 See Lee and Tweedie, *op cit*, p177 for a list of some of these items.

11 This does not mean, however, that private shareholders ought to be relegated to a 'second division' of financial reporting. The idea of simplified financial statements for their use (with warnings about the need to refer to the more complex statements when making decisions) is just as vital as providing more complex information for 'sophisticated' investors. The implication behind the stated assumption is that, in terms of the existing complex system of financial reporting to all shareholders, the needs of the private shareholder necessarily must take second place because of the nature of the reported data.

12 *Ibid*, p22.

13 R. J. Briston and R. Dobbins, *The Growth and Impact of Institutional Investors*, The Institute of Chartered Accountants in England and Wales, 1978, p9.

14 *Ibid, passim*.

15 R. J. Briston, 'The Private Shareholder and the Corporate Report: Some Further Evidence', *The Accountant's Magazine*, December 1977, p507 (emphasis added).

16 R. J. Briston, 'A Final Comment', *The Accountant's Magazine*, July 1978, p298.

17 It certainly does not reside amongst private shareholders, as evidenced in our earlier studies. For example, in Lee and Tweedie, *op cit*, pp18-19, it is shown that only 16% of respondents were in occupations related to accountancy, investment, banking or financial management, and only 14% could be said to have significant accounting and related experience (59% had no experience at all).

18 E. Fama, 'Efficient Capital Markets: A Review of Theory and Empirical Work', *Journal of Finance*, May 1970, pp383-417.

19 R. Ball and P. Brown, 'An Empirical Evaluation of Accounting Income Numbers',

Journal of Accounting Research, Autumn 1968, pp159-77.

[20] For example, D. Downes and T. R. Dyckman, 'A Critical Look at the Efficient Market Empirical Research Literature As It Relates to Accounting Information', *The Accounting Review,* April 1973, pp300-17.

[21] For example, J. R. Boatsman, 'Why Are There Tigers and Things?', *Abacus,* December 1977, pp156-67. In a carefully considered paper, Boatsman argues that the efficient markets hypothesis is only capable of explaining relationships between observed events; and not of predicting what these events will be. His reason is that the available information and share prices used in empirical testing of the hypothesis are not independent variables. The hypothesis is thus irrefutable as it is almost a tautology (p160).

[22] This has recently been argued by G. Whittington, 'Beware Efficient Markets Theory', *The Accountant's Magazine,* April 1979, pp145-6; and T. A. Lee, 'The Role of Accounting and Evidence of Efficient Markets', *The Accountant's Magazine,* June 1979, pp237-40.

[23] R. J. Chambers, 'Stock Market Prices and Accounting Research', *Abacus,* June 1974, pp39-54.

[24] *Ibid,* p42.

[25] *Ibid,* p48.

[26] J. A. Anderson and S. L. Meyers, 'Some Limitations of Efficient Markets Research for the Determination of Financial Reporting Standards', *Abacus,* June 1975, p26.

[27] *Ibid,* p32.

[28] M. C. Findlay, 'On Market Efficiency and Financial Accounting', *Abacus,* December 1977, p110.

[29] *Ibid,* p114.

[30] G. Cochrane, 'The Auditor's Report: Its Evolution in the USA', *The Accountant,* 4 November 1950, p459 (emphasis added).

[31] T. R. Dyckman, M. Gibbins, and R. J. Swieringa, *Experimental and Survey Research in Financial Accounting: A Review and Evaluation,* Paper published at Duke University December 1975, p7.

CHAPTER 2

Research methodology and survey respondents

This chapter outlines the methodology employed in the survey research used for the purposes of this study, and discusses the characteristics of those employed in the participating financial institutions (henceforth — institutional investors) and stockbroking firms (henceforth — stockbrokers). Much of the description will also provide an introduction to the background factors which were used as variables in the cross-analyses made with data derived from the survey.

Following our experience with the earlier private shareholder survey,[1] the method of approach adopted in the study was by interview — that is, a face-to-face meeting with representatives of the financial institutions and stockbroking firms who had agreed to an earlier request to participate in the research, utilising a prepared questionnaire.

The sample

Given the constraints of time and cost, the size of the survey had to be limited. It was, therefore, decided that some 225 respondents should be interviewed. Initially, it was intended to concentrate solely on financial institutions but the involvement of stockbroking firms with many of the institutions, and the finding that 58% of the respondents in the private shareholder study read stockbroker's reports,[2] led to a revision of the research method and the inclusion of stockbroking firms within the survey. It was, however, believed that those *holding* shares should be the prime target of the study, and it was further decided that approximately 60% of the respondents should be institutional investors, with the remaining 40% comprising stockbrokers.

In order to obtain a representative sample of institutional investors, the financial institutions were sub-divided into four different types — insurance companies; pension funds; investment and unit trusts; and merchant banks.

The Royal Commission on the Distribution of Wealth and Income had reported that at the end of December 1973 financial institutions, including banks, held 42% of the quoted ordinary shares in UK companies. The distribution of these holdings among the various financial institutions represented in the above percentage is shown in Table 1.

TABLE 1

Distribution of institutional ownership of quoted ordinary shares in UK companies at 31 December 1973

Institution	Percentage of total ordinary shares in issu %
Insurance companies	39
Pension funds	29
Investment and unit trusts	24
Banks, and other financial institutions	8
	100

Source: The Royal Commission on the Distribution of Income and Wealth, *Report* — No. 2, Cmnd 6171, HMSO, 1975.

The sample frame accordingly was designed to attempt to obtain representatives from financial institutions in the proportions shown in the above table.

It was appreciated that one individual might be unable accurately to represent the views of his organisation but, on the other hand, the time demanded by a lengthy interview (approximately 1¼ hours) could well lead to some organisations refusing to allow many of their staff to participate in the survey. Consequently, it was decided to ask each of the financial institutions and stockbroking firms sampled to allow two of their senior employees to be interviewed independently — in the institutions, preferably a senior investment manager and a senior investment analyst; and in the stockbroking firms, two senior analysts or partners. It was intended that the interviewees should be concerned primarily either with portfolio selection or with the analysis of the financial position and progress of individual enterprises.

A final constraint was the restriction of the sample frame to organisations within reasonable travelling distance from London and Edinburgh. The constraint was, however, relaxed so far as the sampling of stockbroking firms was concerned — firms in the Liverpool and Manchester areas were approached in an attempt to assess whether members of firms outside the two main UK financial centres of Edinburgh and London were different from other stockbrokers in their approach to the use and understanding of reported accounting data. In the event, the response from the Liverpool and Manchester areas was too poor to enable any meaningful comparisons to be made.

The survey response

It was decided to approach the major UK financial institutions within reasonable travelling distance of London and Edinburgh by using the lists of institutions given in the 1975-1976 *Times 1000*. Initially, therefore, letters asking for co-operation were sent to 22 of the top 25 life insurance companies; the pension funds of the 50 largest UK industrial companies and 17 nationalised institutions or industries; the 50 largest investment trusts and 15 of the largest unit trust groups; and the 29 members of the Issuing Houses Association (representing the banks) leading the table of acquisitions and mergers arranged in 1974, and 3 other banks managing pension funds (see below). Ultimately, the *Stock Exchange Official Year Book* was also used to increase the sample of insurance companies by selecting the next 10 largest companies meeting the travel criterion. The response rates to the requests are shown in Table 2.

TABLE 2

Response of financial institutions to requests for assistance with the research

	Number approached	Number accepting	Acceptance rate related to requests for co-operation %	Acceptance rate related to maximum possible acceptances %
Insurance companies	32	29	91	91
Pension funds	67	18	27	45
Investment and unit trusts	65	18	28	30
Merchant banks	32	14	44	47

The response from the insurance companies was exceptionally good — only 3 companies were unable to comply with the request for assistance with the research. The response of the pension funds of the major UK companies and nationalised industries at first sight appears to have been poor. Of the 67 organisations approached, however, the pension funds of 19 were managed by 10 merchant banks (of whom 9 allowed their employees to be interviewed) and the funds of 6 others were operated by 5 different insurance companies (all of whom co-operated in the research). One company refused to disclose the managers of their pension fund, simply stating that the fund was run by 'outsiders' and one other company was involved in a joint scheme with other companies and was unable to offer assistance. The remaining companies not participating in the survey refused to co-operate, either, in the case of 1 company, demanding a fee for co-operation; or, more commonly, failing to answer repeated requests for co-operation. The response rate of the companies and nationalised institutions managing their own pension funds was, therefore, 45%.

The response of the investment and unit trusts was much lower, although it should be said that the possibility of undiscovered interlocking management of some of the funds may mean that the actual response rate of the managers of these trust funds was higher than that shown in Table 2. 3 investment trusts reported that their managers (employed in merchants banks) had already co-operated in the survey, and 2 pairs of trusts indicated that they had the same management. It had been hoped that more funds would inform the researchers of the identity of their managers but most of the non-respondents simply failed to reply to repeated requests for co-operation. Other non-respondents among the investment trust managers stated that they were subjected to frequent pleas from researchers for information and now refused to accede to such requests.

The Times 1000 identifies the managers of unit trusts and, as 5 had already been interviewed in their capacity as employees of a merchant bank or an insurance company, no requests were sent to these managers. Once again, however, the response was poor — judging from the replies received to our requests, the unit trusts also receive what their managers believe are too many requests for research information.

As mentioned above, the 29 members of the Issuing Houses Association responsible for arranging the largest totals of acquisitions and mergers in 1974 were asked to assist in the research. In addition, a

15

further 3 merchant banks not included in the relevant table in *The Times 1000* were also contacted since they operated the pension funds of 3 of the major UK companies already contacted by the researchers.

Two banks reported they were in the process of disbanding their investment departments, and consequently did not believe that they could offer any assistance. Few of the other banks not participating in the survey replied to repeated requests for assistance. Of the 14 banks whose representatives were interviewed, no fewer than 9 managed the pension funds of 15 major UK companies and of 4 nationalised institutions previously contacted by the researchers as part of the survey.

Some of these pension funds were managed by more than one bank. One bank was involved in the management of 5 of these funds, 1 was assisting in the investment policies of 3 funds, and 5 banks helped to run 2 pension funds. All of these banks participated in the survey — the only bank managing a pension fund which refused to co-operate did allow the managers of its own unit trusts to be interviewed. Given that 9 of the top 10 banks in *The Times 1000* allowed their senior staff to be interviewed, and that all of the banks identified as being managers of pension funds previously approached, co-operated in the research (in one case as managers of unit trusts), it could be argued that the low overall response rate of the banks was due to the non-participation of those banks with a lesser influence on the stock market.

The sample frame for the stockbroking firms was drawn from the yellow pages of the Post Office telephone directories for Edinburgh, Glasgow, London (Central), Leeds, Liverpool and Manchester. In the event, the initial response rate was so poor that all suitable firms listed were contacted. The overall response rate and those for the individual areas are shown below in Table 3.

TABLE 3

Response of stockbroking firms to requests for assistance with the research

	London	Edinburgh	Glasgow	Leeds/ Liverpool/ Manchester	Overall
Firms listed	233	10	16	63	322
Less: non-UK firms	11	—	—	—	11
	222	10	16	63	311
Less:					
Firms no longer existing	7	—	—	—	7
Non-stockbroking firms	7	1	1	—	9
	208	9	15	63	295
Less:					
Firms accepting but not interviewed	5	—	—	9	14
	203	9	15	54	281
Firms interviewed	45	7	3	6	61
Acceptance rate	22%	78%	20%	11%	22%

As can be seen from the above table, the acceptance rates varied between areas. In Edinburgh, where the researchers may well have been known to the stockbroking firms, the response was extremely favourable. Despite repeated requests to firms in London and Glasgow, however, only about 1 firm in 5 agreed to co-operate in the survey. In the Leeds/Liverpool/Manchester area, a particular problem (namely the indisposition of an interviewer) arose and because of the time pressure on the other interviewers, the interviews arranged in 9 firms had to be abandoned.

Despite reminders, most of the firms which did not accept the invitation to participate in the study failed to reply to it. A few others, however, wrote back and explained that either they did not have a research department (this was not a precondition for the selection of a firm) or were too small, and consequently did not believe that they could be of sufficient assistance to warrant two members of the firm being interviewed. Other firms stated that their partners and senior partners were too busy to allow the researchers to interview them. In order to ensure that there were no significant differences between the representatives of stockbroking firms responding positively to the request for co-operation and those of the non-responding firms, a brief questionnaire was later sent to a sample of the non-responding firms to compare the background factors of the non-respondents with those of the respondents. This analysis is described towards the end of this chapter. Appendix 1 reproduces the questionnaire used for this purpose.

Even among the organisations willing to participate in the survey, the time pressure on their members frequently resulted in many of the financial institutions and stockbroking firms allowing the researchers access to only one member of the organisation. In other organisations, it was often claimed that one senior employee was an opinion leader with the firm, and that the organisation's view could better be expressed by this one person. In these situations, only one interview was undertaken. Table 4 below shows the number of interviews undertaken in terms of type of organisation and number within each organisation.

TABLE 4
Interviews undertaken

Organisation	Number of organisations visited	Number of interviews undertaken in organisation			Total
		3	2	1	
Financial institutions					
Insurance companies	29	—	22	7	51
Pension funds	18	—	13	5	31
Investment and unit trusts	18	1	12	5	32
Merchant banks	14	—	8	6	22
Total financial institutions	79	1	55	23	136
Stockbroking firms	61	1	32	28	95
Grand total	140	2	87	51	231

It will be noticed that in 2 organisations, 3 employees were interviewed — this occurred when (a) two distinct branches of one of the larger stockbroking firms were approached, and it was discovered that the analysts were quite independent in both policy and research matters; and (b) the analysts in 2 unit trusts under the same overall management were interviewed and, once again, their independence was evident. In effect, in both cases, virtually separate organisations seemed to exist and, consequently, the two additional interviews were included with the others in the study.

The interviewing of more than one individual in an organisation led to problems. Questions were put to the respondents attempting to determine their organisation's policy in particular areas. Occasionally, where more than one employee was interviewed, it became apparent that perceptions of policy differed; the resulting analysis (described in later chapters) has had to outline these areas of disagreement.

Table 5 shows the distribution of the institutional respondents in terms of employing institution compared to the proportion of the ownership of quoted ordinary shares held by the different types of institutions in 1973 (as per Table 1).

TABLE 5
Distribution of institutional respondents by employing institutions

Institution	Distribution of respondents %	Total shares in issue %
Insurance companies	37	39
Pension funds	23	29
Investment and unit trusts	24	24
Merchant banks	16	8
	100	100

n = 136

It can be seen from the table that, with the exception of those respondents employed by pension funds and merchant banks, an almost exact match was obtained. It will, however, be remembered that 9 of the 14 banks which participated in the study managed pension funds for industrial clients.

Consequently, it would seem that the distribution of respondents obtained bears a reasonable similarity to the relative and possible influence of the various financial institutions within the investment community.

The interviews

The interviews were conducted by graduating students at the Universities of Edinburgh and Liverpool. The questionnaire, which is reproduced in Appendix 2, formed the basis for each interview. The interviews were arranged by correspondence or telephone and usually took between 1 and 1½ hours to complete. Interviewing was conducted throughout the

19

Easter and Summer vacations in 1977. Each interviewer was thoroughly briefed prior to interviewing and supplied with a requisite number of questionnaires and printed cards outlining the answers for the limited choice questions. We checked each questionnaire (occasionally an interviewer was asked to contact a respondent again to clarify an answer) and, once all questionnaires were completed and checked, we coded the respondents' answers to enable computation to take place. The analysis was undertaken by us at the University of Edinburgh's Regional Computing Centre, and the program used was the Statistical Package for the Social Sciences.

Background factors

In order to construct an aggregate profile of the 231 respondents, the following background factors were sought: the respondent's sex; number of shareholdings in, and market value of the portfolio(s) to which the respondent's work related; whether the respondent had the final say in investment decisions; the number of years' experience of investment in a financial institution or stockbroking firm; the respondent's experience of using accounting information; and the respondent's accounting knowledge and related experience.

There are other factors which could have been used for the purposes of this profile, and we accept there is a case for examining the factors sought in much greater depth than has been possible in this study. Time pressure, however, imposed restrictions on the number of variables it was possible to examine. In any event, as the subsequent analyses will reveal, many of the factors examined revealed insignificant differences in responses to individual reporting matters covered in the questionnaire.

The following sections discuss each of the background factors utilised in this study. *It should be noted that the relevant tables and appendices are expressed as percentages of 231 respondents. This practice is continued throughout the text unless, for some reason, the number of responses varies from 231. In this case the number of analysable replies will be stated specifically in the table or appendix concerned.*

Respondents' sex

Table 6 reveals that only 2% of the respondents were female.

TABLE 6	
Sex of survey respondents	
	%
Male	98
Female	2
	100

This variable has consequently been ignored in all analyses.

Number of shareholdings in portfolio

Table 7 outlines the number of shareholdings in the portfolios to which the respondents work related.

TABLE 7	
Number of shareholdings in portfolios to which the work of survey respondents related	
	%
1— 100	24
101— 500	33
501—1000	5
1000+	4
'Do not knows'	34
	100

As can be seen from the table, almost three-fifths of the respondents were responsible for portfolios which contained up to 500 different shares. One quarter were responsible for portfolios containing 100 or less different shareholdings. The respondents who did not have information on the number of shareholdings tended to be those who appeared to have little responsibility so far as individual portfolios were concerned — that is, mainly those respondents working for stockbroking firms, the work of over two-thirds of whom did not relate to any particular portfolio. Of the remainder of those employed in stockbroking firms, 71% were involved with portfolios containing 100 or less shareholdings. On the other hand, exactly half of all the institutional respondents were concerned with portfolios containing 101 to 500 shareholdings.

Value of portfolio

TABLE 8

Estimated value of portfolios to which survey respondents' work related

£	%
100,000— 100,000,000	23
100,000,001—1,000,000,000 +	16
'Do not knows' and 'no answers'	28
'Over £1,000,000'	33
	100

As Table 8 reveals, a majority of the respondents were unsure of the worth of, or reluctant to give precise details about, the value of the portfolio(s) to which their work related. Only 39% of those interviewed gave the information specifically requested.

Seven per cent of the total respondents managed portfolios whose value at the time of interviewing was less than £1 million. At the other end of the scale, 10% were concerned with portfolios worth more than £250 million (see Appendix 3).

From the limited evidence available, it appeared that the few stockbrokers (as compared with institutional investors) who valued the particular portfolio(s) with which they worked were less likely to be involved with portfolios worth over £100 million — that is, the work of only 2 of the 14 stockbrokers stating the value of their portfolios was related to portfolios of this size. In contrast the work of 46% of the 77 institutional investors who gave some estimate of portfolio worth was concerned with this type of portfolio. (In terms of type of institution, the percentage of all respondents identifiably concerned with portfolios valued at more than £100 million was as follows — insurance companies (27%); pension funds (32%); investment trusts (14%); unit trusts (27%); and merchant banks (23%).

Final say in investment decision-making

A majority of the respondents stated they made or were involved in the final decision in appraising investments. 60% stated that they had some responsibility for the buy or sell decision (see Appendix 4). Not surprisingly, only 33% of those employed by stockbroking firms claimed to make (or be involved in) these decisions, whereas 79% of those working in the financial institutions gave a similar answer. This involvement in the decision-making process must often lead to the respondents concerned having a major impact on the stock market. 70% of those whose work related to portfolios valued at over £100 million claimed to have a say in the final investment decision.

TABLE 9
Final say in investment decisions

	%
Yes	60
No	35
'Do not knows' and 'no answers'	5
	100

Experience of institutional investment

A majority of the respondents had spent 10 years or less in the investment world (see Table 10).

TABLE 10
Survey respondents' experience of institutional investment

Years	%
1— 5	24
6—10	34
11—20	28
21 +	12
None	2
	100

Depite this, all groups appeared to be equally involved in the investment decision making process. Indeed, 63% of those who had 5 years or less experience were involved in the final decision — a figure which was marginally higher than that of any other group. Experience, too, appeared to be virtually unrelated to the value of the portfolios to which the respondents' work related. The work of those who had more than 10 years' experience of institutional investment was marginally more likely to relate to more valuable portfolios than that of respondents with lesser experience, but the results were found not to be significant at the 0.05 level when using the chi square test. Little difference was noted in the experience levels of the employees of financial institutions and stockbroking firms, although more of the former's employees (15%) than those of the latter (6%) had more than 20 years of experience.

Experience of using accounting information

Most of the respondents, as shown by Table 11, had a minimum of five years' experience of using accounting information.

TABLE 11
Survey respondents' experience of using accounting information

Years	%
1— 5	11
6—10	36
11—20	34
21 +	19
None	—
	100

Indeed, almost 1 in 5 of the respondents had been using such information for more than 20 years. Perhaps, not unexpectedly, there was a close relationship between experience in the investment world and the use of accounting data. For example, 75% of those with under 10 years' experience in the investment community had a similar length of experience in using accounting data. For those with more than 10 years' experience, the relationship was even closer — 92% had equivalent experience of using accounting statements.

Those who had more than 10 years' experience of using accounting data were marginally more likely to be involved in investment decision making (62%) than those whose experience was less than 10 years (55%). Little difference was, however, noted in the accounting experience of those employed in stockbroking firms or in the financial institutions.

Accounting training

Despite the experience of respondents in using accounting information, relatively few were found to hold accounting qualifications or to have attended courses in accounting (see Appendix 5).

24

TABLE 12

Accounting and related experience or knowledge of survey respondents

	%
Significant	25
Little	16
None	59
	100

Table 12 reveals that only 25% of respondents had undertaken any training such as that mentioned above. Only 16% admitted to having attended short courses in accounting, the remainder stated that any accounting skills they had acquired had been picked up 'on the job'. Not surprisingly, those respondents who had greater experience in using accounting information tended to be more likely to have received formal accounting training. For example, 37% of those whose experience of using accounting data spanned more than 20 years had received significant training in accounting, whereas only 8% of those who had used accounting data for no more than five years had received similar training. Once again, no major difference in the training of those employed by stockbroking firms or financial institutions was noted.

Summary of background factors

It is obviously difficult to come to an accurate conclusion about the typical respondent in this study, but the following seems to be a reasonable summary. The typical institutional investor was male, and was likely to be involved in the final investment decision; to have had between 6 and 20 years of experience of the investment community, and of handling accounting information; to have had little or no formal training in accounting; to have been involved with portfolios containing 500 or fewer shareholdings but with a value likely to range from £1 million to £1,000 million. The typical stockbroker was likely to have similar personal characteristics but was unlikely to relate his work to any particular portfolios or to be involved in investment decision-making.

Respondents and non-respondents

As mentioned earlier in the chapter, in order to ensure that the survey respondents were representative of the group of investors sampled, it was necessary to ascertain the main background characteristics (outlined in the previous sections) pertaining to the non-respondents. For this reason, a brief questionnaire covering these matters was sent at the beginning of 1979 to the 220 non-responding stockbroking firms. (It was decided not to approach the institutional investors since, as Table 2 and the subsequent comments reveal, the institutional response rates were much higher than that of the stockbroking firms. Additionally, the problem of interlocking managements meant that institutions whose employees had already co-operated in the study could have been approached again inadvertently and, because of the time lapse between the receipt of the initial request for co-operation and that of the questionnaire for non-respondents, could have also responded to the latter).

Questionnaires sent to 37 stockbroking firms were returned because the firms could no longer be traced; 2 other firms refused to take part in the supplementary survey; and replies were received from only 15 others, of whom all but one returned questionnaires from two senior members of the firm. The response rate (involving only possible responses) from the stockbroking firms of 8% was disappointingly low — especially as each firm received a reminder and additional questionnaires some three weeks after the initial mailing.

Because of the low response rate, no statistical comparison between respondents and non-respondents has been undertaken. Comparing the two groups, however, it can be seen that, broadly, the background characteristics of respondents and non-respondents appeared to be reasonably similar.

TABLE 13
Respondents and non-respondents (stockbrokers)

BACKGROUND VARIABLES	*Respondents* % n = 95	*Non-respondents* % n = 29
Number of shareholdings		
1— 100	20	55
101— 500	8	14
501—1000	3	7
1001 +	2	7
'Do not knows' and 'no answers'	67	17
	100	100
Use of accounting information (years)		
1— 5	11	14
6—10	29	21
11—20	42	55
21 +	17	10
'No answer'	1	—
	100	100
Experience of institutional *investment (years)*		
1— 5	26	14
6—10	27	48
11—20	37	31
21 +	6	7
'No answer'	4	—
	100	100
Accounting and related experience		
Significant	18	17
Little	20	45
None	62	38
	100	100

18% of respondents had a significant experience of accounting compared to 17% of non-respondents. Similarly, 40% of respondents had used accounting information for 10 or less years and 53% of this group had worked in the investment world for a similar period of time. The corresponding figures for non-respondents were 35% and 62% respectively. Only one major difference between the groups was

27

revealed, and this related to the number of shareholdings in the portfolio to which the stockbrokers' work related. The work of 55% of the non-respondents, as opposed to 20% of the respondents, was concerned with portfolios which contained 100 or less different shareholdings. It should, however, be noted that two-thirds of the respondents did not give any information on shareholdings. (The non-respondents were asked about the value of these portfolios but, as so few answers were forthcoming, no comparison with the respondents has been shown).

It would seem from the limited evidence available that the respondents and non-respondents were likely to have relatively similar backgrounds in terms of accounting experience, use of accounting information and experience in the investment world. The overall conclusion would seem to be that there is no hard evidence to show that the respondents were not broadly representative of the total sample. Only in the case of portfolio size was there any apparent difference between respondents and non-respondents — the former tending to claim that their work did not relate to any particular portfolio.

Approach to analysis

In our earlier study of the private shareholder, it became clear that the comprehension of financial reporting practice of the respondents was the key factor from which all subsequent examinations and analyses could be made. For this reason, the remainder of this text has been structured as follows:

(1) *An examination of the overall levels of understanding of the survey respondents* (Chapters 3, 4, 5 and 6). This analysis is concentrated initially on five specific areas of financial reporting practice and outlines whether, in aggregate, the respondents' comprehension was reasonable, vague or almost non-existent. Having considered each specific area of reporting practice, the results are aggregated in Chapter 5 into an overall index of individual respondents' understanding which reveals the distribution of the respondents' comprehension. A further index relating to understanding of inflation accounting is constructed in Chapter 6, and both indices are then used in later analyses.

(2) *A review of the use made of financial information in the respondents' organisations* (Chapters 7, 8, 9 and 10). This section

not only outlines the way in which financial institutions and stockbroking firms approached the analysis of company financial information, but also considers the individual respondents' own use and assessment of financial information provided both by companies and by other external sources. A main aim of this section was to categorise the respondents in terms of their reading pattern of company annual reports. The financial experts were divided into three reading pattern groups (very thorough, thorough, and less thorough readers of the annual report — Chapter 8) which were used in later analyses. A secondary but nevertheless important objective of this section was to establish the relative importance to, and influence on, respondents of the various sources of financial information.

(3) *An analysis of those respondents who both understood and read sources of financial information* (Chapter 11). This chapter uses the index of comprehension constructed in Chapter 5 and the reading pattern categorisation obtained in Chapter 8, and relates these factors to the background characteristics of the individual respondents in an attempt to identify those persons who had a high level of understanding and use of financial information. It examines the use and comprehension of conventional financial reporting of the individual respondents; summarises the analysis of comprehension in terms of financial statements adjusted to take account of changes in the levels of general and specific prices; and provides a further summary of the specific areas of traditional reporting practice not understood by the respondents. The overall conclusions of the study and recommendations for future action are presented in Chapter 12.

REFERENCES

[1] T. A. Lee and D. P. Tweedie, *The Private Shareholder and the Corporate Report*, Institute of Chartered Accountants in England and Wales, 1977.
[2] *Ibid*, p68.

CHAPTER 3

Understanding financial information

As indicated in Chapter 1, it is essential to evidence the expertise of the so-called 'sophisticated' investor. In particular, it is important to demonstrate that he is capable of understanding the financial messages contained in the various sources of corporate information of which he makes use. Unless his level of understanding is high, there are obvious risks associated with his investment decision making — that is, other than those inherent in the investments concerned. Lack of proper understanding of available financial information could result in inadequate or improper assessments of alternative investments, to the detriment of the hundreds of thousands of individuals relying on the investment expertise concerned to provide necesary levels of income and capital appreciation (as in pension funds, life assurance companies, investment trusts, and unit trusts).

With this in mind, this and subsequent chapters will analyse the research results pertaining to certain tests of understanding given to the survey respondents. It must be emphasised that these tests have not been designed to evidence absolute levels of comprehension amongst respondents. Rather, they provide broad guidelines as to the potential understanding of persons who carry a considerable investment responsibility. Thus, they give important initial evidence of whether or not these respondents should be capable of using complex financial information with an understanding of the underlying principles which would be sufficient to allow for its effective use in investment decision making. In no way can these tests therefore be seen as evidencing a guarantee of adequate information understanding in investment decisions. The tests underlying this and subsequent chapters will, therefore, concentrate only on producing results of aggregate levels of understanding applied to relatively straightforward and basic notions associated with reported financial information. They are an essential starting point only in the complex process of conclusively determining shareholder understanding.

Assessing actual understanding

The survey respondents were asked to state their perceived understanding of reported accounting information, prior to being tested in seven specific areas in order to construct an aggregate profile of comprehension for the respondents as a group. The questions asked related mainly to the traditional system of accounting but, in addition, several were asked which concerned the contemporary problem of accounting and reporting for changing prices and price levels. Thus, respondents were required to evidence an understanding of both familiar and less well-known features of the corporate financial reporting system.

It is almost impossible to devise tests of comprehension of reporting practices which would satisfy every person interested or involved in the area. If tests are conducted specifically on the use of accounting figures then difficulties arise in attempting to assess whether they have been used effectively and, if so, whether this has been as a result of luck, experience, understanding, or some combination of each of these things. On the other hand, if the tests are limited to questions of broad principle and convention, then their critics are quick to respond that levels of understanding achieved may be poor indicators of understanding when actual accounting figures are used in practice.

Of the two possible approaches, it was felt in this study that the second one of examining for understanding in a broad sense was more meaningful at this stage of accounting research, rather than pursuing the exceedingly problematic first approach of testing on the use of accounting data. The existing lack of specific criteria with which to test in the latter area leaves the alternative 'broad-brush' approach to be used. In any case, the results from questions of principle and convention provide the basis of understanding necessary for comprehension of more pragmatic issues in accounting.

The comprehension tests were conducted in two main·categories — the first relating to traditional financial reporting practice (which had been used in the previous study of private shareholder comprehension[1]); and the second relating to inflation accounting practice (an area hitherto not researched in this way). The traditional category concentrated on five main areas — the general nature of reporting; the general contents of specific financial statements; accounting terminology commonly used in financial reports; the main valuation bases appropriate to particular assets; and certain key financial ratios. With the exception of the addition of funds statements to the 'general contents of specific financial statements' area, the topics covered in this category were the same as those contained in the aforementioned private shareholder study. In the latter, these had been found to provide a reasonable coverage of private shareholder comprehension, and it is believed that the same would apply to the more expert institutional investor or stockbroker.

The inflation accounting category was included in order to provide some early evidence of how well 'sophisticated' investors were coping with the problem of financial reports on the effects of price changes on accounting results. This is a topic of growing importance, and it is essential that such financial information users are thoroughly familiar with the system. Two main areas were covered in the interviews — the nature of inflation accounting statements and adjustments; and the inflation accounting valuation bases appropriate to particular assets. The inflation acounting system used for this purpose was mainly that of current cost accounting as had been advocated by the Accounting Standards Committee prior to the interviews.[2]

Perceived understanding of respondents

At the outset, it was felt to be useful to ask the respondents what they believed to be their level of understanding of financial reporting practice, particularly in relation to investment decision making. Table 14 summarises their views on this matter, and Appendices 6 to 12 inclusive, provide cross-analyses of these views with the 7 main background variables used throughout this study.

TABLE 14
Perceived understanding of reported accounting information

	%	%
Respondents indicating that they understood reported accounting information		
and found it relevant to their investment decisions	87	
and found it irrelevant to their investment decisions	8	
and found it only sometimes relevant to their investment decisions	1	96
Respondents indicating that they did not understand reported accounting information		2
'Do not knows' and 'no answers'		2
		100

Almost all of the 231 respondents believed they understood reported accounting information (96%), and of the latter group, almost 9 out of every 10 stated they also found it relevant to their investment decisions. Only 2% of respondents perceived a personal lack of understanding. Given the type of respondents (institutional investors and stockbrokers), it should not be surprising to read that so many felt they understood such information, and found it relevant. On the contrary, it is surprising to find 8 respondents not providing such perceptions. For further analysis, these respondents have been omitted from the cross-tabulations as they represent such a small sub-group.

When relating respondents' perceptions to their background characteristics, it is found that none of the latter appear to have influenced the two main perceptions (understand and find relevant; and understand and find irrelevant or only sometimes relevant). Indeed, for each of the variables, the results show that approximately 9 out of every 10 respondents believed they understood reporting accounting information and found it relevant; with the remainder forming the other category of 'irrelevant or only sometimes relevant'. This lack of difference in the results (none of which were statistically significant at the 0.05 level using the chi square test) means that the relevant null hypotheses cannot be rejected.

These results reveal quite clearly that the perceptions of the individual

33

respondents concerning their understanding and use of accounting information were formed irrespective of their background — that is, irrespective of what they were responsible for, and what experience they had had. Almost all felt they could understand and use such information. The following chapters will attempt to evidence the reality of the perceptions — first, in the area of traditional reports and, secondly, in the area of inflation accounting.

REFERENCES
[1] T. A. Lee and D. P. Tweedie, *The Private Shareholder and the Corporate Report*, The Institute of Chartered Accountants in England and Wales, 1977.
[2] At the time of the survey, the practices used in the tests were taken from 'Current Cost Accounting', *Exposure Draft 18*, Accounting Standards Committee, 1976.

CHAPTER 4

Assessing actual understanding of traditional financial information

The previous chapter provides evidence of respondents' perceived understanding. This chapter concentrates on their actual understanding of five areas of financial reporting practice — that is, the general nature of reporting; the nature of financial statements; accounting terminology; accounting valuation bases; and financial ratios. Obviously, these are not the only areas suitable for testing the comprehension of institutional investors and stockbrokers. Nevertheless, they appear to cover the main areas of financial reporting practice and, as such should provide investors with a foundation for understanding the more quantitative aspects of accounting. The following sections will explain the research results in each area in the order stated above.

General nature of reporting

Financial statement users ought to have a reasonable understanding of the main features of company financial reporting, mainly as a background to their understanding of more detailed and precise financial reporting matters. In this sense, it is felt that they should have a general understanding of the legal responsibilities, objectives, and nature of data associated with published financial statements. Thus, in this study, respondents were asked to state who they thought are responsible for these statements; what the aims of the statements are; and whether reported data can be regarded as being of an approximate or precise nature.

Before commenting on the research results obtained, however, it is important to specify what were regarded as reasonable, vague or incorrect responses (these being the three main categories into which answers were placed). So far as legal responsibility was concerned, responses indicating company boards of directors were classified as reasonable answers. All others were classified as incorrect, unless coupled with the correct answer (in which case they were usually reclassified as vague answers). Answers relating to reporting objectives were somewhat more difficult to classify due to the existing lack of agreement on this topic within the accountancy profession, but those specifying accountability, or the provision of data for investment decision making, were taken as reasonable responses. Vague understanding was attributed to responses indicating reported data which could be used to justify dividends or to those giving vague descriptions of shareholder accountability. All other responses were regarded as incorrect. Certain multiple responses required to be reclassified as vague or incorrect, depending on the nature of the individual answers provided. Finally, with regard to the nature of accounting data, reasonable responses were regarded as those indicating its approximate nature. Those responses stating such data were either accurate or inaccurate were classified as having no understanding. The overall response to these matters is contained in Table 15, and the more detailed supporting data are contained in Appendices 13 to 15 inclusive.

TABLE 15
Actual understanding of the general nature of reported financial statements

LEVEL OF UNDERSTANDING	Legal responsibility for financial statements %	Objectives of financial statements %	Accuracy of reported data %
Reasonable	75	20	51
Vague	4	56	—
Poor or none	21	24	49
	100	100	100

Overall, the results in Table 15 evidence a distinct split in the comprehension of the responding group in this matter. In none of the areas covered was there a convincing portrayal of understanding. Three out of every 4 respondents gave a reasonable answer to the question of legal responsibility (but 21% had poor or no understanding); but only 1 in 5 respondents had a reasonable understanding of reporting objectives (a very low response given the type of respondent), although more than

50% had vague notions of this matter; and there was an almost equal split in the total group between those believing in the approximation of reported data (51%) and those believing in its accuracy or inaccuracy (49%). These results are disappointing, given their fundamental nature and the background of the respondents concerned. However, it must be remembered that an understanding of these issues is not absolutely essential to the proper use of reported financial information. It is worrying, nevertheless, to see 13% of respondents believing company secretaries to be responsible for financial statements; 15% of respondents indicating financial statements provide a valuation of the reporting company as a whole; and 27% of respondents stating that reported accounting data are accurate.

Nature of financial statements

This section is concerned with respondents' understanding of the general nature of 6 main financial statements — the chairman's report, the directors' report, the profit and loss account, the balance sheet, the auditor's report, and the sources and application of funds statement. Each is usually contained in company annual financial statements (particularly of large companies and groups) and, as each contains information of potential use to the institutional investor and stockbroker, it is reasonable to suggest these persons ought to have a reasonable understanding of their general nature and content.

The questions asked in relation to each of these financial statements were relatively open-ended, resulting in a variety of responses (which have been analysed in detail in Appendices 16 to 21 inclusive). However, for purposes of further analysis, it was necessary to categorise these answers into groupings indicating reasonable, vague and poor or no understanding. How this was undertaken, is noted at the end of each of the relevant Appendices. The overall results, following this regrouping, are contained in Table 16.

TABLE 16

Actual understanding of the nature of individual parts of the annual financial report

LEVEL OF UNDERSTANDING	Chairman's report %	Directors' report %	Profit & loss account %	Balance sheet %	Auditor's report %	Funds state- ment %
Reasonable	85	29	57	74	65	23
Vague	11	31	28	15	18	13
Poor or none	4	40	15	11	17	64
	100	100	100	100	100	100

Most respondents understood the content of the chairman's report (85% gave reasonable responses, and a further 11% indicated vague understanding). Comprehension of the directors' report, on the other hand, was very much poorer — approximately 3 out of 10 respondents only having a reasonable grasp of the topic, and 40% having a poor or no understanding of it. A somewhat better response was given to the profit and loss account — but little more than one-half of the respondents (57%) could provide reasonable answers, and 15 out of every 100 respondents had poor or no understanding.

Almost 3 out of 4 respondents (74%) had a reasonable understanding of the contents of the balance sheet, the remainder either having a vague (15%) or poor understanding (11%). These results reveal that this was the best understood of the main financial statements by this particular group of respondents. The auditor's report content was less well understood on the whole (approximately two-thirds of the group providing a reasonable response), but the funds statement was the least understood statement of all — 64% of respondents having a poor or no understanding, and just over 1 in 5 having a reasonable understanding. The relatively recent appearance of this statement to the reporting scene may have had something to do with this result, but it is worrying to evidence such a poor overall understanding of the nature of the contents of such an important accounting report.

Taken together, the responses of these financial experts to the questions relating to the content of the 6 main statements in the annual financial report of a company reveal a reasonable but not outstanding understanding. Only in the case of the chairman's report (usually qualitative rather than quantitative in approach) did more than three-quarters of the respondents evidence reasonable understanding. The balance sheet was the only accounting statement which attracted relatively similar responses — the directors' report and the funds statement being relatively very poorly understood; and the profit and loss account and auditor's report being, for the type of respondent, only moderately understood. It may be that respondents were lazy in their responses to what they regarded as relatively simple questions on familiar topics. However, precautions were taken to guard against this as interviewers were instructed to encourage respondents to provide fuller answers when the initial response was too vague.

Accounting terminology

Accounting and the financial reports which are produced from it involve the use of a highly complex and technical language. As such, it is essential that potential report users are fully conversant with accounting jargon — especially as many of the terms used by accountants may have an accounting meaning different from their everyday meaning (for example, as with 'profit' and 'reserves'). This section therefore examines the results of respondents' answers to questions about the meaning of 6 well-known, often used accounting terms — profit, depreciation, equity capital, current assets, reserves, and accrued charges. Table 17 contains a summary of such results, the details of which are provided in Appendices 22 to 27, inclusive.

TABLE 17
Actual understanding of terminology used widely in reported financial statements

LEVEL OF UNDERSTANDING	Profit %	Depreciation %	Equity capital %	Current assets %	Reserves %	Accrued charges %
Reasonable	15	23	29	56	50	45
Vague	47	70	60	33	12	3
Poor or none	38	7	11	11	38	52
	100	100	100	100	100	100

In general terms, respondents' understanding of these accounting terms was much less than for the content of the main accounting and related statements. Indeed, in several instances, only a small minority of respondents had what could be termed a reasonable understanding.

There was, however, a number of aggregate responses of a vague nature to indicate the possibility of respondent laziness in answering.

With the commercial and investment sectors of a mixed economy such as that of the UK, the term 'profit' is a very familiar and very important indicator. It is used for a variety of purposes and decisions and, therefore, it is exceedingly surprising to discover, first, only 15% of respondents having a reasonable understanding of it and, secondly, that nearly 4 out of 10 respondents had poor or no understanding of it. The number of vague responses (47%) goes some way to mitigating this overall impression of lack of comprehension by institutional investors and stockbrokers.

The position is only slightly improved with the reponses to 'depreciation' and 'equity capital'. Less than one-quarter of respondents (23%) could give a reasonable definition of the very familiar term of depreciation (70% giving a vague answer, however); and 29% reasonably defined the term of equity capital, with a further 60% being vague about it. The size of the 'vague' response to these two terms indicates that respondents may have been too casual in their responses. This is arguably confirmed in the answers to what may be considered to be less well-used and more definite terms of current assets, reserves, and accrued charges. In each case, approximately one-half of the respondents were able to give a reasonable response (56%, 50% and 45% respectively), although, in the case of reserves, nearly 4 out of 10 financial experts had little or no understanding and, in the case of accrued charges, more than one-half lacked even a vague understanding.

Considering the type of respondent being used in this study, the responses to the questions on accounting terminology cannot be viewed as anything other than disappointing. Perhaps the familiarity of terms caused a certain casualness in response (for example, 39% stating that profit was a sum or surplus remaining after deducting expenses; and 34% stating that depreciation was an amount written off assets). This might explain the vagueness in responses to terms such as profit, depreciation, and equity capital. However, it does not explain the inability of certain respondents to define 'reserves' (7% saying they were monies set aside for contingencies; and 15% not defining them by stating they were 'equity minus share capital') or 'accrued charges' (36% not knowing or not giving an answer to this term).[1]

UNDERSTANDING OF TRADITIONAL FINANCIAL INFORMATION

Accounting valuation bases

An essential ingredient of traditional accounting practice is asset valuation. Even within the historic cost system there are variations of and to historic costs which require understanding if the full meaning of reported accounting data is to be properly appreciated. The present debate on current cost accounting enlarges and emphasises this problem. In this section, the results of respondents' answers to questions relating to the existing system of accounting will be considered; particularly within 3 areas — plant and machinery, stock and work-in-progress, and quoted investments. These are assets which are to be found in most published balance sheets, and each involves a somewhat different valuation approach (plant being depreciable; stock often involving complex allocation procedures, as well as the use of the 'lower of cost or market value' convention; and investments requiring some disclosed note of their market value). Table 18 summarises the results, and Appendices 28 to 30, inclusive, provide the analysed responses in some detail.

TABLE 18
Actual understanding of traditional accounting valuation bases

LEVEL OF UNDERSTANDING	Plant and machinery %	Stock and work-in-progress %	Quoted investments %
Reasonable	62	81	67
Vague	29	3	1
Poor or none	9	16	32
	100	100	100

Nearly two-thirds of respondents (62%) had a reasonable understanding of the traditional plant valuation basis, with only 9% giving 'poor or no understanding' responses (7% not providing any positive response). Once again, there was a sizeable vague response (29%). By way of contrast, the aggregate responses to stock and to quoted investments were far more definite (that is, lacking in any appreciable vague response). More than 8 out of 10 respondents had a reasonable understanding of stock and work-in-progress valuations (only 16% had a poor or no understanding); and two-thirds (67% had a similar understanding of quoted investment values (with 32% having a poor or no understanding).

41

The level of understanding of these valuation principles exhibited by respondents was generally good. The level of understanding was somewhat higher than for the more conceptual matters of the general nature of reporting, and the nature of financial statements and even the practical area of terminology. The relative lack of vagueness about valuations also highlights the difference in response between this area and that of terminology. In other words, there are indications in this section that respondents had a clearer understanding of more practical matters than they did of matters of general concept.

Financial ratios

In order to make best use of the available financial information of companies, the user-decision maker will require to reduce it to a form which maximises its information content. One of the most generally accepted ways of doing this is to produce a series of financial ratios which, when compared inter and intra-company, indicate key matters in corporate activity and performance. Investors form one such group of financial ratio producers and users, and it was felt that the respondents in this study (all of whom are connected in some way or another with company investment) ought to be tested on their comprehension of certain of the most familiar ratios in share investment. The ratios chosen were the price-earnings ratio, the dividend yield, and the dividend cover. Each is included in the *Financial Times* quotations list, and each is often included in the annual report of quoted companies. Table 19 summarises the findings which are detailed in Appendices 31 to 33, inclusive.

TABLE 19
Actual understanding of financial ratios

LEVEL OF UNDERSTANDING	Price-earnings ratio %	Dividend yield %	Dividend cover %
Reasonable	47	13	68
Vague	45	80	26
Poor or none	8	7	6
	100	100	100

One of the most familiar and used financial ratios must undoubtedly be the price-earnings ratio. Yet, on the evidence of this survey, the financial experts concerned did not have a completely clear understanding of its meaning. Only 47% could give a reasonable definition, with an almost similar number (45%) having a vague understanding only, and the remainder (8%) giving incorrect answers or no answers. This result is very surprising although it does not necessarily mean the ratio is badly used in practice.

The dividend yield was apparently misunderstood to an even greater extent — a very small minority of 13% giving a reasonable response; and 8 out of 10 respondents only able to provide a vague answer. In contrast, the response to dividend cover was somewhat better — two-thirds of respondents having a reasonable understanding and only 6% having a poor or no understanding.

Overall, the response in this area was not expected. The very small 'poor or no understanding' figures for each item indicates that respondents did have some understanding but were unable, in a great many cases, to convey it to the interviewer. It is to be presumed that this vagueness was limited to definitional understanding, and did not extend to the practical use of data relating to the ratios concerned.

Summary

The conclusions to be drawn from the findings outlined in this chapter are reasonably straightforward. First, in each of the 5 areas covered, the level of understanding by respondents was not as high as might perhaps have been expected from financial experts. This was particularly the case in the areas of accounting terminology and financial ratios (topics in each of them lacking sufficient 'reasonable' responses — for example, in relation to definitions of profit, depreciation, price-earnings ratio, and dividend yield), but is also to be seen in parts of each of the other areas (for example, in relation to the objectives of financial statements, the directors' report, and the funds statement).

Secondly, there is relatively consistent evidence of a general vagueness in the responses indicating either incomplete understanding or casualness in providing the answer or possibly a mixture of both. As interviewers guarded against vague responses, it appears possible that the respondents may have lacked reasonable understanding in many of these areas because the relevant items were so familiar as never to be questioned so far as meaning was concerned (this could particularly be the case with topics such as profit and the price-earnings ratio). Thirdly, despite the respondents having usually at least a vague understanding of the topic in question, there was, in response to particular questions, a considerable number of respondents with poor or no understanding — this ranged from 4% for the chairman's report and 6% for dividend cover to 52% for accrued charges and 64% for the funds statement.

The existence of such responses from these respondents is a potential cause for concern. Equally of concern is the variability of response — for example 85% understanding reasonably well the content of the chairman's report but only 23% being in the same category *vis-à-vis* the funds statement. In other words, the understanding of these financial experts was not as high as might have been expected (although few respondents revealed a total lack of knowledge), and was exceedingly variable, depending on the area of comprehension concerned. Such a conclusion must be interpreted within the context of the nature of the questions asked and the bases for the categorisation of responses. Within these constraints, however, a picture of the overall understanding of the group of respondents concerning certain aspects of the financial reporting process has emerged. An analysis of overall understanding and individual respondent's comprehension would, however, provide more definitive conclusions. This will be done in the next chapter.

REFERENCE

[1] For further comment on this issue, see T. A. Lee, 'Sandilands and User Comprehension', *Journal of Business Finance and Accounting*, Spring 1976, pp85-96; D. P. Tweedie, 'The Psychological Background to Financial Reporting', *The Accountant's Magazine*, December 1976, pp470-74; and D. P. Tweedie, 'ED18 and User Comprehension — the Need for an Explanatory Statement', *Journal of Business Finance and Accounting*, Autumn 1977, pp285-98.

CHAPTER 5

Further assessment of actual understanding of financial information

Following the establishment of absolute levels of understanding of the survey respondents in the findings of the previous chapter, this chapter attempts to determine more precisely their levels of understanding in relation to a defined group average. Following its use in a previous study of shareholder comprehension,[1] an index of understanding has been constructed from which can be determined different levels of understanding.[2] It is based on points scores attributable to respondents' answers to the questions asked in each of the 5 areas of financial reporting practice analysed in Chapter 4. Responses classified as indicating reasonable understanding were given a points score of 2; those indicating vague understanding were given a points score of 1; and those indicating no understanding were given a points score of 0. Thus, the maximum possible scores for each of the 5 areas were as follows: general nature of reporting — 3 questions, maximum score = 6; nature of financial statements — 6 questions, maximum score = 12; accounting terminology — 6 questions, maximum score = 12; accounting valuation bases — 3 questions, maximum score = 6; and financial ratios — 3 questions maximum score = 6. This gave a total maximum score for understanding of 42.

Understanding scores

The overall analysis of understanding in each of the five reporting areas is contained in Appendix 34. The above points scores have been applied to the responses given by each interviewed financial expert. From the data contained in Appendix 34, it can be seen that the conclusions given in Chapter 4 have been generally confirmed — that is, for each of the 5 areas, the distribution is skewed by the respondents' knowledge of the items concerned. This is particularly the case with accounting valuation bases (skewness coefficient = −1.23) and financial ratios (skewness coefficient = −1.22). It is least so in the most conceptual area in which testing was conducted — the general nature of reporting (skewness coefficient = −0.25). These differences can also be evidenced in the calculated means (accounting valuation bases = 4.52 out of 6; and financial ratios = 4.06 out of 6: compared with general nature of reporting = 3.52 out of 6; nature of financial statements = 7.83 out of 12; and accounting terminology = 6.61 out of 12). In addition, there is a certain amount of dispersion associated with the mean for all areas — ranging from a standard deviation of 1.20 and a mean of 4.06 (for financial ratios) to a standard deviation of 1.56 and a mean of 3.52 (for general nature of reporting). These results can be put in context more clearly as in Table 20.

TABLE 20

Understanding scores for individual financial reporting matters

UNDERSTANDING SCORE RANGE*	General nature of reporting %	Nature of financial statements %	Accounting terminology %	Accounting valuation bases %	Financial ratios %
Upper range	32	44	22	62	44
Middle range	43	44	60	25	47
Bottom range	25	12	18	13	9
	100	100	100	100	100

*Respondents' scores were expressed as a percentage of the maximum possible score in each area — see Appendix 34. For each of the 5 areas, the scores were cut at the 33 and 67 percentiles.

The data in Table 20 have been constructed from those in Appendix 34. By grouping the points score scales into (approximately) a bottom third, a middle third, and a top third, the response rates can be examined more easily in aggregate. The lack of precision, and the corresponding presence of vagueness, is to be seen in all areas — a minority of responses being in the upper range in each area, with the exception of the upper range of accounting valuation bases into which 62% of respondents fell. The vagueness was greatest with accounting terminology with 60% of respondents coming into the middle range and only 22% in the upper range. Relatively similar aggregate responses were achieved with the nature of financial statements and financial ratios (a small minority of respondents in the bottom range, and the remainder split relatively equally between the upper and middle ranges). Only with the general nature of reporting was there a significant response in the bottom range — in this case, 25%. Overall, therefore, the best understood area appeared to be accounting valuation bases; the worst was the conceptually-orientated general nature of reporting; and the remaining areas exhibited a great deal of vagueness, coupled with small groups of respondents lacking understanding.

Constructing the index of understanding

By aggregating the levels of respondents' understanding still further, an overall index of understanding can be constructed, revealing those survey respondents with an understanding above and below an average for the group as a whole.

Prior to this being done, two relative matters were considered. First, whether all 5 reporting areas, and their related points scores, should be included in the index. Secondly, whether any of the areas so included should be weighted on account of their relative importance. The first consideration related to the possible inclusion in the index of topics which were not a proper test of respondents' understanding of financial reporting practice, and which could therefore distort the index unduly. The second matter was concerned with whether certain of the areas tested were more significant aspects of financial reporting practice than others. Again, the crucial point of debate was the possible distortion of the index.

The 5 areas of reporting practice were examined with a view to establishing their appropriateness in an overall index of understanding. From this examination, it was felt that the area dealing with the general nature of financial reporting (that is, legal responsibilities, reporting objectives, and data accuracy) was one which, although important to a proper understanding of reporting practice, was not absolutely essential to it. For this reason, there appeared to be sufficient doubt about this area (and not about the other areas) to necessitate further testing to prove the point — that is, to evidence whether respondents' understanding or lack of understanding of the general nature of reporting was repeated consistently in their responses to the other 4 areas tested. If it was consistently repetitive then the argument for excluding it from the index would not be strong.

The test applied was Kendall's tau which was considered in this case to be superior to Spearman's coefficient of rank correlation because of the relatively large numbers of responses associated with relatively few individual points scores. In order to conduct the tests of correlation, an overall index of understanding was constructed from the points scores in each of the 5 areas covered in the survey. The points scores of respondents in each of these areas were correlated with each other, as well as with the overall index, and Table 21 summarises the results.

TABLE 21

Significance of relationship between various parts of the index of understanding

	PART 1	PART 2	PART 3	PART 4	PART 5	INDEX
	r	r	r	r	r	r
PART 1	—					
PART 2	.04	—				
PART 3	.06	.17 **	—			
PART 4	.00	.08	.17 **	—		
PART 5	.10 *	.21 **	.17 **	−.01	—	
INDEX	.28 **	.54 **	.53 **	.33**	.34 **	—

PART 1 = understanding of general nature of reporting; PART 2 = understanding of nature of financial statements; PART 3 = understanding of accounting terminology; PART 4 = understanding of accounting valuation bases; PART 5 = understanding of financial ratios; INDEX = overall index of understanding containing each of the previously-mentioned parts. Each based on points scores outlined in Appendix 34.

r = Kendall's coefficient of rank correlation
* = significantly different from 0 at p $<$ 0.05
** = significantly different from 0 at p $<$ 0.01

With the exception of accounting valuation bases when correlated with financial ratios, the various parts of the index and the overall index were positively correlated to each other — although not strongly in most instances. This positive correlation was weakest, and also least significant statistically, in the case of the general nature of reporting.

The inevitable conclusion about these results is that the various points scores in the index did not correlate too well, although most did correlate positively. The responses to the questions on the general nature of reporting appear to be far less correlated with the other areas, and, for that reason, have been excluded from the final construction of an index of understanding.[3] A further conclusion of the rank correlation statistics reveals that the level of understanding achieved by the survey respondents in one particular area of financial reporting practice was not consistently repeated in other areas. The level of understanding achieved in each area was generally in the same direction, as indicated previously in the review of the skewness coefficients. Thus, there is typically in this study a small but positive correlation between different areas with the exception of the general nature of reporting with its very low positive correlations. This is not inconsistent with the previous analyses of individual responses to particular reporting areas—the levels of understanding varying between one area and the next.

Finally, there is no evidence to indicate that one particular area of financial reporting practice was more important to the responding financial experts than any other area. Judging by the responses given to the questions asked, all areas appeared to be treated with equal importance. For this reason, no extra weighting has been applied to the 4 areas contained in the index (the general nature of reporting having been excluded as above) except so far as has been predetermined in the balance of interview questions — 6 being asked in relation to each of the nature of financial statements and accounting terminology; and 3 being asked in relation to each of accounting valuation bases and financial ratios. It is believed that, given the nature of individual topics questioned, there is a reasonable balance between the different areas covered in the eventual index of understanding.

The index of understanding

The 4 areas represented in the index gave a maximum score of 36. Respondents' scores were aggregated, and a distribution resulted from a score of 1 to a maximum score of 35. The mean score was 23.02, with a standard deviation of 5.40, and a skewness coefficient of -1.18. For purposes of further analysis, it was decided that respondents with the greatest and least understanding of these topics should be identified and, thus, the overall distribution required to be grouped into what could be described as above average, average and below average understanding. The average index was decomposed as reasonably as possible into 3 segments — the bottom 25%, the middle 50%, and the top 25% of respondents (bottom relating to low scores; top relating to high scores). It was then possible to decompose the data further by introducing categories approximating to the bottom 10% and top 10% of the distribution. Thus, the overall distribution was broken at the following percentiles — 11, 24, 73 and 86. Because of the cumulative frequency achieved, it was not possible to break at the 10, 25, 75 and 90 percentiles. Table 22 details the 'split' distribution.

TABLE 22
Overall index of actual understanding of financial reporting

OVERALL UNDERSTANDING SCORE*	%	%
Much above average understanding		
29—35	14	
Above average understanding		
27—28	13	27
Average understanding		
21—26		49
Below average understanding		
18—20	13	
Much below average understanding		
1—17	11	24
		100

*Maximum possible score obtainable from the four reporting areas covered in the index was 36.
mean = 23.02; standard deviation = 5.40; skewness coefficient = −1.18

On the basis of the chosen cut-off points, 27% of respondents were deemed to have above average understanding — that is, 27 or more points out of 36 or 75% or more of the maximum score. In addition, more than one-half of this group (14% of total respondents) gained 81% or more of such a maximum (29+ points out of 36). Given the background of the survey respondents, such results are not surprising. However, the scores in the other categories are relatively disappointing — 49% of respondents obtaining the deemed average score range of between 21 and 26 points (between 58% and 72% of the maximum score); and 24% of respondents falling below what had been judged to be average performance with 56% or less of the maximum. Indeed, 11% of respondents could only muster between 3% and 47% of the 36 points maximum.

Having established this analysis of the group's understanding, the newly-created variable of understanding can be used for later cross-analyses, particularly against respondents' readership of available financial information, and their various background characteristics. An initial comparison, however, is now made between respondents' perceived relevance of reported accounting information and their deemed actual understanding of it — that is, did those who perceived its relevance also evidence an understanding of it; and, conversely, did those who perceived its irrelevance also evidence a lack of understanding of it?

Perceived relevance and actual understanding

In Table 14 of Chapter 3, it was shown that 96% of respondents believed they understood reported accounting information, of which 90% stated they found it relevant to their investment decisions. Ignoring the very small number of respondents (8) who either indicated no such understanding or did not give a statement reflecting their perception of this matter, these positive perceptions of information relevance have been cross-tabulated with the distribution of actual understanding (as detailed in Table 23).

TABLE 23
Perceived and actual understanding of survey respondents

PERCEIVED UNDERSTANDING	n*	LEVEL OF UNDERSTANDING					
		Much above average %	Above average %	Average %	Below average %	Much below average %	Total %
Understand and find relevant	200	13	13	50	14	10	100
Understand and find irrelevant or only sometimes relevant	23	18	17	43	13	9	100

*5 respondents gave no indication of their perceived understanding; and 3 respondents stated they did not understand accounting information. These have been omitted from the analysis in order not to distort the results unduly.
(Not statistically significant at $p = 0.05$ using the chi square test)

In order to make sense of the data in Table 23, it was used to test a hypothesis (these will be labelled H throughout the remainder of the text, and will be given numerical subscripts in series, that is, H_1, H_2 . . . . H_n):

H_1 Those respondents who believed they understood reported accounting information and found it relevant to their investment decisions, had a significantly better understanding of traditional accounting topics than those who believed they understood it but found it irrelevant (or only sometimes relevant).

The test of this hypothesis was used to evidence whether or not respondents' perceptions of information relevance to investment decisions and their deemed actual understanding were compatible. In the event, the null hypothesis cannot be rejected as the differences were not significant at the 0.05 level, using the chi square test. Therefore, respondents' perceptions of the relevance of reported accounting information to investment decisions were not significantly related to their levels of actual understanding (as determined by the specific understanding tests used in this survey).

Summary

The evidence of this chapter reveals that the responding financial experts had a variable understanding of the 5 main areas of financial reporting covered by the survey. The overall level of understanding was reasonably high for the group as a whole, with accounting valuation bases being best understood, and the general nature of reporting the least understood. A significant feature of the analysis undertaken to this point is the vagueness attributable to many of the responses, particularly in areas in which respondents should have a great deal of familiarity — for example, with accounting terminology.

The correlation of the various responses in each of the main reporting areas revealed, first, evidence to support the exclusion of responses to the general nature of reporting from the construction of an overall index of understanding; and, secondly, relatively low positive correlations between the remaining parts of such an index. The latter, once constructed, facilitated the categorisation of the respondents in terms of above average, average, and below average understanding for the group as a whole. The initial use of this index (when cross-tabulated with perceived understanding) provided evidence that, in this particular study, there was no obvious and significant relationship between respondents' actual understanding of the matters questioned and their prior perceptions of the relevance of reported information to investment decisions. Further comprehension analyses concerning respondents' backgrounds, as well as specific areas of misunderstanding, will be examined in later chapters.

REFERENCES

[1] See T. A. Lee and D. P. Tweedie, *The Private Shareholder and the Corporate Report*, Institute of Chartered Accountants in England and Wales, 1977, pp43-51.
[2] See A. N. Oppenheim, *Questionnaire Design and Attitude Measurement*, Heinemann, 1966, pp100-102.
[3] See also Lee and Tweedie, *op cit*, pp46-7.

CHAPTER 6

Assessment of actual understanding of inflation accounting

One of the most vexing of practical accounting issues in recent times has been the search for an acceptable system of accounting for the effects of inflation. This is a matter which has occupied a great deal of the accountancy literature over the last few years and, consequently, it is not intended to repeat in this text what has been more than adequately covered elsewhere.[1] Instead, the aim of this chapter is to provide what is believed to be the first evidence from the UK of the levels of understanding attributable to the topic of inflation accounting by persons with the financial expertise and experience to acquire such an understanding. In a recently published study, it has been shown that financial analysts and chartered accountants in Canada do not perceive themselves in general to have a reasonable understanding of current value accounting (at least, so far as 4 of its main variants were concerned).[2] Due to the relative novelty of the topic to practitioners and users, this would appear to be intuitively the position in the UK as well. Thus, given the potential importance of inflation accounting, this study provides some necessary UK evidence.

The interview survey of the various respondents included certain questions relating to their understanding of contemporary inflation accounting matters. With one exception, the questions related to the system of accounting based on current costs (hereafter CCA). At the time of conducting the survey, the UK inflation accounting debate had switched its initial attention from current purchasing power accounting (hereafter CPPA)[3] to current cost accounting (mainly due to the report of the Sandilands Committee[4]). The main questions asked were derived from the CCA recommendations contained in the then recently published *Exposure Draft 18* — 'Current Cost Accounting'. The one exception to this was a question on the contents of CPPA statements which, at the time of the survey, were still being published by some UK companies as a result of the recommendations contained in *Provisional Statement of Standard Accounting Practice 7.*[5]

The areas into which the questions asked of respondents fell were as follows: the nature and content of CPPA and CCA-based financial statements; the nature and meaning both of specific adjustments and of aspects of CCA financial statements (revaluation surpluses resulting from the use of current costs; the cost of sales adjustment to revise the historical cost of sales to a current cost equivalent; and the statement of change in the shareholders' net equity interest to reflect the extent to which the restatement of shareholders' capital in current cost terms has kept pace with the general level of inflation); and, finally, the definition of the CCA valuation bases used for specific assets (plant, raw materials stock, contract work-in-progress, and quoted investments). It was felt that this would provide sufficient evidence to draw some initial conclusions about the degree to which a system such as CCA was understood by the financially expert sector of the investment community. The following sections analyse the results in detail, prior to the construction of an index of understanding on these matters similar in principle to the main index outlined in Chapter 5.

Nature of inflation accounting statements

First, the respondents were examined on the nature of inflation accounting statements. Table 24 contains the overall analysis, and Appendices 35 and 36 provide the underlying detail (including explanations of how the responses were categorised into the 'reasonable', 'vague' and 'no or poor' understanding groupings).

TABLE 24
Actual understanding of the nature of inflation financial statements

LEVEL OF UNDERSTANDING	*CPPA* statements %	*CCA* statements %
Reasonable	9	8
Vague	44	19
Poor or none	47	73
	100	100

The above results reveal just how poorly the contents of both CPPA and CCA statements were understood by the survey respondents. Only 9% (for CPPA statements) and 8% (for CCA statements) had a reasonable understanding; but 47% and 73%, respectively, had poor or no understanding. On the whole, CPPA statements tended to be the better understood (with 44% of respondents having a vague understanding of them compared with just less than 1 out of every 5 (19%) for CCA statements). It is to be appreciated that the use of CPPA systems in practice should have made respondents more familiar with it as compared with CCA, but there was obviously a confusion between the two systems at the time of interview — 34% of respondents stating CCA was a form of accounting for inflation or current purchasing power (as distinct from accounting for specific price changes on particular assets).

Inflation accounting terminology

As with traditional accounting terminology, it is vital that potential accounting information users nowadays have a reasonable understanding of the terminology associated with inflation accounting (in this case, in terms of CCA). Table 25 summarises the results achieved in this regard, and these are supported by the data contained in Appendices 37 to 39, inclusive.

TABLE 25
Actual understanding of individual parts of CCA financial statements

LEVEL OF UNDERSTANDING	Revaluation surpluses %	Cost of sales adjustment %	Statement of change in shareholders' net equity interest %
Reasonable	57	19	2
Vague	6	38	42
Poor or none	37	43	56
	100	100	100

As was the case with the previous results on the nature of inflation financial statements, the data in Table 25 reveal poor levels of overall comprehension. Only in the case of revaluation surpluses is there a sizeable number of reasonable responses (57%) — but even in such a familiar area as this, more than one-third of respondents (37%) had no or poor understanding (it is felt this would have been a familiar area to respondents because of the revaluing of assets such as property in historical cost-based financial statements). As Appendix 37 shows, the influence of CPPA is evident, even in straightforward matters such as revaluation, with 4% of respondents stating it was a current purchasing power adjustment.

The cost of sales adjustment was the next-best understood item in this section — approximately 1 in 5 respondents having a reasonable understanding, and approximately a further 2 in 5 having a vague understanding. Nevertheless, 43% of respondents had little or no understanding of the meaning of the cost of sales adjustment. Indeed, 3% confused it with some form of CPPA adjustment.

The meaning of the statement of change in shareholders' net equity interest was very poorly understood, with a meagre 2% of respondents having a reasonable grasp of it, and a further 42% having only a vague understanding. It was to be expected that this controversial and new financial statement would attract the least favourable response, but it was surprising to discover more than half of the respondents (56%) in the no or poor understanding category (indeed, 38% gave 'do not know' responses or no answer at all).

CCA valuation bases

CCA usually involves a variety of differing valuation bases dependent on the asset being valued.[6] In a sense, this was an extension of the revaluation approach adopted in historical cost accounting — that is, both systems adopt multiple valuation bases. In the case of *Exposure Draft 18,* this could involve replacement costs, net realisable values, economic values, and even historical costs. This results in complications in CCA, and it is of importance to evidence the degree to which these complexities are understood by potential CCA report users. With this in mind, Table 26 summarises the results of the answers to questions asked of the survey respondents in relation to 4 specific asset types. Appendices 40 to 43, inclusive, provide the detailed analyses.

TABLE 26
Actual understanding of CCA valuation bases

LEVEL OF UNDERSTANDING	Plant and machinery %	Raw materials stock %	Specific contract work-in-progress %	Quoted invest-ments %
Reasonable	57	47	1	60
Vague	15	16	16	—
Poor or none	28	37	83	40
	100	100	100	100

Despite the relative poverty of response in the two earlier areas of CCA, the respondents evidenced a far better understanding of the more practical matter of valuation. 57% had a reasonable understanding of plant values, and the corresponding figures for raw materials stock and quoted investments were 47% and 60%, respectively. On the other hand, virtually no respondents (1% only) had a reasonable understanding that specific contract work-in-progress was valued at its value to the business until its date of consumption, and thereafter at its actual cost. In the cases of plant, raw materials stock, and contract work-in-progress, a small minority had a vague understanding (15%, 16% and 16%, respectively), but, in all cases, a sizeable number of respondents had poor or no understanding (nearly 3 out of 10 with plant; over one-third (37%) with stock; more than 8 out of 10 with contract work-in-progress; and exactly 4 out of 10 with investments). With the exception of the rather complex provisions in *Exposure Draft 18* for contract work-in-progress, these results are much more encouraging indicators of the respondents' understanding of CCA in comparison to the other areas examined in this study.

Understanding scores

By combining respondents' answers to the questions on the nature of inflation financial statements and inflation accounting terminology, two main financial reporting areas concerned with inflation were created for further analysis — that is, the nature of inflation accounting statements and adjustments (for which 5 questions were asked) and inflation accounting valuation bases (for which 4 questions were asked). As with the traditional accounting practice responses in Chapter 5, the aim of this chapter is to determine more precisely the individual respondent's actual understanding in relation to some group average. The construction of an index of understanding on inflation accounting matters was used for this purpose, revealing above average, average, and below average levels of understanding for the group as a whole. Points scores were attributed as before to each response in each reporting area — 2 for reasonable understanding; 1 for vague understanding; and 0 for no or poor understanding. Thus, the maximum score for the first of the 2 areas mentioned above was 10 points, with a maximum of 8 points for the second area — giving a maximum total of 18 points.

Appendix 44 outlines the overall analysis of respondents' scores in each of the 2 reporting areas, following the application of the above points scores to each response. From this data, it can be seen that the conclusions from the individual analyses in this chapter are largely confirmed. In the case of the nature of inflation accounting statements and adjustments, only 21% of respondents obtained more than 50% of the available points, and 18% obtained nil scores. The mean of 3.39 out of 10, the large standard deviation of 2.41, and the slight skew towards lack of understanding (coefficient = 0.17), all indicate that, generally speaking, respondents were floundering in this area of inflation accounting.

By way of contrast, responses to the valuation questions were better — 45% of respondents obtaining one-half or more of the available points, although 21% obtained no score. The mean (3.77 out of 8) and the skew to understanding (−0.40) both reflect this better performance, although the standard deviation of 2.46 indicates the extent of spread of response.

These results can be seen more clearly in the simplified distributions in Table 27. Using the data contained in Appendix 44, the total distribution in each of the 2 main areas of inflation accounting covered in the survey were separated into an upper, middle and bottom range of scores (in the first area, the scores were cut at the 30 and 70 percentiles, and in the second area at the 37 and 63 percentiles — these being deemed the most appropriate given the 10 point and 8 point scales used).

TABLE 27
Understanding scores for individual inflation accounting matters

UNDERSTANDING SCORE RANGE*	Nature of inflation accounting statements and adjustments %	Inflation accounting valuation bases %
Upper range	9	37
Middle range	40	26
Bottom range	51	37
	100	100

*Respondents' scores were expressed as a percentage of the maximum possible score in each area — see Appendix 44. For the first area, the scores have been cut at the 30 and 70 percentiles due to the 10 point scale involved. For the second area, the scores have been cut at 37 and 63 percentiles due to the 8 point scale involved.

The overall impression to be gained from these score ranges confirms the previous more detailed analyses. First, in the case of responses to the nature of inflation accounting statements and adjustments, only 9% of respondents were in the upper range but a majority (51%) fell into the bottom range, thereby indicating a poor overall response in this area. The equivalent response to the questions on inflation accounting valuation bases was considerably better, with 37% of respondents in both the upper and lower ranges.

Constructing the index of understanding

The results in Table 27 only explain in general terms respondents' understanding of certain inflation accounting issues. By constructing an overall index of understanding from the relevant distributions, however, an individual respondent's understanding can be compared with a group average. None of the 9 matters contained in the overall distributions in Appendix 44 appeared to be capable of unduly biasing or distorting the index which can be constructed from them. It will be remembered that 2 items concerned the nature of inflation accounting statements; 3 items covered inflation terminology and accounting adjustments or measurements (making 5 items in all of a general nature); and a further 4 items dealt with the valuation bases used in CCA.

Both areas of inflation accounting were analysed in order to consider whether or not there was a similarity between them to justify their combination in an overall index of understanding. The way in which this was done was by correlating the responses in each area against each other and against the overall index. Kendall's tau was used for this purpose and, as can be seen in Table 28, there was a positive and significant correlation, at least sufficient to reveal a positive relationship between the two areas of inflation accounting, and to justify their combination in an overall index of understanding.

TABLE 28
Significance of relationship between various parts of the index of understanding of inflation accounting matters

	PART 1	PART 2	INDEX
	r	r	r
PART 1	—		
PART 2	.40 *	—	
INDEX	.75 *	.73 *	—

PART 1 = nature of inflation accounting statements and adjustments; PART 2 = inflation accounting valuation bases; INDEX = overall index of understanding containing each of the previously-mentioned parts. Each based on points scores outlined in Appendix 44.

r = Kendall's co-efficient of rank correlation
* = significantly different from 0 at p $<$ 0.01

The 2 areas of inflation accounting surveyed provided responses giving a maximum possible score of 18. The mean score of 7.15 (with a relatively large standard deviation of 4.28), despite a distribution skewed slightly to respondents' understanding (coefficient = −0.26), further confirm the relatively poor comprehension of respondents in this area and indicate the need to improve report user understanding of CCA particularly. The distribution was decomposed into 5 approximate segments — roughly a bottom 10%, a bottom 25%, a middle 50%, a top 25%, and a top 10%. To do this, the distribution was cut at the 13, 23, 75, and 93 percentiles because the particular cumulative frequency did not allow breaks at the 10, 25, 75 and 90 percentiles. Table 29 outlines this five-way split.

TABLE 29
Overall index of actual understanding of inflation accounting

OVERALL UNDERSTANDING SCORE*	%	%
Much above average understanding		
12—16	7	
Above average understanding		
11	18	25
Average understanding		
4—10		52
Below average understanding		
1—3	10	
Much below average understanding		
0	13	23
		100

*Maximum possible score obtainable from the two accounting areas covered in the index was 18.
Mean = 7.15; standard deviation = 4.28; skewness co-efficient = −0.26

Once again, the index indicates respondents' relative lack of understanding of inflation accounting matters — the top 25% of respondents obtained more than 61% of the maximum possible score of 18, and the top 7% achieved two-thirds or more of the maximum (67%). But 13% of respondents obtained a 0 score, and nearly a quarter (23%) could only obtain a score of less than 17% of the maximum. In other words, although the overall distribution of responses was skewed towards understanding, this was because respondents could be divided into 2 relatively distinct groups — one having a reasonable if not outstandingly high understanding, and the other having little or no understanding.

Perceived relevance and actual understanding

Table 30 outlines the comparison of respondents' perceptions of the relevance of reported accounting information and their actual understanding of the inflation accounting matters surveyed (as was the case with the earlier equivalent analysis with traditional accounting topics, 8 respondents failed to state their perception in this regard, and have been omitted from the cross-tabulation).

62

TABLE 30

Perceived understanding and level of understanding of inflation accounting matters of survey respondents

| PERCEIVED UNDERSTANDING | n* | LEVEL OF UNDERSTANDING | | | | | |
		Much above average %	*Above average* %	*Average* %	*Below average* %	*Much below average* %	*Total* %
Understand and find relevant	200	7	20	52	10	11	100
Understand and find irrelevant or only sometimes relevant	23	13	4	61	13	9	100

*5 respondents gave no indication of their perceived understanding; and 3 respondents stated they did not understand accounting information.
(Not statistically significant at p = 0.05 using the chi square test)

A specific hypothesis has been stated for purposes of this analysis:

H$_2$ Those respondents who believed they understood reported accounting information, and found it relevant to their investment decisions, had a significantly better understanding of inflation accounting topics than those who believed they understood it but found it irrelevant (or only sometimes relevant).

Although there are some differences in the data in Table 30, the results are insufficient to support the rejection of the null hypothesis (not statistically significant at the 0.05 level). In other words, respondents' perceptions of the relevance of reported accounting information for investment decision were not significantly related to their understanding of the inflation accounting topics surveyed.

Summary

The level of understanding of inflation accounting (particularly CCA) matters raised in this survey was in many ways very poor. This is perhaps not surprising given, at the time of interviewing, the then relatively recent introduction of inflation accounting statements. However, the absolute levels of understanding on specific CCA topics were disappointing and, in the case of those of general principle, somewhat weak. Understanding of the CCA valuation conventions was markedly better but, overall, there were a considerable number of respondents who had little or no understanding of inflation accounting matters. This is a situation which will have to be remedied given the potential importance of CCA in relation to investment decisions, generally, and to the work of many of these financial experts, particularly.

REFERENCES

[1] See the extensive bibliographies in T. A. Lee, *Income and Value Measurement*, 2nd Edition, Nelson, 1980.

[2] W. Falk, 'How Well-known is CVA?', *CA Magazine*, March 1979, pp39-44.

[3] 'Accounting for Changes in the Purchasing Power of Money', *Provisional Statement of Standard Accounting Practice 7*, Accounting Standards Committee, 1974.

[4] 'Inflation Accounting', *Report of the Inflation Accounting Committee*, Cmnd 6225, HMSO, 1975.

[5] *op cit.*

[6] See, for example, 'Current Cost Accounting', *Statement of Standard Accounting Practice 16*, Accounting Standards Committee, 1980.

Respondents' views on the use made of financial information in their organisations

Having considered the general understanding of reporting practices revealed by the financial experts interviewed, the next 4 chapters are concerned with the use made of available financial information by the respondents' employing organisations. This chapter considers the processing of such information within these organisations. The next 3 chapters consider the use made of particular sources of information and deal in turn with (a) the annual company report; (b) other sources of published financial information; and (c) company visits.

Useful financial information

After an introductory question to ensure that the organisation employing the interviewee was involved in stock market dealings, each respondent was asked which pieces of financial information were found to be of the greatest assistance to his organisation in its investment activities. The answers are given in Table 31.

(Table 31 is on the next page.)

TABLE 31
*Financial information found to be of greatest assistance
in investment activities*

	Percentage of respondents mentioning item %
Earnings per share	31
Financial status; financial position; capital structure	28
Profitability	27
Dividend yield	21
Price-earnings ratio	19
Dividend per share	14
Dividend cover	10
Cash flow	5
Future prospects of a company	2

n = 229

Note: The 2 respondents who used a chartist approach to investment analysis were not asked the question.

It can be seen from Table 31 that the piece of information mentioned most frequently was earnings per share (by 31% of respondents). Earnings or profits undoubtedly were of great importance to the respondents as profitability was mentioned by 27% and the price-earnings ratio was mentioned by 19%. In all, 57% of respondents considered earnings in some form to be of the greatest assistance in their organisations' investment activities.

While, from Table 31, a company's financial position appeared to be the next most important single aspect of financial information sought after earnings, dividend information was considered to be of greater overall importance. In all, 31% of respondents mentioned dividend information in some form — dividend yield being considered rather more important than dividend per share or dividend cover. It was interesting to note that, despite the attention paid in recent years by the accounting profession to inflation accounting, few respondents mentioned that such information was of the greatest assistance to them in investment activities. In only 10 cases were any pieces of financial information considered in terms other than historical cost data.

USE MADE OF FINANCIAL INFORMATION

The use of external financial advisers

In most organisations the investment decision maker did not act in isolation. Table 32 reveals that only 21% of respondents declared that those responsible for the investment decision in their organisation also read and analysed the financial information relevant to it without reliance on other analysts. (The data in Tables 32 to 34 relate to both annual and interim reports. Due to the very close similarity between the results for the two types of report, no specific reference is made to the interim report.)

TABLE 32

Information flow to investment decision makers in the respondents' organisations

	Percentage of respondents mentioning flow pattern	
	Annual reports %	Interim reports %
The decision maker analyses financial information himself and receives reports from analysts within, and external to, the organisation.	10	10
The decision maker analyses financial information himself and receives reports from analysts within the organisation.	21	20
The decision maker analyses financial information himself and receives reports from analysts external to the organisation.	6	6
The decision maker analyses financial information himself.	21	21
The decision maker receives reports from analysts within the organisation.	33	34
The decision maker receives reports from analysts external to the organisation	7	7
The decision maker receives reports from analysts within, and external to, the organisation.	2	2
n = 229	100	100

Note: The 2 respondents who used a chartist approach to investment analysis were not asked the question.

67

Whereas, in all, 58% of the respondents believed that decision makers undertook some form of analysis of company annual reports, in the view of a majority of these respondents (37% of all respondents) decision makers generally received assistance. 66% of respondents stated that some of the analysis of annual reports was made by other analysts within their organisation — half of this group declared that the decision maker relied entirely upon internal analysts, and undertook no analysis himself. External advice was considered by one-quarter of the respondents to be used by their organisations' decision makers.

Differences were noticed in the information flow existing in financial institutions and in stockbroking firms. 62% of respondents employed by financial institutions were of the opinion that investment decisions were made by employees of the organisation without outside assistance. On the other hand, no fewer than 96% of those employed by stockbroking firms held the same view about the operating procedures within their firms. Only 4 of the 61 stockbroking firms surveyed appeared to use outside assistance for investment decision making. Analysing the responses of institutional investors in terms of the type of organisation employing them, it would seem that insurance companies appeared to have relied least on outside assistance. Taking the respondents' replies as indicating the use made of internal and external advisors in investment decision making in their organisations, it was evident that 45% of the 29 insurance companies covered in the survey, 61% of the 18 pension funds, 55% of the 18 unit or investment trusts, and 50% of the 14 merchant banks relied on such external assistance. (It should be noted, however, that, on occasion, the organisation's two representatives being interviewed disagreed about its policy. Disagreements over the use of external advisors were noted in over half of the unit or investment trusts and merchant banks in which one respondent stated that the organisation used outside assistance for investment decision making purposes. Employees of insurance companies and pension funds were somewhat more in agreement — in only 4 of the 13 insurance companies in which one employee was of the opinion that outside advisors were used was such disagreement evident. The corresponding figure for pension funds was 5 out of 11 funds).

Information analysis

Having been questioned about the flow of information within their organisation, the respondents were then asked several questions about the type of financial analysis undertaken or sought by their organisation. First, they were presented with a card giving pre-selected answers to a question asking whether analysed financial information relating to all companies or only to particular companies was examined within their organisation. The answers to this question are given in Table 33.

TABLE 33
Companies for which financial information is read and analysed

	Percentage of respondents mentioning item	
	Annual reports %	*Interim reports* %
Companies in existing portfolio and potential additions to the portfolio	63	61
All companies	29	29
Companies in existing portfolio	3	4
Potential additions to existing portfolio only	2	2
Other and 'no answers'	3	4
	100	100

n = 229

Note: The 2 respondents who used a chartist approach to investment analysis were not asked the question.

Table 33 shows that 63% of respondents stated that in their organisation the analysis of company annual reports extended not only to those of companies whose shares were currently held by it or by its clients, but also to reports of companies whose shares were considered to be potential additions to existing holdings. 29% of respondents went further, and claimed that in their organisations the annual reports of all major companies were examined. Merely 3% stated that only the annual reports of companies in the portfolios of their organisation or of its clients were examined.

Marked differences were evident in the approaches adopted by stockbroking firms from those of the financial institutions. 60% of those employed by the former declared that their firms examined the annual reports of all major companies — only 7% of those employed by the institutions gave the same answer. 84% of the latter group stated that

69

their organisations were concerned with companies whose shares were currently held or were considered to be potential additions to the portfolio — the corresponding figure for those employed by stockbroking firms was 34%.

Similar differences were revealed when the responses of these financial experts were analysed in terms of their organisation. Respondents in 37 (61%) of the 61 stockbroking firms surveyed declared that their firms analysed the annual reports of all major companies — in only 5 of these firms were there disagreements between their survey representatives on this point. By way of contrast, in only 8 of the 79 financial institutions surveyed did a respondent state that his employer adopted the same approach to financial analysis and, in all bar 2 of these organiations, the other respondent disagreed. In 75 (95%) of the financial institutions, however, at least one respondent stated that his organisation's approach was to examine only companies whose shares were either existing holdings or specific potential additions. (In 14 of these institutions the other representative interviewed disagreed with this view.) Representatives of 25 (41%) of the stockbroking firms surveyed stated that their firms adopted the same approach as most of the financial institutions. In only 6 of these firms was any disagreement between respondents apparent.

Whichever approach to financial analysis was adopted, little time appeared to be lost in analysing published financial information provided by companies.

TABLE 34
Time of analysis of reported financial information

	Percentage of respondents mentioning time of analysis	
	Annual reports %	Interim reports %
Within one month of receipt of report	55	48
Immediately on receipt of report	33	41
Between one and three months of receipt of report	7	5
Other answers	5	6
n = 229	100	100

Note: The 2 respondents who used a chartist approach to investment analysis were not asked the question.

Table 34 reveals that 88% of respondents stated that annual reports received by their firms were read and analysed within one month of receipt. Indeed, 33% of respondents were of the opinion that in their organisations such reports were analysed as soon as they arrived. 56% of the 126 respondents who stated that their organisation did not analyse reports immediately upon receipt, but ensured that they were examined within one month, also gave an impression of internal urgency by adding that analysis of annual reports was undertaken at the first available opportunity within one month of their receipt.

Stockbroking firms appeared to analyse companies' annual reports rather more quickly than financial institutions. 47% of those respondents who were employed by the former stated that analysis of the reports took place in their firms without delay — only 24% of those employed by the financial institutions expressed the same opinion.

The respondents gave the impression that their employing organisations adopted a wide range of practices so far as the detailed analysis of company reports was concerned. Two distinct approaches were disclosed — one relating to the type of analysis undertaken, and the other concerned with the period analysed. In all, 78% of respondents commented that a ratio analysis of company financial statements was generally undertaken in their organisations. 56% of respondents mentioned that usually funds flow statements were either constructed or examined for each company analysed — only 2%, however, admitted to using funds flow data without also undertaking ratio analysis. A few respondents (17%) remarked that for analysis purposes their organisations were content to relate the analyses of companies' current year's results to those of the preceding year. A much larger group (56%), however, stated that their organisations took a longer time perspective and examined companies' financial data over a period of several years. (No material differences in the type of analysis undertaken in stockbroking firms and financial institutions were apparent.)

TABLE 35

Acceptance of analysis provided in financial reports

	Percentage of respondents mentioning item	
	Ratio %	Funds Flow %
Accepted after verification	43	44
Accepted without verification	24	35
Ignored and separate internal computation undertaken	30	17
Ignored and separate external verification undertaken	2	2
'No answers'	1	2
n = 229	100	100

Note: The 2 respondents who used a chartist approach to investment analysis were not asked the question.

Approximately one-quarter of the respondents admitted that their employers accepted, without verification, ratios provided in the companies' financial reports (see Table 35), although a slightly larger proportion (35%) stated that their organisations appeared to be willing to accept company source and application of funds statements at their face value.

30% of respondents employed by the financial institutions (in 39% of the individual institutions) indicated that their organisations would normally accept any financial ratio produced by companies in their published financial statements. Stockbroking firms, however, seemed less willing to accept any ratio provided by companies. Only 17% of those employed in such firms (in 21% of the individual firms) admitted to this practice. (Disagreements about the acceptance of companies' analyses were noted in 18% of the individual financial institutions and in 7% of individual stockbroking firms.)

So far as the source and application of funds statement was concerned, the respondents employed by financial institutions once again evidenced that their organisations would appear to be more willing to accept company figures than would stockbroking firms. 39% of those respondents employed in the former organisations (representing 51% of the institutions surveyed) compared to 29% of those employed in the latter (representing 39% of the firms surveyed) stated that their organisations did not verify this financial statement. (In 18 of the 40 financial institutions in which at least one respondent stated that the organisation relied on companies' source and application of funds statements, another respondent disagreed. For stockbroking firms the corresponding figure was 10 out of 24 firms.)

Forecasting of results

In only 5 of the 79 financial institutions, and 6 of the 61 stockbroking firms surveyed was there unanimity from respondents in the view that the reported financial information of companies was not used to make predictions of their financial results. The predictions stated to be made by respondents in the other responding organisations are shown in Table 36.

TABLE 36
Financial results predicted by analysts in respondents' organisations

	Percentage of respondents mentioning item %
Earnings per share	67
Profits or profits before tax	57
Dividends per share	31
Sales	18
Price-earnings ratio	13
Financing; indebtedness	13
Balance sheet	8
Funds flow	7
Cash flow	7
Dividends	3
Share price	1

n = 229

Note: The 2 respondents who used a chartist approach to investment analysis were not asked the question.

Two closely-related items dominate Table 36. Two-thirds of the respondents stated that, in their organisations, corporate earnings per share were predicted, while 57% were of the opinion that estimates were made of the future profits of companies. Combining the respondents who gave these answers with those who stated that their organisations were concerned with the prediction of price-earning ratios, it transpired that no fewer than 81% of respondents mentioned that forecasting of profitability in some form was undertaken by their organisations.

By combining other groups of answers, it was discovered that 32% of respondents mentioned that dividends were predicted; 14% stated that estimates of future share prices were made; and 13% confirmed that tables outlining future funds or cash flows of companies were constructed. Not unexpectedly, virtually no differences were noted in the types of predictions made between those respondents employed in financial institutions and those working for stockbroking firms.

Only 6% of respondents stated that their employing organisation made any attempt to forecast information in other than historical cost terms. All of these respondents, however, commented that their firms also produced current cost or current purchasing power estimates of corporate progress or financial position in addition to historical cost projections of results. The current value forecasts made by the employing organisations of these respondents were either concerned with earnings adjusted to take account of changing prices or the dividends which could be distributed from such earnings.

Just under one-half of the forecasts, according to the respondents, apparently achieved an accuracy of within 10% of the actual outcome — the modal answer indicating that an accuracy of between 6 to 10 per cent of the final results was obtained (see Table 37).

TABLE 37
Estimated accuracy of predictions

	Percentage of total predictions recorded in Table 36 %
Accurate to within ± 5%	15
Accurate to within ± 6 to 10%	32
Accurate to within ±11 to 20%	10
Accurate to within ±21 to 30%	3
Impossible to assess accuracy	7
Accuracy never checked or monitored	10
Other answers	1
No response given	22
	100

n = 485

Many respondents were, however, unable to answer the question put to them concerning the accuracy of forecasts. An explanation for this was perhaps revealed in the answers of several respondents who commented that it was extremely difficult to give an estimate of accuracy because differing degrees of success were experienced in different industrial sectors. 10% of respondents admitted that in their organisations the accuracy of forecasts was never checked.

One-half of the forecasts of profit or earnings per share and 53% of the estimates of future dividends were judged by the respondents concerned to have been within 10% of the eventual outcome. Other estimates, however, apparently did not normally achieve this level of accuracy. Only one-third of the forecasts of sales and (possibly more importantly for these respondents) estimates of future price-earnings ratios were considered by the respondents whose organisations made such forecasts to have fallen within the 10% range of accuracy. Slightly lower levels of forecast success were estimated for funds or cash flow (28% within 10% of the actual outcome) and future financing (23% within 10% of the actual outcome). (It should, however, be remembered that the figures given in this paragraph relate to the percentages of forecasts made. For 40% of all forecasts, as Table 37 indicates, the respondents were unable or refused to give an indication of the accuracy of the forecasts made — fewer indications of accuracy were given for forecasts unconnected with earnings or dividends.)

Summary

This chapter has given an indication of the ways in which the responding financial institutions and stockbroking firms approached the analysis of financial information reported by companies. The financial data which appeared to give greatest assistance to respondents were those related to corporate profitability and dividends.

Stockbroking firms apparently were far more independent in analysing available financial data — the financial institutions appeared to rely rather more heavily on analysts external to such organisations. A further difference between the institutions and stockbroking firms lay in the scope of financial analysis undertaken. Many stockbroking firms appeared to analyse the financial statements of all major companies — institutional analysts seemed to be more concerned with specific companies whose shares were held or were being considered as potential additions to the portfolio.

It was most noticeable that the responding organisations typically analysed available financial information either as soon as it was received or within one month of its receipt. Stockbrokers were somewhat quicker in such use than institutional investors. The majority of respondents were employed in organisations in which financial ratios and funds flows were either verified or recomputed rather than reliance placed entirely on those disclosed by companies in their financial reports. Most responding organisations used available financial information for predicting future financial results (mainly relating to profitability), and a considerable proportion of respondents believed these predictions to be within 10% of actual results.

Having obtained this overview of the form of financial analysis undertaken by the responding organisations, our investigation turned to the source of financial information used in the analyses described in the previous sections. These sources, and the actual information obtained from each, are discussed in the next 3 chapters.

CHAPTER 8

Individual respondents' use and assessment of the annual report

The previous chapter was concerned with the respondents' perceptions of the use made of reported financial information within their organisations. This chapter examines the individual respondent and his use and assessment of the corporate annual report.

Respondents' reading of the annual report

Each respondent was presented with a card containing 12 sections commonly found in corporate annual reports, and was required to state whether or not he read each of these sections. If the answer for any section was in the affirmative, the respondent had then to state whether he considered that he read the section thoroughly or read it briefly for interest. Table 38 reveals the results of these questions.

(Table 38 is on the next page.)

TABLE 38

Parts of annual reports read by survey respondents

PART OF ANNUAL REPORT (n = 229)	Read thoroughly %	Read briefly for interest %	Not read at all %	Total %
Profit and loss account	91	7	2	100
Balance sheet	90	7	3	100
Notes to accounts	80	16	4	100
Chairman's report	76	22	2	100
Composition of activities statement	71	21	8	100
Source and application of funds statement	67	26	7	100
Directors' report	55	36	9	100
Statistical information	55	35	10	100
Statement of accounting policies	55	34	11	100
Supplementary CCA statement	43	42	15	100
Auditor's report	38	38	24	100
Supplementary CPPA statement	37	44	19	100

Note: Respondents who did not answer a particular part of this question were deemed not to have read that section of the report. The rank correlation between 'no answers' and 'did not read' was 0.78. This was considerably higher than the rank correlations of 'no answers' and the other two categories of response. The 2 respondents who claimed to have relied on the chartist approach to investment analysis were not asked this question, and were omitted from the analysis.

The two principal financial statements were the most thoroughly read sections of the annual report. Only 2% of respondents failed to read the profit and loss account, while only 3% paid a similar lack of attention to the balance sheet. Both statements were read thoroughly by 9 out of every 10 of the financial experts. The section of the annual report which forms the main support for these two statements — the notes to the accounts — was the next most thoroughly read section. 8 out of every 10 respondents studied this part of the report carefully, and only 4% failed to read it. Even fewer (2%) failed to read the chairman's report, although the proportion of respondents reading it thoroughly (76%) was slightly lower than for the notes to the accounts.

The source and application of funds statement which, following the introduction of *SSAP 10,* [1] is now a major feature of a company's financial statements, was not read as intensively as the two traditional statements. Only two-thirds of the respondents read it thoroughly, and 7% failed to examine it at all. Even the statement of accounting policies, which to many observers of the financial world is as important as the notes to the accounts (giving as it does a guide to the accounting methods used in the production of the major financial statements), was ignored by 11% of respondents and was read thoroughly only by just over one-half of them.

On the whole, however, most statements were read thoroughly by more than one-half of the responding financial experts. Only 3 sections of the annual report were read intensively by less than one-half of the respondents and, of these sections, 2 were statements about which considerable controversy has existed in recent years — that is, the two inflation accounting statements. The remaining statement — the auditor's report — is, however, of a non-controversial nature, and it is disturbing to discover that almost one-quarter of the respondents apparently were prepared to take the financial statements and the supporting sections of the annual report at face value without seeking to ascertain whether or not the auditor agreed with the directors' disclosures and presentation of the company's results. Indeed, 20% both of those who claimed to read the profit and loss account thoroughly, and of those who stated that they paid equal attention to the balance sheet, apparently did not read the auditor's report. By way of contrast, it is also interesting to note that respondents did not simply accept the presentation of the main financial statements without some examination of the figures. Only 1% both of those who read the balance sheet thoroughly, and of those who examined the profit and loss account with equal care, failed to read the notes to the accounts. Accounting policies were also examined closely. Only 8% of those respondents reading the balance sheet thoroughly and 9% of those according the same treatment to the profit and loss account, failed to read the statement of accounting policies.

Certain types of respondent read sections of the annual report more thoroughly than other respondents. For example, those who had achieved a level of understanding of reporting practices rated as above or much above the average of the respondents as a whole, read all sections (with the sole exception of the supplementary CPPA statement) more intensively than those who had obtained a rating of below or much below average understanding. In addition, those who had greater experience in investment tended to read the main financial statements produced in the annual report less thoroughly than those with lesser experience. For example, while 94% of those with 10 or fewer years' experience read the profit and loss account thoroughly, and 96% of the same group paid similar attention to the balance sheet, the corresponding figures for those

79

respondents with more than 10 years' experience for the two financial statements were, respectively, 86% and 82%. More emphasis, however, was placed by the latter group than the former on the directors' report, the auditor's report, the statement of accounting policies, and the two supplementary inflation accounting statements.

Stockbrokers paid far more attention to the chairman's and directors' reports than did respondents employed by financial institutions. 88% of the stockbrokers read thoroughly the chairman's report, and 67% of them paid a similar degree of attention to the directors' report. The corresponding figures for those employed in the financial institutions were 68% and 47%, respectively. (These differences were significant at the 0.01 level using the chi square test.) Those employed in the institutions, however, paid somewhat more attention than those employed by stockbroking firms to the supplementary inflation accounting statements but, generally, the latter read most statements more intensively than the former. (The profit and loss account and balance sheet were studied equally closely by both groups.)

Perceived importance of sections of the annual report

Thorough reading of a section of the annual report does not necessarily mean that it was considered to be vital in the investment decision-making process — interest may have been the main or only motivating factor for any section being read. Consequently, each respondent was asked what degree of influence each section had in relation to investment decisions within his organisation. Each respondent was therefore requested to rank each section on a 5 point scale relating to its degree of influence. The scale was as follows: 1 = maximum influence; 2 = considerable influence; 3 = moderate influence; 4 = slight influence; and 5 = no influence. The means and standard deviations of the respondents' perceptions of the degree of influence of each section of the annual report are shown in Table 39.

TABLE 39
*Survey respondents' views on the degree of influence of parts
of the annual report on their organisations' investment decisions*

RANKING (n = 215)	PART OF ANNUAL REPORT	MEAN°	STANDARD DEVIATION
Of maximum to considerable influence			
1	Profit and loss account	1.45	0.82
1	Balance sheet	1.45	0.69
Of considerable to moderate influence			
3	Chairman's report	2.10	1.05
4	Notes to accounts	2.34	1.24
5	Source and application of funds statement	2.69	1.20
6	Composition of activities statement	2.74	1.25
Of moderate to slight influence			
7	Statistical information	3.17	1.17
8	Statement of accounting policies	3.21	1.24
9	Directors' report	3.33	1.11
10	Supplementary CCA statement	3.49	1.13
11	Supplementary CPPA statement	3.81	1.07
12	Auditor's report	3.92	1.23

Note: The 3 respondents who did not read any section of the annual report; the 2 respondents who used a chartist approach to investment analysis were not asked the question; and those respondents (11) who did not answer any part of the question, have been omitted from the analysis. Respondents who did not assess the influence of any particular section of the report were deemed to have considered it to be of no influence. The rank correlation between 'no answers' and 'no influence' was 0.95. This was considerably higher than the rank correlation of 'no answers' and the other categories of responses.

Table 39 reveals that, generally speaking, the degree of influence of each section of the annual report on investment decisions was comparable to the intensity with which each section was read by the respondents. The two principal financial statements, the profit and loss account and balance sheet were considered to be of far greater influence than the other sections — both being rated as being of maximum to considerable influence. The next 4 sections ranked as being of considerable to moderate influence were also the parts of the annual report read most thoroughly after the two principal financial statements, although there were slight differences between reading intensity and influence on investment decisions. For example, the notes to the accounts, which ranked third in terms of the proportion of respondents reading them thoroughly, were ranked fourth in terms of influence, exchanging places with the chairman's report which had been ranked fourth in terms of reading intensity. The remaining sections of the annual report were all ranked as being of moderate to slight influence on investment decisions. It would seem that the provision of supplementary inflation accounting financial information did not have a major impact on investment decisions — they were ranked below all other parts of the annual report with the sole exception of the auditor's report.

A check on the respondents' perceptions about the influence of each section of the annual report was made by asking them to rank each part of the annual report in relation to the others. The results are shown in Appendix 45. In some cases, sections were considered to be equally important; therefore the same rating was given to the two sections concerned (for example, if two sections were ranked equal third they would both be given rank 3, and the next section following would be ranked fifth and so on). Consequently, some columns of Appendix 45 will sum to more than 100% and others will aggregate to less than 100%.

The only major difference in ranking the sections of the annual report in terms of influence or relative importance concerned the statistical information section which dropped from seventh position in influence to ninth in relative importance. It is interesting to note the importance accorded the profit and loss account — no fewer than 57% of respondents believed it to be of prime importance and, in total, just over three-quarters of the respondents believed it to be one of the two most important parts of the annual report. The balance sheet, too, was rated as being of major importance — 71% of respondents rating it as one of the two most important sections, and 39% stating it was the most important part of the report (or ranked first with another section). The other parts of the annual report lagged far behind in terms of importance — only the chairman's report and the notes to the accounts were considered by 15% or more of the respondents to be of prime importance.

Despite the differing backgrounds of the financial experts interviewed, only a few differences between the various types of respondent were found in their ratings of the various sections of the annual report. With only a minor exception, all groups assessed the importance of the various sections in the same order as the overall sample of respondents (shown in Appendix 45). All groups ranked the profit and loss account as being the most important section of the report, and the balance sheet as the second most important section. The chairman's report was ranked third by all groups with the sole exception of those respondents who did not have any final say in investment decisions — this group rated the notes to the accounts as being marginally of greater importance. All other groups ranked the latter section in fourth position.

While, in general, the background characteristics of the respondents appeared to have little effect on their assessment of the ranking of the various sections of the annual report, some groups more than others emphasised the prime importance of certain sections. For example, 68% of those whose comprehension of reporting practices was deemed to be above or much above average rated the profit and loss account as being of the utmost importance, compared to only 51% of those whose understanding was deemed to be below or much below average.

Similar results were found when cross-analysing the respondents' assessments of the influence of the various sections of the annual report on investment decisions with the various background variables. In all groups bar one, the section which was rated by most respondents as being of maximum influence was the profit and loss account. The other sections were almost invariably rated in the same order as shown in Table 39. 71% of the respondents employed by financial institutions (and especially those employed by insurance companies, pension funds and merchant banks), however, rated the balance sheet as being of maximum influence compared to 68% of the same group attributing the same degree of importance to the profit and loss account. (The corresponding figures for those employed by stockbroking firms were balance sheet — 54%; profit and loss account — 71%). The institutional investors were also inclined to attribute more influence to the notes to the accounts (35% rated this section as being of maximum influence) than to the chairman's report which was rated by 28% as being of maximum influence. 42% of the stockbrokers, on the other hand, considered the chairman's report to be of the utmost influence, surpassing the assessment made by this group of the notes to the accounts. This latter section was only considered by 27% of stockbrokers to be of equal influence.

Useful information in annual reports

The reason for the rating of the profit and loss account as the most important section of the annual report was not difficult to discover. Table 40 reveals that no fewer than 48% of respondents believed that, of the information contained in companies' annual reports, profitability was of particular relevance to their firms.

TABLE 40

Information in annual reports perceived by the respondents to be of particular relevance to their organisations

	%
Income information (current profits; trends of profits)	48
Capital structure	40
Future prospects	39
Liquidity or solvency	27
Sales (excluding future sales prospects)	14
Dividend information	5
Company development or expansion	5

n = 229; the 2 respondents who used a chartist approach to investment analysis were not asked this question.

This demand for earnings information corresponded with the respondents' earlier comments when 57% stated that earnings were of the greatest assistance in their organisation's investment activities. The demand for dividend information, however, was not so consistent. Only 5% of respondents mentioned that information on dividends found in the annual report was of particular relevance to their organisations, whereas 31% had previously stated that details about dividends were of the greatest assistance in the latter's investment activities.

A large proportion of respondents was consistent in seeking data on capital structure (40% found such information in the annual report to be relevant, while previously 28% had stated that it was of the greatest assistance in investment activities). A similar percentage of respondents, however, commented on information previously unmentioned by all bar 2% — no fewer than 39% of respondents believed details of a company's future prospects were of particular relevance to their organisation, despite their earlier failure to mention the assistance of such information in investment decisions.

Those respondents seeking information on a company's future prospects usually sought it in the chairman's report. Only 8% of respondents searching for such information stated that they obtained it in other sections of the annual report. Not unexpectedly, most of those mentioning that earnings data were particularly relevant (82%) scanned the profit and loss account. 11% of those seeking information on profitability, however, appeared to be concerned with earnings trends and used the statistical information provided in the annual report. A further 10% obviously were interested in an analysis of overall profitability. These respondents looked for information about earnings in the composition of activities statement rather than in the profit and loss acount. The respondents interested in the capital structure or liquidity of a company, not surprisingly, used the balance sheet to obtain such information — just under 94% in both cases utilised this statement for this purpose.

Reading pattern of the individual respondent

So far, this chapter has been concerned mainly with respondents' overall use of individual sections of corporate annual reports. While the use made of individual sections is in itself of utility in highlighting those sections of the report deemed by the respondents to be relevant to their needs, it does not reveal which combination of sections are used to produce an overall impression of a company's financial affairs. The remainder of this chapter considers the individual respondents' *overall* use of the annual report, and reveals which sections were used in conjunction with others to provide the information they desired. In the following analysis of the individual respondents' annual report reading patterns, no account was taken of supplementary inflation accounting statements as not all companies produced such information in their annual report, whereas most other sections about which the respondents were questioned were commonplace features of company reports.

The first stage in the analysis involved the division of respondents into groups based on their reading of the annual report. Those who read all sections of the report (24% of all respondents) and those who did not read any section at all (1%) were easy to identify, and are shown as Groups 1 and 6, respectively, in Table 41.

TABLE 41

Annual report reader groups

	%
1. Thorough readers of both quantitative and qualitative data (all sections of the annual report read thoroughly)	24
2. Thorough readers of quantitative data (at least profit and loss account *and* balance sheet read thoroughly)	65
3. Thorough readers of qualitative data (chairman's report and/ or directors' report read thoroughly)	6
4. Readers of quantitative and qualitative data not falling into Groups 1, 2, 3 or 5	1
5. Brief readers of quantitative data not falling into Group 3 (profit and loss account and balance sheet read briefly)	3
6. Non-readers of annual reports	1
	$\overline{100}$

n = 229; the 2 respondents who used the chartist approach to investment analysis have been omitted from this analysis.

The division of the remaining respondents into other patterns of reading of the annual report was not so straightforward. Few respondents had absolutely identical reading patterns and, consequently, it was necessary to concentrate on assessing the intensity of reading of a combination of particular statements by grouping respondents in broad, although not identical, annual report reading patterns. It was decided to base the groups mainly on the reading of the sections of the annual report which had been those read most thoroughly by respondents; namely, the profit and loss account, balance sheet and the chairman's report. (See Table 38 — the notes to the accounts were ignored for this purpose being in effect an appendix to the two main financial statements.)

The respondents who read thoroughly either the chairman's report or the directors' report, but who did not pay the same degree of attention to both the profit and loss account and balance sheet, were categorised as Group 3. This group, therefore, consisted of those who were concerned mainly with the qualitative (i.e. narrative) sections of the annual report. This group consisted of only 6% of respondents. Most of them read thoroughly the chairman's report alone—a mere 4 respondents read both statements thoroughly, and only 1 read thoroughly the directors' report to the exclusion of the chairman's report.

Having separated those interested in the more qualitative aspects of the annual report from the remainder, attention was now centred on those who concentrated on the more quantitative sections of the report — the profit and loss account and balance sheet. Those who did not read thoroughly all sections of the annual report but who read thoroughly the two main financial statements were identified as Group 2. This was the largest of the reading pattern groups. No fewer than 65% of all respondents fell into this category. Some respondents (3%), not included in any reading pattern group above, had read both the profit and loss account and balance sheet briefly and were categorised as Group 5—these being respondents who recognised the importance of quantitative data but who paid less attention to it than the respondents in Group 2. The remaining 1% of the respondents were designated as Group 4 — the residual group.

Looking at the overall picture, it can be seen that only a minute proportion of the respondents did not read the annual report at all. Almost one-quarter, however, examined all parts of the report thoroughly, while a further 65% read thoroughly at least the two main financial statements. In all, therefore, only 11% of respondents did not read thoroughly both the profit and loss account and balance sheet. Indeed, only 4 (2%) of the 229 respondents questioned about their reading of the annual report admitted that they did not read at least one of the two main financial statements.

For purposes of further analysis, the reading pattern groups were considered to be rather cumbersome to use — especially in view of the small numbers in some of the groups. The original intention had been to divide the respondents into two main types of annual report reader — thorough readers and less thorough readers. Thorough readers were to be Groups 1 and 2, and the remaining respondents would have been termed less interested readers. Two complications, however, arose. First, the thorough reader group would have consisted of almost 9 out of every 10 respondents, leaving only a tiny proportion as a group for purposes of contrast. Secondly, while those in Group 2 had read thoroughly the two main financial statements, analysis revealed that a few of the respondents in Group 2, while reading thoroughly the profit and loss account and balance sheet, appeared to be ignoring other sections of the annual report and could scarcely be deemed to be termed thorough readers. To meet these two points, it was decided (a) to keep Group 1 as a separate category to be termed very thorough readers; and (b) to adopt another criterion for a thorough reader which would be applied to those respondents in Group 2.

Each respondent was, therefore, awarded 2 points for each section of the annual report read thoroughly, and 1 point for each section read briefly. The new criterion to determine thorough readers of the annual report demanded that, in addition to reading thoroughly the profit and loss account and balance sheet, the respondent should have amassed 12 points. This, in effect, meant that a thorough reader should have read thoroughly the two main financial statements and, on average, have read all 8 other sections of the annual report included in this analysis at least briefly.[2] If the respondent had omitted to read any section of the report then, to be deemed a thorough reader, he would, to compensate, have had to have read thoroughly not only the profit and loss account and balance sheet but, in addition, another section of the report. The new criterion necessitated the division of Group 2 into Groups 2a and 2b. The latter group consisted of the 7 respondents in Group 2 who did not meet the definition of a thorough reader, while Group 2a consisted of the 142 respondents in the former Group 2 who had scored 12 points or more.

Appendix 46 (which shows the reading patterns of all groups with the exception of Groups 1 and 6 whose reading patterns were obvious) reveals the major differences between Groups 2a and 2b. Only a few respondents in Group 2a failed to read any section at least briefly — although it is interesting to note that 22% did not read the auditor's report. By way of contrast, significant proportions of Group 2b failed to read the directors' report (43%); the statement of accounting policies (86% — as opposed to 8% in Group 2a); the auditor's report (100%); the source and application of funds statement (28%); the statistical information (29%); and the composition of activities statement (14%).

The other reader groups were composed of only a few of the respondents and do not warrant much detailed comment. A few points, however, are of interest. Of the 14 respondents in Group 3 (readers of qualitative data), most read the main sections of the annual report at least briefly, 57% failed to read the auditor's report, and 50% and 43%, respectively, paid no attention to the statistical information and the composition of activities statement.

The 7 respondents who read the profit and loss account and balance sheet briefly (Group 5) all also paid similar attention to the chairman's report. The auditor's report and the statement of accounting policies were the sections of the annual report which received least attention from this group.

Appendix 46, therefore, clearly shows that Group 2 read the annual report more intensively than the other groups, with the sole exception of the group of responding financial experts who read thoroughly every section used in the analysis. Table 42, which is derived from Appendix 46, shows *on average* each group's pattern of reading for each section of the annual report. The table was constructed by averaging the reading intensity for all sections of the annual report read — that is, by averaging the percentages shown in each line of Appendix 46.

TABLE 42
Level of intensity of reading of company annual financial reports

	READER GROUPS						
LEVEL OF INTENSITY OF READING	*Very thorough readers*	*Thorough readers*	*Less thorough readers*				
	1	2a	2b	3	4	5	6
	%	%	%	%	%	%	%
Read thoroughly	100	66	30	32	15	3	—
Read briefly	—	29	40	43	40	74	—
Do not read	—	5	30	25	45	23	100
	100	100	100	100	100	100	100
n =	54	142	7	14	2	7	3
% of 229	24	62	14				

From the above table, it can be seen that differences in the average reading intensity of the very thorough readers, thorough readers and less thorough readers were quite marked. On average, 66% of the thorough readers (Group 2a) read thoroughly each section of the annual report, while only 21% of the less thorough readers (Groups 2b, 3, 4, 5 and 6) paid the same degree of attention to each section. By definition, of course, the very thorough readers all read each section of the annual report thoroughly.

Supplementary inflation accounting statements

Using the newly-defined thorough reader groups, it can be seen which type of respondent appeared to be interested in supplementary inflation accounting statements. Table 38 had previously shown that less than one-half of the respondents had read these statements thoroughly, but Table 43 below goes further, and highlights which particular type of reader showed most interest in such sections of the annual report.

TABLE 43
Thorough reader groups and the use of supplementary
inflation accounting statements

	READER GROUP		
	Very thorough readers (Group 1) (n = 54)	*Thorough readers* (Group 2a) (n = 142)	*Less thorough readers* (Groups 2b, 3, 4, 5, 6) (n = 33)
CCA statement	%	%	%
Read thoroughly	93	33	6
Read briefly	7	56	42
Not read at all	—	11	52
	100	100	100
CPPA statement	%	%	%
Read thoroughly	93	23	6
Read briefly	7	58	39
Not read at all	—	19	55
	100	100	100

Respondents were questioned about both current cost and current purchasing power accounting statements. At the time the interviews were conducted in mid-1977, CCA statements were commonly appearing in company reports, although a few companies retained the CPPA style of statements which had been used in previous years (especially after the introduction of *PSSAP7*). Table 43 evidences that clear differences in the intensity of reading of such statements existed between the thorough reader groups (the differences were significant at the 0.01 level using the chi square test). Almost all of those who were very thorough readers of the annual report read the supplementary statements thoroughly. Indeed, none of this group failed to study inflation accounting statements. In contrast, a majority of the thorough readers read the statements only briefly for interest, while over one-half of the less thorough readers of the report paid no attention to such information. (Further details of this analysis are given in Appendix 47.)

Summary

The evidence presented in this chapter reveals that the responding financial experts appeared to obtain a great deal of relevant information from the annual report. Data on company income, capital structure, liquidity and future prospects all seemed to be gleaned from the report. Much of this information came from 6 sections of the annual report which were studied more carefully than other sections by the respondents — namely, the two main financial statements, the notes to these statements, the chairman's report, the composition of activities statement, and the source and application of funds statement. Only a few respondents failed to read any section of the annual report — by way of contrast, 89% of respondents studied both the balance sheet and the profit and loss account thoroughly. Indeed, almost one-quarter read thoroughly all sections of the annual report (excluding the optional inflation accounting statements).

Based upon their stated pattern of reading of the annual report and the intensity of their reading of its contents, the respondents were divided into 3 reading pattern groups (very thorough, thorough and less thorough readers of the annual report). The following chapter uses this variable of intensity of reading to assess whether or not those respondents who appeared to be less interested in the annual report used other sources to obtain the information relevant to their needs.

REFERENCES AND FOOTNOTES

[1] 'Statements of Source and Application of Funds', *Statement of Standard Accounting Practice 10*, Accounting Standards Commitee, 1975.
[2] It should be remembered that inflation accounting statements were not included in the analysis. The respondents were categorised on the basis of their reading of the 10 remaining sections of the annual report.
[3] 'Accounting for Changes in the Purchasing Power of Money', *Provisional Statement of Standard Accounting Practice 7*, Accounting Standards Committee, 1974.

CHAPTER 9

Individual respondents' use of other sources of information

Use of other sources of financial information

Table 44 below shows the use made by respondents of published sources of financial information about companies, other than the annual report. The sources shown in this table were pre-selected by the authors although the respondents were invited to state other sources used. Only a few diverse responses were, however, forthcoming, and these have been ignored for the purposes of analysis.

USE OF OTHER SOURCES OF INFORMATION

TABLE 44

Use made by survey respondents of other sources of
financial information about companies

SOURCE OF INFORMATION	Read thoroughly %	Read briefly for interest %	Not read at all* %	Total %
Occasional merger reports	85	12	3	100
Financial press reports	77	23	—	100
Interim financial reports	75	22	3	100
Stockbrokers' reports	71	22	7	100
Moodie's or Extel cards	67	24	9	100
Economy data and reports	58	35	7	100
Industry data and reports	53	36	11	100
Company reports to employees	13	58	29	100

n = 228

1 respondent who did not answer any part of the question, and the 2 respondents who claimed to have relied on the chartist approach to investment analysis have been omitted from the table.

*Included in this column are respondents who failed to answer the particular part of this question. The rank correlation between the 'do not read' answers and 'no answers' for the 8 sources of information was 0.33. The correlations between 'do not read' and the other two categories of response were considerably less, and in the case of 'read thoroughly' the correlation was negative.

It is interesting to note from Table 44 that all sources, with the sole exception of employee reports, were read thoroughly by a majority of the respondents. Employee reports are, however, seldom sources of primary information, but invariably repeat, in a simplified form, data available in companies' annual reports to shareholders. Consequently, the relative lack of interest in employee reports shown by the respondents concerned is understandable.

Of the remaining sources, occasional acquisition and merger reports were read by the respondents more thoroughly than any other source. This, too, is not surprising given that such reports can reflect the beginnings of major changes in the companies concerned. For the same reason, it would seem that financial press reports were studied thoroughly by more than three-quarters of the respondents — indeed, none of them stated that he failed to read the financial press. Only 3% did not read companies' interim reports and, again, these were read thoroughly by three-quarters of these financial experts. It should be noted, however, that despite sources of information other than the annual report being read thoroughly by large proportions of the respondents, none of the sources were studied as thoroughly as the profit and loss account and balance sheet presented in corporate annual reports (see Table 38) which were read thoroughly by 9 out of every 10 respondents.

Little difference was noted in the answers of different types of respondents. Stockbrokers, however, read all sources more thoroughly than institutional investors with the sole, though not surprising, exception of stockbrokers' reports. Only 50% of the stockbrokers read thoroughly reports from other stockbroking firms, whereas 86% of the respondents employed by institutions claimed to read such reports with the same degree of attention. Those respondents who had significant experience of accounting tended to read all sources of information less thoroughly than those who had little or no experience of accounting. (The differences between the groups were not, however, significant at the 0.05 level when the chi square test was applied.) The only information which those respondents who had significant experience in accounting read more thoroughly than either of the other two accounting experience groups was contained in occasional merger or acquisition reports. Interestingly, this was the only source which revealed statistically significant differences between the comprehension groups ($p < 0.01$). 90% of those with much above, or above average understanding of reporting practices read these reports thoroughly, compared to 86% and 78%, respectively, of those with average comprehension and below or much below average comprehension.

Perceived importance of other sources of financial information

The respondents' thorough reading of the various sources of information about companies other than annual reports did not, however, imply that their employing organisations put the same degree of emphasis on the value of these sources when investment decisions were being made by them.

TABLE 45

Survey respondents' views on the degree of influence of other sources of information about companies other than the annual report on their organisations' investment decisions

RANKING	SOURCE OF INFORMATION	MEAN*	STANDARD DEVIATION
Of maximum to considerable influence			
1	3 or 6 monthly reports from companies	1.85	1.00
Of considerable to moderate influence			
2	Financial press reports	2.25	0.99
3	Occasional acquisition or merger reports	2.33	1.24
4	Stockbrokers' reports	2.49	1.33
5	Economy data and reports	2.52	1.18
6	Industry data and reports	2.55	1.18
Of moderate to slight influence			
7	Moodie's or Extel cards	3.26	1.39
Of slight to no influence			
8	Company reports to employees	4.21	0.86

n = 217

The 2 respondents who used a chartist approach to investment analysis were not asked the question. Those respondents (12) who did not answer any part of the question have been omitted from the analysis. Respondents who did not assess the influence of any particular source of information were deemed to have considered it to be of no influence. The rank correlation between 'no answers' and 'no influence' was 0.55. The correlations between 'no answers' and the other categories of responses were considerably less and, in the cases of 'maximum' and 'considerable' influence, were negative.

Table 45 reveals that, while occasional merger reports and financial press reports were more widely read by the respondents than interim financial statements from companies, the same respondents estimated that the latter source had more influence on their organisations' investment decisions. Using the same 5 point scale to measure influence as had been used in connection with Table 39 in the last chapter, the respondents rated company interim financial statements as having more influence than any other source of information; that is, as being of maximum to considerable influence — a rating which, in connection with the annual report, they had only awarded to the profit and loss account and balance sheet. It is interesting to note, however, that the latter two statements were rated as being higher on the influence scale than interim statements.

The influence of the interim report could also be gauged by the fact that 47% of respondents answering the question rated this report as being of maximum influence on their organisations' investment decisions. Indeed, 76% considered the report to be of at least considerable influence. In contrast, to this, only 31% believed occasional merger reports exerted maximum influence on decision making in their organisations, while similar views about stockbrokers' reports and financial press reports were held by 29% and 23%, respectively, of the respondents.

The importance of the interim report to the respondents' organisations was further emphasised when those surveyed were asked to rank the sources of financial information (excluding the company annual report) in terms of their relative importance in their organisations' investment decisions. No fewer than 50% of respondents rated the interim report as being the most important of the given sources of information (see Appendix 48). Only 25% rated stockbrokers' reports as being the most important source, and even financial press reports and occasional merger reports were only given this rating by 16% and 15%, respectively, of the financial experts concerned.

Some respondents rated certain sources more highly than did their colleagues. For example, 42% of those employed by institutional investors rated stockbrokers' reports as being of prime importance, and 46% rated these reports as being of maximum influence. The corresponding figures for those employed by stockbroking firms were 2% and 4%. The overall difference was revealed by the means of the influence ratings of the two groups — the institutional investors rated the reports at 1.85 (that is, of maximum to considerable influence); whereas the mean of the stockbrokers' responses was 3.4 (of moderate to slight influence). It is not unduly surprising that the differences between the two groups ($p < 0.01$) were so great. Many of those employed by the institutions appeared to use stockbrokers' reports as a primary source of data, whereas those employed by stockbroking firms tended to rely on other data in compiling such reports. For instance, 66% of the latter rated interim accounts as being of maximum influence, whereas only 35% of the former held the same opinion. Similarly, 70% of the stockbroking group of respondents rated three or six monthly reports as being of prime importance, compared to 36% of the institutional group ($p<0.01$). Therefore, interim reports appeared to be the major source of published information for stockbrokers — the sources rated next most important by them (each by only 17%) were financial press reports and Moodies or Extel cards.

The interim report was the prime source of other published information about companies for very thorough and thorough readers of the annual report. 62% of the former and 48% of the latter rated such reports as being of maximum influence. Only 21% of the less thorough readers of the annual report rated the interim reports so highly ($p<0.01$). The sources rated as being of maximum influence by the less thorough readers of the annual report were stockbrokers' reports (61%) and financial press reports (43%) — both of which were generally 'second-hand' sources. The corresponding percentages for the very thorough readers were 20% and 18%, respectively. (Similar results were obtained in analysing the relative importance ratings of the above sources.) Few major differences were apparent in the analysis of the responses of the other categories of respondents.

Use of all sources of published information

The categorisation of respondents into groups based on reading intensity had been based on their reading of corporate annual reports. The possible reasons for some of these professional analysts and investment managers merely skimming through these reports will be investigated in depth in the following chapters. One reason, however, could be that those who did not study the annual report as intensively as other respondents used other published sources of financial information to obtain the facts they required.

This section examines whether or not the less thorough readers and the thorough readers did compensate for their failure to use company annual reports as thoroughly as the very thorough readers. Specifically, the following hypothesis was tested:

H_3 Those respondents who were less thorough readers, and those respondents who were thorough readers of the annual report, read other sources of financial information more thoroughly than those who read the annual report very thoroughly.

Table 46 shows the reading of other published financial information analysed by the three report reading groups.

TABLE 46

Extent of survey respondents' use of other sources of information in relation to the thoroughness of their reading of the annual report

READER GROUPS		SOURCES OF INFORMATION																							
		OMR			FPR			IFR			SR			MEC			EDR			IDR			CRE		
		t	b	n	t	b	n	t	b	n	t	b	n	t	b	n	t	b	n	t	b	n	t	b	n
	n	%	%	%	%	%	%	%	%	%	%	%	%	%	%	%	%	%	%	%	%	%	%	%	%
Very thorough readers of the annual report	54	98	—	2	91	9	—	93	5	2	74	19	7	68	26	6	70	28	2	68	28	4	22	58	20
Thorough readers of the annual report	142	86	13	1	72	28	—	78	20	2	69	24	7	66	23	11	56	40	4	53	39	8	10	60	30
Less thorough readers of the annual report	32	56	31	13	75	25	—	34	53	13	75	16	9	72	22	6	47	25	28	28	38	34	12	47	41

n = 228

The respondent who did not answer any part of the question assessing the use of other sources of published financial information apart from the annual report, and the 2 respondents who claimed to have relied on the chartist approach to investment management, have been omitted from the analysis.

OMR = occasional merger reports;   FPR = financial press reports;   IFR = interim financial reports;
SR = stockbrokers' reports;   MEC = Moodies or Extel cards;   EDR = economic data and reports;
IDR = industry data and reports;   CRE = company reports to employees;
t = thorough reading;   b = brief reading;   n = no reading
(All percentages in each section equal 100 in aggregate)

Table 46 shows that in all cases, with the exception of stockbrokers' reports and Moodies and Extel cards, the very thorough readers of the annual report also read other published sources of financial information more intensively than other respondents. The differences in the reading patterns of the 3 groups in respect of stockbrokers' reports and Moodies and Extel cards were slight but, in the case of other sources, were statistically significant using the chi square test ($p < 0.05$) — with the exception of company reports to employees. The less thorough readers tended to use financial press reports, stockbrokers' reports and Moodies or Extel cards most intensively whereas the very thorough readers and thorough readers were more concerned with primary sources of data — namely, occasional merger and acquisition reports and interim reports.

Very thorough readers also paid a great deal of attention to the financial press.

Given the above results, it would seem that hypothesis H_3 has to be rejected. Indeed, it would seem that very thorough readers of company annual reports study other sources of financial data about companies or the economy (with the exceptions of stockbrokers' reports and Moodies and Extel cards) with at least equal but generally more intensity than those who pay less attention to company annual reports.

As a check on this finding, two further tests were employed. To conduct these tests, an index of the intensity of reading of other sources was calculated for each respondent by awarding 2 points for every published source of financial information shown in Table 44 which he read thoroughly and 1 point for each source read briefly. The maximum 'score', therefore, was 16 points. To enable a comparision to be made with the respondents' reading of the annual report, they were divided into 3 groups:

(a) the very thorough readers of other published sources of financial information who read all other sources thoroughly;

(b) the thorough readers of other sources who read *on average* 6 sources briefly and 2 thoroughly (that is, those who amassed 10 points on the intensity of reading index) — a similar criterion had been used for assessing the respondents' intensity of reading the annual report; and

(c) the remaining respondents who were considered to be less thorough readers of other sources of financial information.

Only 9 respondents (of whom 4 were very thorough and 4 thorough readers of annual reports) read all other sources of financial information thoroughly. Consequently, for the purposes of further analysis, these respondents have been included with 194 other respondents termed thorough readers of other sources of financial information. The first test, whose result is shown in Table 47, compared the groupings of respondents determined by their reading (a) of the annual report; and (b) of all other sources of published information.

TABLE 47
*Comparison of intensity of reading of annual report
and intensity of reading of other sources of financial information*

READING OF ANNUAL REPORT		READING OF OTHER SOURCES OF FINANCIAL INFORMATION		
		Very thorough and thorough readers	*Less thorough readers*	*Total*
	n	%	%	%
Very thorough readers	54	98	2	100
Thorough and less thorough readers	174	86	14	100

n = 228

The respondent who did not answer any part of the question assessing the use of other sources of published financial information apart from the annual report, and the 2 respondents who claimed to have relied on the chartist approach to investment management, have been omitted from the analysis.

This analysis again reveals that those respondents who read the annual report very thoroughly were more likely than those who read it less intensively to read other published sources of financial information thoroughly. (The differences shown in Table 47 were significant at $p < 0.01$ using the chi square test.) The second test involved a rank correlation between the indices constructed for respondents' reading of the annual report and their reading of other sources of published information. (It will be remembered that the indices were based on the awarding of 2 points if a section of the annual report or source of information other than the annual report was read thoroughly, and 1 point if the section or other source was read briefly.) If some respondents compensated for reading the annual report less thoroughly than other respondents by studying other sources of financial information more intensively than their colleagues, it would be expected that a negative correlation between the two indices would result. The correlation, however, which again indicates that hypothesis H_3 must be rejected, was positive. Using Spearman's rho a result of $+0.45$ (significantly different from 0 at $p < 0.01$) was obtained. It would therefore seem that those who studied the annual report very thoroughly were more likely than other respondents who paid a lesser degree of attention to the annual report to study, in depth, other published sources of financial information — that is, a consistent interest in published information was revealed.

Useful information found in published sources other than the annual report

From the evidence presented in Chapter 8, it appeared that the annual report did not satisfy all the information needs of the respondents. It could be expected, therefore, that other sources of financial data would contain information of use to financial experts which was unavailable in corporate annual reports. Consequently, the respondents were asked what information derived from these other sources they believed was of particular relevance to their organisations.

TABLE 48

Information derived from sources other than annual reports perceived by the survey respondents to be of particular relevance to their organisations

	%
Income data (profit performance; trends; earnings per share)	38
Future prospects (future demand; contracts; plans)	32
General view of economy	16
General trend information (past record; growth; past trends — unspecified but excluding income and dividend trends)	15
General view of industry	14
Surprising (that is, not already known) information about a company	12
Solvency; liquidity	11
Attitude in stock market towards company	10
General information about a company (activities; labour; geographical spread)	9
Dividend information	6

n = 229

The 2 respondents who claimed to have relied on the chartist approach to investment analysis have been omitted from this table.

It can be seen from Table 48 that the future prospects of a company was a piece of information mentioned frequently by respondents. 32% of them stated that such information derived from a source other than the annual report was relevant to their organisation. Given that, in Table 40, 39% of respondents had mentioned that such relevant information was to be found in the annual report, it seems surprising that only 2% of respondents had earlier declared that details of a company's future prospects were of the greatest assistance in their organisations' investment activities. The same could not, however, be said for information on corporate earnings. In answer to earlier questions, 57% of respondents had declared that such data were of the greatest assistance in their organisations' investment activities, and 48% had perceived income information in the annual report to be of particular relevance to their organisations. 38% of respondents now suggested that income data found in sources other than the annual report were also useful to their employers.

No other single piece of information was sought by more than one-sixth of the respondents. It would seem from Table 48 that, apart from details about future prospects and income, the financial experts concerned were mainly using sources other than the annual report to obtain background information about the company and, consequently, were seeking more general knowledge about the industry in which it operated or attitudes in the City towards it.

Not unexpectedly, the main source of income information was interim reports. 52% of those seeking such information used this medium, although stockbrokers' reports (23%), acquisition and merger reports (17%) and the financial press (17%) were also used but to a lesser extent. While interim reports were also used by 35% of those seeking information on a company's future prospects, slightly more of the respondents (43%) obtained guides to a company's future by means of stockbrokers' reports. Financial press reports were obviously used as a good source of background information as 32% of respondents seeking to assess a company's prospects used these ubiquitous reports. In addition, the financial press was used by 54% of those looking for what they termed 'surprising information' about companies — that is, previously undisclosed information of immediate interest.

Summary

This chapter has given an indication that most of the main published sources of financial information about companies other than the annual report are likely to be read thoroughly by a majority of investment managers and financial analysts. While merger reports and the financial press were read more thoroughly than companies' interim reports by the respondents, the latter source was considered to be far more influential in terms of investment decision making than were the others.

Part of the reason for this was undoubtedly the desire for both current information on a company's earnings and hints about a company's future prospects. These two pieces of information appeared to be the reason for many respondents scanning sources of information other than the annual report. The annual report seemed, however, to be extremely influential. The annual profit and loss account and balance sheet were rated by respondents as having more influence on their organisation's investment decision making than any other published source of information. In addition, those who did not read the annual report thoroughly did not seem to compensate by using other sources of published information. It would seem that a financial expert who studied the annual report intensively also paid a great deal of attention to other sources of information. In other words, evidence of a consistent interest (either higher or lower relative to other respondents) in all published financial information seemed to exist.

CHAPTER 10

Respondents' views on company visits

Chapters 8 and 9 were concerned with the respondents' use of both formal accounting information provided by companies, and other published information dealing with corporate performance and financial position. This chapter considers a third source of information about companies — the receipt of information obtained from visits to companies. This source of information is quite distinct from the other sources. Any information obtained during a visit to a company may well be unique in the sense that it may not be shared by other investors (both existing and potential), whereas published sources provide knowledge for all users. Consequently, company visits would seem at first sight to be an extremely useful means of obtaining information in advance of other investors.

Companies visited by respondents' organisations

To commence this investigation into company visitations, respondents were questioned about the extent to which such visits were made to companies by their organisations. Table 49 reveals that only 6% of respondents believed that members of their organisations did not make any such visits.

TABLE 49

Respondents' views on the extent to which visits are made by members of their organisation to companies in which it has invested (or intends to invest)

COMPANIES VISITED	FREQUENCY OF VISITS	%
Selected companies	Infrequently	43
Selected companies	Frequently	27
All companies	Frequently	21
None		6
All companies	Infrequently	3
		100

n = 229

The 2 respondents who claimed to have relied upon the chartist approach to investment analysis were not asked this question, and were omitted from the analysis.

Forty-six per cent of respondents stated that members of their organisation only visited on an infrequent basis — a vast majority of these respondents stating that only selected companies were visited. 48% of those surveyed, however, were of the opinion that their organisation arranged frequent visits to companies — 21% answering that all companies in which their organisation (or its clients) had invested or possibly intended to invest were visited.

In general, the visits were made mainly to both existing and potential investments. In the few cases, however, where visits were only made either to existing investments or to companies whose shares were potential additions to the organisation's or its clients' portfolios, visits to existing investments were more numerous — 14% of respondents stated that members of their organisation only visited companies whose securities had already been purchased, and only 2% declared that visits made solely to those companies in which an investment might be made. The type of visits made differed markedly depending upon whether the visiting organisation was a stockbroking firm or a financial institution. 44% of those respondents who were employed by stockbroking firms declared that their firms visited all companies frequently whereas only 4% of those employed by the financial institutions held this view. 61% of the latter respondents stated that their organisation arranged only infrequent visits to companies and then only in selected cases — the corresponding figure for respondents employed by stockbroking firms was 15%.

There appeared, therefore, to be a distinct difference in the nature and frequency of company visitations organised by institutions and stockbroking firms. This was confirmed when the replies of respondents were analysed in terms of their employing organisations. Taking these replies as being true reflections of the policies of the organisations concerned, it was found that 76% of the 29 insurance companies surveyed; 67% of the 18 pension funds; 72% of the 18 investment or unit trusts; and 64% of the 14 merchant banks arranged only infrequent visits to selected companies. (It should be noted that, as usually more than one member of an organisation was interviewed, occasionally opinions were divided but, so far as the above analysis is concerned, these differences were minimal.)

Only 5 of the 79 (6%) financial institutions were said to arrange on a frequent basis visits to all companies in which they were interested and, in 4 of these institutions, there was disagreement on this matter between the 2 respondents concerned. A completely different picture was given by those working in stockbroking firms. Respondents in 46% of the 61 such firms surveyed declared that their organisation visited, on a frequent basis, all companies in which it was interested. (In one-quarter of these firms, however, respondents' opinions were divided.) In all, respondents employed in 72% of stockbroking firms declared that their firms visited, on a frequent basis, either all companies in which they were interested or only selected companies. (In one-quarter of these cases, there was dissension over the responding view expressed.) Only 20% of stockbroking firms were said by their employees to arrange infrequent visits to selected cases. (In two-fifths of these firms a different view existed between the employees interviewed.) Even allowing for disagreements between those interviewed in each organisation it is clear that, in general, there appears to be quite a different attitude towards company visitations existing in financial institutions and stockbroking firms. The institutions seemed to be interested in visiting companies only rarely and even then only if clarification of certain matters was required. Stockbroking firms, however, appeared to visit companies more as a matter of course. This, perhaps, is a reason for the high rating by respondents employed by financial institutions of stockbrokers' reports (as was seen in Chapter 9) — these reports possibly being used as a substitute for company visits.

The objectives of company visits

As Table 50 reveals, the major reason for visiting companies appeared to be the obtaining of a first-hand impression of the calibre of company management. 56% of respondents indicated that their organisations believed in the need to examine management, not necessarily by the financial results published in corporate reports but by an assessment of potential. Indeed, not surprisingly, most of the reasons given by the respondents for company visits were concerned with the assessment of the future prospects of companies (including the initiation of new products) — that is, either directly or indirectly by assessing such matters as a company's progress to date, its management, products and markets. The overall aim of a visit could, therefore, be deemed to be an aid to the interpretation of a company's financial results by the construction of a frame of reference of future expectations. The background data sought by 48% of respondents could be considered to be useful to construct part of such a framework of future potential but could also be used to give explanations of recent financial results.

The 216 financial experts who declared that their organisations conducted company visits were asked with whom relevant matters were discussed during such visits. Not unexpectedly, two key executives were identified. 88% of respondents stated that talks were held with the company's chairman or managing director, while an almost identical percentage (86%) indicated that the finance director was also a vital member of the management team, and consequently was sought out during company visits. Other directors were only mentioned by 11% of respondents, and no other member of management was mentioned by more than 10% of respondents.

TABLE 50

Respondents' views on the reasons for company visits

	%
To assess the company's management	56
To obtain background information about the company	48
To assess the company's future prospects	35
To monitor the company's progress	19
To maintain good relations with the company	18
To learn about new projects initiated by the company	12
To increase understanding of the company's products or markets	11
To discover the answer to a specific problem in assessing the company	7

n = 229

The 2 respondents who claimed to have relied upon the chartist approach to investment analysis were not asked this question, and were omitted from the analysis.

Perceived importance of company visits

While a great deal of information, relating particularly to the company's future, could possibly be obtained during company visits, the overall relevance of visits can be judged by ascertaining how vital the respondents perceived this source of information to be. Consequently, they were asked to assess the degree of influence which company visits, published financial information from companies, and other sources of information about companies had in relation to the investment decisions made within their organisations. In addition, they were asked to rank in order of importance to their organisation the 3 sources of information mentioned above.

TABLE 51

Survey respondents' views on the degree of influence of the major sources of information about companies on their organisations' investment decisions

RANKING	SOURCE OF INFORMATION	MEAN*	STANDARD DEVIATION
Of maximum to considerable influence			
1	Formal published accounting information from companies	1.61	0.75
2	Other sources of information about companies and their industries	1.89	0.76
Of considerable to moderate influence			
3	Company visits	2.17	1.19

n = 216

The 2 respondents who used a chartist approach to investment analysis were not asked the question. Those respondents (13) who did not answer any part of the question have been omitted from the analysis. Respondents who did not assess the influence of any particular source of information were deemed to have considered it to be of no influence. The rank correlation between 'no answers' and 'no influence' was 0.63. The correlations between 'no answers' and the other categories of response (with the marginal exception of 'moderate influence') were considerably less and, in the case of 'maximum influence', negative.

Table 51 indicates that company visits were considered, as an overall source of information for investment decision making, to be of the least influence, although such a source still rated as being of considerable to moderate influence. Indeed, 38% of respondents answering the question stated that their organisations considered such visits to be of maximum influence. (The same 5 point scale which has been described in Chapter 8 was used.) Formal published financial information from companies was considered to be the most influential source of information, being rated as being of maximum to considerable influence in investment decision making. The same overall rating was accorded to other sources of financial information about companies and their industries (henceforth referred to as 'outside sources'), but the differences in influence between information received direct from companies, and that received from sources external to companies, was quite marked. 52% of respondents were of the opinion that formal published accounting information from companies was of maximum influence, whereas only 31% held the same view about the influence of outside sources. The latter respondents were even fewer in number than those who rated company visits as being of maximum influence, but far more respondents considered outside sources to be of considerable influence than held this view about company visits (53% as opposed to 29%).

Similar results were obtained when respondents were asked to rank relatively the 3 basic sources of information in terms of the perceived importance accorded to them by the respondents' organisations. The results, which are shown in Appendix 49, reveal that 64% of respondents rated formal published accounting information from companies as being of prime importance, whereas only 36% and 26%, respectively, rated outside sources and company visits as being of equal importance. Only 11% of respondents rated formal published accounting information from companies as being of least importance, while no fewer than 48% held this view about company visits.

Both those respondents working in stockbroking firms and those employed by the financial institutions rated published accounting information from companies as, relatively, the most important of the 3 sources to their firms. 59% of the latter, and 68% of the former, judged such information as being of prime importance. The two groups, however, divided when deciding which of the other two sources were of more importance to their firms — those employed by institutions rated outside sources higher than company visits, whereas the opposite was the case with those employed by stockbroking firms. As an illustration of the contrast between the two groups, 62% of the institutional respondents rated company visits as being of least importance, while only 29% of the stockbrokers held the same view. Indeed, 37% of the latter respondents believed that such visits were of prime importance whereas only 17% of those employed by financial institutions held a similar opinion.

The results were confirmed when an analysis was undertaken of respondents' views on the degree of influence of the 3 sources of information on the investment decisions of their employing organisations. The results in Table 52 below illustrate, once again, the greater emphasis on company visits by those employed by stockbroking firms in comparison with their colleagues employed by the financial institutions.

TABLE 52

Influence of the major sources of information on organisations' investment decisions about companies analysed by type of employing organisation

STOCKBROKING FIRMS			FINANCIAL INSTITUTIONS		
RANKING	SOURCE OF INFORMATION	MEAN	RANKING	SOURCE OF INFORMATION	MEAN
Of maximum to considerable influence			*Of maximum to considerable influence*		
1	Formal published accounting information from companies	1.54	1	Formal published accounting information from companies	1.66
2	Company visits	1.77	2	Other sources about companies and their industries	1.82
3	Other sources about companies and their industries	1.99			
			Of considerable to moderate influence		
			3	Company visits	2.45
n = 90			n = 126		

Those respondents eliminated for the purposes of Table 51 have also been eliminated in the above analysis.

Unlike stockbrokers who rated company visits as being of maximum to considerable influence, such visits were rated by the remaining respondents as having only considerable to moderate influence on the investment decisions of the financial institutions surveyed.

Similar results were obtained when respondents' views were analysed in terms of their individual employing organisations. While representatives of 62% of stockbroking firms stated that company visits were of maximum influence on their firms' investment decisions (in 37% of these firms, the respondents' colleagues did not rate company visits so highly), only in the case of pension funds did the representatives of more than one-third of the institutions surveyed hold the same view. Even then, only respondents employed in 44% of pension funds believed that company visits were of maximum influence on the investment decision making of their organisations. (In three-quarters of these pension funds the respondents' colleagues did not assess the influence of company visits so highly.) As would have been expected from earlier results, the representatives of the financial institutions surveyed rated formal published accounting information from companies as being generally of much greater influence than company visits.

Part of the reason for the emphasis given by respondents to published accounting information from companies can be judged from Tables 53 and 54 below.

111

TABLE 53

Overall assessment of the relevance of particular pieces of information

INFORMATION	RELEVANCE		
	Item mentioned at any time by respondent as being of assistance or relevance in investment decisions	*Item mentioned as being of greatest assistance in investment decisions*	*Item mentioned as being of relevance and derived from published company accounting information, outside sources or company visits*
	%	%	%
Profitability or earnings of a company	82	57	63
Future prospects of a company (including information on major new projects and developments)	73	2	73
Financial status, solvency or liquidity of a company	65	28	56
General information about a company	52	—	52
Dividend information about a company	36	31	10

n = 229

The 2 respondents who used a chartist approach to investment analysis were not asked the question analysed in this table.

Table 53 shows the items of information apparently most frequently desired by the respondents' organisations. The left-hand column of the table indicates the percentage of respondents mentioning on any occasion during the interview that the piece of information concerned was relevant to, or of assistance in, investment decision making.

There are obvious inconsistencies within the table. For example, while 57% of respondents stated that information about company profitability was of the greatest assistance in investment decision making to their organisations, 19% of respondents, having said this, never mentioned that such information was sought from published company reports, outside sources or during company visits. (The corresponding figures for other pieces of information were financial status, 9%; and dividend information, 26%.) An even greater inconsistency can be found when considering information on future prospects. While only 2% of respondents stated at the commencement of the interview that such information was of the greatest assistance in their organisations' investment decision making, no fewer than 73% later stated that indications about a company's future were sought from the various sources about which they were questioned.

Despite these inconsistencies, Table 53 indicates clearly the apparent importance of the pieces of information shown. 82% of respondents believed company income information was useful to their organisations; 65% held the same view about data concerning the financial status of companies; and 36% believed dividend information was of assistance in their organisations' investment decision making. Each of these 3 items are obtainable from corporate financial statements. On the other hand, two pieces of information — future prospects (mentioned by 73% of respondents) and general information about a company (mentioned by 52%) are by no means compulsory insertions in a company's financial reports. Not surprisingly, therefore, the 3 items of information which are legally required, or can be derived from statutorily prescribed information, were apparently sought by the respondents' organisations mainly from formal published information from companies (Table 54).

TABLE 54
Major sources of particular items of information

INFORMATION	SOURCE OF RESPONDENT'S ORGANISATION'S INFORMATION			
	Formal published information from companies (annual & interim reports) %	*Other sources of information about companies and their industries* %	*Company visits* %	*Information sought from at least one of the three sources (as per Table 53)* %
Profitability or earnings of a company	55	27	—	63
Future prospects of a company (including information on major new projects and developments)	47	29	38	73
Financial status, solvency or liquidity of a company	53	8	—	56
General information about a company	—	9	48	52
Dividend information about a company	7	4	—	10

n = 229

The 2 respondents who used a chartist approach to investment companies were not asked the questions analysed in this table.

For example, the right-hand column of Table 54 reveals that 63% of respondents believed that their employing organisation derived information on a company's profitability from at least 1 of the 3 sources about which they were questioned (that is, published accounting information from companies, outside sources and company visits). Yet of all the respondents, only 8% stated that their organisations sought such information from outside sources alone — the remaining 55%

consisted of 36% of respondents whose organisations obtained such information from published company sources alone, and 19% whose organisations used both published company data and outside information. No respondent admitted that the employees of his organisation sought information on profitability during company visits. Similarly, while 56% of all respondents stated that their organisations derived information on the financial status of a company from at least one of the 3 sources, company visits were not used to obtain such information, and only 3% of respondents asserted that their organisations used an outside source without consulting published company information. 5% of those surveyed believed that their organisation used both published company data and outside sources, but most (48%) stated that it solely used information provided by companies. Only 10% of respondents were of the opinion that their organisation sought information about dividends from at least one of the 3 sources, yet Table 54 shows that none of these organisations apparently obtained such information during company visits. 6% of respondents believed their organisations used company reports in isolation for dividend information; 3% felt outside sources were used; and 1% stated that both company and outside sources were utilised to satisfy the need for such information.

Published company reports were still used as a prime source of news about corporate future progress (as shown in Table 54). In all, 73% of respondents said their organisations sought such information — 20% of respondents believing the data came from published company sources alone; 6% stating they were derived from outside sources; 16% claiming they were obtained during company visits; 9% mentioning that all 3 sources were used; and the remainder being of the opinion that their organisations obtained such information from 2 of the sources (the most frequent combination mentioned being published company reports and outside sources).

Most of the background information about a company appeared to be obtained during a visit to the enterprise itself. Only 4% of respondents claimed that their organisations solely used outside sources to obtain background data about a company, whereas 43% asserted that company visits alone were utilised for this purpose. 5% of respondents stated that both sources were used.

The Companies Act 1980 may well curb the practice of seeking information on the future prospects of a company during visits to companies — information which obviously can be of a price-sensitive nature. The Act prohibits an insider knowingly in possession of unpublished price-sensitive information from dealing or consulting another person to deal in the company's securities or even communicating that information to another person if he has reasonable cause to believe that he would make use of that information.[1] (The term 'insider' includes an individual who has knowingly obtained information from an individual connected with a company and who knows or should know that the information has only been disclosed for the proper performance of the insider's functions.)

Summary

This chapter has considered the role of company visitations in investment decision making by the financial institutions and stockbroking firms. It was clear that the representatives of these two groups of organisations rated the importance of such visits very differently. Respondents employed by stockbroking firms were more enthusiastic about visits to companies and, in general, it could be said that their firms organised frequent visits to companies in which they were interested. The institutions were apparently more inclined to undertake visits rarely, and then only to selected companies. The different attitudes towards company visitations could, in part, explain the apparent interest of institutional investors in stockbrokers' reports which presumably would contain information obtained from companies during such visits.

While the institutions' interest in stockbrokers' reports could possibly explain their greater reliance (by comparison with stockbroking firms) on sources other than the company itself from which to obtain financial information, it should be 'stressed that the source of financial information rated most highly by representatives of both stockbroking and financial institutions was quite clearly financial reports (both annual and interim) published by companies. The respondents indicated very strongly that the information contained in these reports was the most vital source of information for investment decision making in their employing organisations.

REFERENCE

[1] See Institute of Chartered Accountants of Scotland, *Guide to the Companies Act, 1980*, Gee & Co., 1980, Chapter 5.

CHAPTER 11

Understanding, reading behaviour and respondents' background

In Chapters 4 and 5 it was demonstrated that the survey respondents had a reasonable (if, on occasion, disappointing) level of understanding of traditional accounting topics. By analysing their responses, however, it was possible to divide those surveyed into categories deemed to be demonstrating above average, average and below average understanding for purposes of this study. In Chapter 8, the reading patterns associated with company annual reports were examined in detail, and these were divided into 3 categories of reader — that is, very thorough, thorough, and less thorough readers.

With the respondents thus separated into various 'understanding' and 'readership' sub-groups, it was possible to examine the composition of these groups in relation to the background characteristics of respondents — that is, the type of respondent; the number of shareholdings for which he was responsible; whether or not he had a final say in investment decisions; his investment experience; his experience in using accounting information; and his accounting background.

The remainder of this chapter is concerned with providing these cross-analyses in order to test the validity of the following hypotheses (using the chi square test throughout, with $p \leqslant 0.05$):

H_4 Those respondents who were very thorough readers of annual reports had a substantially better understanding of traditional accounting topics than those who were thorough readers, and those who were less thorough readers.

H_5 Institutional investors read annual reports more thoroughly and had a substantially better understanding of traditional accounting topics than stockbrokers.

H_6 Those respondents whose work related to larger portfolios read annual reports more thoroughly and had a substantially better understanding of traditional accounting topics than those whose work related to smaller portfolios.

H_7 Those respondents whose work related to more valuable portfolios read annual reports more thoroughly and had a substantially better understanding of traditional accounting topics than those whose work related to less valuable portfolios.

H_8 Those respondents with a final say in investment decisions read annual reports more thoroughly and had a substantially better understanding of traditional topics than those with no such say in investment decisions.

H_9 Those respondents with significant investment experience read annual reports more thoroughly and had a substantially better understanding of traditional accounting topics than those with less investment experience.

H_{10} Those respondents with significant experience of using accounting information read annual reports more thoroughly and had a substantially better understanding of traditional accounting topics than those with less experience of such use.

H_{11} Those respondents with significant accounting experience read annual reports more thoroughly and had a substantially better understanding of traditional accounting topics than those with little experience and those with no experience.

Summarising on these hypotheses, therefore, it was hoped to provide evidence to support the following assertion — that, because of differences in the respondents' investment occupation, portfolio size and value, investment decision function, investment experience, use experience, and accounting experience, there were differences in their use and understanding of traditional accounting statements and topics surveyed in this study.

Readership and understanding

In order to test hypothesis H_4, it was necessary to compute the data described in Table 56. But, prior to examining this, it is interesting to compare respondents' perceptions of information relevance with their reading behaviour (detailed in Table 55).

TABLE 55
Perceived relevance and readership of annual reports

PERCEIVED RELEVANCE	n*	Very thorough readers of annual reports %	Thorough readers of annual reports %	Less thorough readers of annual reports %	Total %
Understand and find relevant	199	23	67	10	100
Understand and find irrelevant or only sometimes relevant	22	27	27	46	100

*2 respondents have not been included in the readership analysis; 5 respondents gave no indication of perceived relevance; and 3 respondents stated they did not understand accounting information.
(p<0.01)

The above analysis clearly shows that those respondents believing in their understanding, and finding reported information relevant to their investment decisions, tended to be far more thorough readers of annual reports when compared with those with perceived understanding but who found such information irrelevant (or only sometimes relevant). 90% of the first group were at least thorough readers, compared with 54% of the

TABLE 56
Reading of annual report and level of understanding of survey respondents

READING OF ANNUAL REPORT	n*	Much above average %	Above average %	Average %	Below average %	Much below average %	Total %
				LEVEL OF UNDERSTANDING			
Very thorough readers	54	17	15	41	11	16	100
Thorough readers	142	14	13	53	14	6	100
Less thorough readers	33	9	9	43	15	24	100

*2 respondents have not been included in the readership analysis.
(Not statistically significant at the 0.05 level)

second group, thus lending credence to their prior perceptions (p<0.01).

The comparison of actual readership with actual understanding in Table 56 is less straightforward than was the case in Table 55. Very thorough readers had 32% of their group in the above average understanding categories, compared with 27% of thorough readers, and only 18% of less thorough readers. The equivalent results for these groups in the below average categories were 27%, 20%, and 39%, respectively. It is particularly interesting to note the sizeable proportion of very thorough and thorough readers in the below average category (especially the 16% of very thorough readers who had much below average understanding). However, the null hypothesis cannot be rejected although, in certain categories of understanding, there do appear to be differences (results not significant using the chi square test). It must therefore be concluded that readership of annual reports does not provide any substantial explanation of differences in understanding by these respondents (or vice-versa). Hypothesis H_4 is not supported by the available evidence.

Understanding, readership and type of respondent

The analysis of respondent type and actual understanding is contained in Table 57.

TABLE 57
Type of survey respondent and level of understanding of survey respondents

TYPE OF SURVEY RESPONDENT		LEVEL OF UNDERSTANDING					
		Much above average	*Above average*	*Average*	*Below average*	*Much below average*	*Total*
	n*	%	%	%	%	%	%
Institutional investors	136	13	12	52	14	9	100
Stockbrokers	95	15	14	43	13	15	100
(Not statistically significant at the 0.05 level)							

25% of respondents from financial institutions had above average understanding and 23% were below average; the equivalent stockbroker statistics being 29% and 28% respectively. Thus, there appears to be

120

little to choose between the groups, and the understanding part of the null hypothesis based on H_5 cannot be rejected. It cannot therefore be accepted that a relationship exists between respondents' actual understanding and the nature of their investment occupation.

TABLE 58
Type of survey respondent and readership of annual reports

TYPE OF SURVEY RESPONDENT	Very thorough readers of annual reports		Thorough readers of annual reports	Less thorough readers of annual reports	Total
	n*	%	%	%	%
Institutional investors	135	26	58	16	100
Stockbrokers	94	20	68	12	100

*2 respondents have not been included in the readership analysis.
(Not statistically significant at the 0.05 level)

The same general conclusion can be reached in relation to the analysis of respondent type and readership (Table 58). Institutional investors appeared to be slightly more very thorough readers of annual reports than stockbrokers, but the statistical insignificance of these results indicates that there is no significant difference between the two groups on the basis of the available evidence, and the null hypothesis based on H_5 cannot be rejected in so far as it relates to readership.

Understanding, readership and shareholdings

Many of the respondents in this survey were responsible for portfolios containing a large number of individual shareholdings. However, despite the nature of their employment, and despite the large size of most portfolios, it was felt that differences in such numbers could result in differences to respondents' understanding and readership. Tables 59 and 60 summarise the results.

121

TABLE 59
Number of shareholdings and level of understanding of survey respondents

NUMBER OF SHAREHOLDINGS FOR WHICH SURVEY RESPONDENTS RESPONSIBLE		Much above average	Above average	Average	Below average	Much below average	Total
	n*	%	%	%	%	%	%
1—100	56	12	14	45	13	16	100
101—500	75	10	15	47	17	11	100
501 +	22	4	5	73	9	9	100

LEVEL OF UNDERSTANDING

*78 respondents did not know the number of shareholdings for which they were responsible.
(Not statistically significant at the 0.05 level)

Table 59 cross-tabulates the number of shareholdings with respondents' understanding, and evidences little difference in the latter until the number of shareholdings exceed 500, when understanding tends to be less in the above and below average categories, and falls more into the average group (73% of respondents, as compared with 45% and 47% of the other two shareholding groups). This may well be explained by the factor of seniority — the more senior the respondent, the more shareholdings for which he may have been responsible, and the less he may therefore have been involved in having to understand accounting

TABLE 60
Number of shareholdings and readership of annual reports

NUMBER OF SHAREHOLDINGS FOR WHICH SURVEY RESPONDENTS RESPONSIBLE		Very thorough readers of annual reports	Thorough readers of annual reports	Less interested readers of annual reports	Total
	n*	%	%	%	%
1—100	55	22	60	18	100
101—500	74	19	63	18	100
501 +	22	36	50	14	100

*78 respondents did not know how many shareholdings they were responsible for, and a further 2 respondents have not been included in the readership analysis.
(Not statistically significant at the 0.05 level)

information (possibly relying on subordinates in this respect). With no significant differences, this part of the null hypothesis relating to H_6 cannot be rejected.

The same general conclusions can be made about hypothesis H_6 in relation to portfolio size and readership in Table 60, with the differences between the groups being statistically insignificant at the 0.05 level (size therefore not explaining differences in readership, and the null hypothesis not being disproved). 82% of each of the first two 'size' groups were at least thorough readers but, paradoxically considering the equivalent results in Table 59, the '501+' group had 86% of its respondents as at least thorough readers, and 36% as very thorough readers (as compared with 22% and 19% for the other groups). Thus, the '501+' group had the least understanding but contained the most thorough readers.

Understanding, readership and portfolio valuation

Another way of judging portfolio size against understanding and readership is to compare the latter factors with different categories of portfolio values in order to test hypothesis H_7 (the results of these cross-analyses are contained in Tables 61 and 62).

TABLE 61

Value of portfolios and level of understanding of survey respondents

VALUE OF PORTFOLIOS		LEVEL OF UNDERSTANDING					
		Much above average	Above average	Average	Below average	Much below average	Total
£	n*	%	%	%	%	%	%
100,000— 100,000,000	54	8	6	54	16	16	100
100,000,001—1,000,000,000+	37	15	17	48	11	9	100

*64 respondents gave 'do not know' or 'no answer' responses, and 76 respondents did not specify portfolio values sufficiently accurately.
(Not statistically significant at the 0.05 level)

As with the results in the previous section, portfolio valuation appears to provide little explanation of differences in levels of understanding.

The £100m to £1,000m category appears to contain more above average respondents (32%) and less below average respondents (20%) than the other range of portfolios values analysed but the understanding part of the null hypothesis related to H_7 cannot be rejected.

TABLE 62
Value of portfolios and readership of annual reports

VALUE OF PORTFOLIOS		Very thorough readers of annual reports	Thorough readers of annual reports	Less interested readers of annual reports	Total
	n*	%	%	%	%
£					
100,000— 100,000,000	54	17	65	18	100
100,000,001—1,000,000,000 +	37	35	46	19	100

*64 respondents gave 'do not know' or 'no answer' responses; 74 respondents did not specify portfolio values sufficiently accurately; and a further 2 respondents have not been included in the readership analysis.
(Not statistically significant at the 0.05 level)

Table 62 also reveals a poor connection between portfolio values and readership, although the £100m to £1,000m category contains more very thorough readers than does the other category (35% against 17%). Despite this, the readership part of the null hypothesis based on H_7 cannot be rejected on the basis of the available evidence.

Understanding, readership and final say

Tables 63 and 64 contain the cross-analyses of understanding levels,

TABLE 63
Final say in investment decisions and level of understanding of survey respondents

FINAL SAY IN INVESTMENT DECISIONS		LEVEL OF UNDERSTANDING					
		Much above average	Above average	Average	Below average	Much below average	Total
	n*	%	%	%	%	%	%
Yes	138	12	11	50	13	14	100
No	81	17	19	47	11	6	100

*12 respondents gave 'do not know' or 'no answer' responses.
(Not statistically significant at the 0.05 level)

124

readership and whether or not respondents had a final say in investment decisions.

The results in Table 63 suggest that those respondents having no say in investment decisions had, on the whole, a better understanding of traditional accounting topics than those with such a say (36% of the former, compared with 23% of the latter, had above average understanding; and the equivalent much above average statistics were 17% and 12%, respectively. Thus, there were differences in the levels of understanding of these two groups of respondents, but these were statistically insignificant and the understanding part of the null hypothesis related to H_8 cannot be rejected.

TABLE 64

Final say in investment decisions and readership of annual reports

FINAL SAY IN INVESTMENT DECISIONS	n*	Very thorough readers of annual reports %	Thorough readers of annual reports %	Less thorough readers of annual reports %	Total %
Yes	136	25	58	17	100
No	81	22	73	5	100

*12 respondents gave 'do not know' or 'no answer' responses, and a further 2 respondents have not been included in the readership analysis.
($p < 0.05$)

There does, however, appear to be a significant relationship between the final say in investment decisions and readership of annual reports. Table 64 reveals that those respondents with no say in investment decisions (presumably therefore supplying data to the decision makers) were more thorough readers of the annual reports (95% coming into this category) than those making decisions (83%). There was little to choose between the respondents in the very thorough readership group. With $p < 0.05$, the readership part of the null hypothesis based on H_8 can be rejected — but it would seem that those respondents who made investment decisions were, on the whole, less thorough readers than those who did not make decisions (that is, the antithesis of hypothesis H_8).

125

Understanding, readership and investment experience

Hypothesis H_9 was tested by using the data contained in Tables 65 and 66.

TABLE 65

Investment experience and level of understanding of survey respondents

INVESTMENT EXPERIENCE (years)		LEVEL OF UNDERSTANDING					
		Much above average	Above average	Average	Below average	Much below average	Total
	n*	%	%	%	%	%	%
1 —10	135	18	15	45	15	7	100
11 +	92	8	10	53	12	17	100

*4 respondents who had no investment experience have been omitted from this analysis.
($p < 0.05$)

The above results ($p < 0.05$) evidence clearly that those respondents with less investment experience (1 to 10 years) had significantly more understanding of traditional accounting topics than those with more experience (11 + years) — 33% of respondents with less experience, and only 18% with more experience, had above average understanding (18% and 8%, respectively, for much above average understanding). Thus, the understanding part of the null hypothesis related to H_9 does not hold and can be rejected. From these results, therefore, it could be argued that the less experienced respondents' knowledge of accounting matters was more

TABLE 66

Investment experience and readership of annual reports

INVESTMENT EXPERIENCE (years)		Very thorough readers of annual reports	Thorough readers of annual reports	Less thorough readers of annual reports	Total
	n*	%	%	%	%
1 —10	134	18	72	10	100
11 +	91	32	47	21	100

*2 respondents have not been included in the readership analysis; nor have the 4 respondents with no investment experience.
($p < 0.01$)

up to date than that of their seniors who may have been growing out of touch so far as reporting practices were concerned (that is, the antithesis of H_9).

The antithesis part of the second part of hypothesis H_9 is also supported by the available evidence — that is, the less experienced respondents (in investment terms) were, on the whole, the more thorough readers of annual reports — 9 out of 10 in the 1 to 10 years category being at least thorough readers, compared with approximately 8 out of 10 in the 11 + years category. However, 32% of the latter (compared with 18% of the former) were very thorough readers. In other words, most of the least experienced respondents were thorough readers, but a sizeable proportion of the most experienced respondents made very thorough use of annual reports. With $p < 0.01$, these results lead to the rejection of the readership part of the null hypothesis based on H_9.

Understanding, readership and use experience

The experience of respondents in using accounting information is analysed for purposes of hypothesis H_{10} in Tables 67 and 68.

TABLE 67

Experience of using accounting information and level of understanding of survey respondents

USE EXPERIENCE (years)		LEVEL OF UNDERSTANDING					
		Much above average	Above average	Average	Below average	Much below average	Total
	n*	%	%	%	%	%	%
1 —10	109	17	18	46	13	6	100
11 +	121	12	8	51	14	15	100

*1 respondent with no experience of using accounting information has been omitted from this analysis.
(p = 0.05)

It can be seen that the understanding part of the null hypothesis based on H_{10} is not supported by the evidence, and can be rejected (p = 0.05); but those respondents with the least use experience (1 to 10 years) had a better understanding as a group than those with more experience (11 +

years). 35% of the former group had above average understanding, and 19% below average understanding, compared with 20% and 29%, respectively, of the latter group. This result is similar to that of investment experience in the previous section.

TABLE 68
Experience of using accounting information and readership of annual reports

USE EXPERIENCE (years)		Very thorough readers of annual reports	Thorough readers of annual reports	Less thorough readers of annual reports	Total
	n*	%	%	%	%
1 —10	108	19	70	11	100
11 +	120	27	55	18	100

*1 respondent with no experience of using accounting information has been omitted from this analysis, and 2 respondents have not been included in the readership analysis.
(p = 0.05)

Again with results significant at $p = 0.05$ the null hypothesis based on the readership part of hypothesis H_{10} could be rejected — that is, the 2 use experience groups did not have similar reading behaviour. The least experienced group, however, contained more thorough readers (89% as against 82%) while the more experienced group had a greater proportion of very thorough readers (27% as against 19%). Again, these results are similar to those concerned with investment experience.

Understanding, readership and accounting experience

The final background variable to be tested was respondents' specific accounting experience. Hypothesis H_{11} relates to this, and the data used are in Tables 69 and 70.

TABLE 69
Accounting experience and level of understanding of survey respondents

ACCOUNTING EXPERIENCE		LEVEL OF UNDERSTANDING					
		Much above average	*Above average*	*Average*	*Below average*	*Much below average*	*Total*
	n	%	%	%	%	%	%
Significant	58	15	9	55	12	9	100
Little	37	22	13	49	8	8	100
None	136	11	15	46	15	13	100

(Not statistically significant at the 0.05 level)

There appears to be little relationship between the respondents' accounting experience and their levels of understanding (the results were not statistically significant). Indeed, the results show that those respondents with no experience as a group had 26% of their number in the above average understanding category, compared with 35% of those with little experience, and 24% of those with significant experience. Since the null hypothesis could not be rejected, this part of hypothesis H_{11} cannot be accepted.

TABLE 70
Accounting experience and readership of annual reports

ACCOUNTING EXPERIENCE		*Very thorough readers of annual reports*	*Thorough readers of annual reports*	*Less thorough readers of annual reports*	*Total*
	n*	%	%	%	%
Significant	56	25	59	16	100
Little	37	30	59	11	100
None	136	21	64	15	100

*2 respondents have not been included in the readership analysis.
(Not statistically significant at the 0.05 level)

A similar conclusion about hypothesis H_{11} can be reached in relation to the readership behaviour of respondents. Those with little accounting experience appeared to be more thorough readers of annual reports, with 30% of such a group classed as very thorough readers, and only 11% as less thorough readers. But the null hypothesis based on H_{11} cannot be rejected on this evidence (hypothesis H_{11} cannot therefore be accepted).

Summary

In this chapter, 8 specific hypotheses have been tested by cross-tabulating the various understanding and readership categories produced in earlier chapters with the various background characteristics of the survey respondents. In particular, the hypotheses suggested that these characteristics ought to create significant differences in the levels of understanding and readership of the respondents as evidenced in this study. In the event, the results provided mixed support for the specific hypotheses.

The following broad conclusions can be stated. Differences in respondents' reading of the annual corporate report did not appear to be related to their understanding of traditional accounting topics. No explanation of differences in such comprehension or in annual report reading patterns could be explained by a respondent's occupation, differences in his responsibilities measured in terms of portfolio size or valuation, or by his experience of accounting. On the basis of the evidence of this survey, only experience in the investment world and experience in using accounting data appeared to be significantly related (albeit inversely) to annual report reading and to comprehension of traditional reporting practices.

The results of this chapter should not be unexpected. The respondents were financial experts employed in the investment sector of the economy. Very few do not make extensive use of (or place reliance on) several relevant information sources and they are all responsible (directly or indirectly; partly or wholly) for very large portfolios involving regular and significant decision making. It is not surprising, therefore, that the crucial factors should be the extent of their experience in investment and information usage. What is less predictable is the evidence that such experience and understanding are inversely related — presumably because the more experienced respondents are less directly involved with detailed accounting information, and have a knowledge of accounting which is growing obsolete as they get older. This is one conclusion which, if confirmed by further research, ought to give some concern to the investment community — that is, the need to ensure that its more experienced members remain conversant with accounting matters which impinge on the investment decisions and portfolios for which they may well be responsible.

Understanding of inflation accounting and respondents' background

Similar hypotheses to H_4 to H_{11}, inclusive, were formulated in relation to respondents' background characteristics and their understanding of inflation accounting topics. The relevant tabulations are given in Appendices 50 to 58, inclusive, but are not commented on in full in this chapter. The following paragraphs are given as a brief summary.

The results relating to understanding of the inflation accounting practices pertaining at the time of interviewing are in some ways similar to the cross-analyses affecting traditional accounting practice — that is, several of the background characteristics of the responding financial experts proved to be unrelated factors vis-à-vis their understanding of inflation accounting practices. Indeed, respondents' occupation, portfolio size, say in investment decisions, and accounting experience were not statistically significant characteristics in this respect (applying the chi square test with $p \leqslant 0.05$). However, the extent to which respondents read annual reports, portfolio valuation, investment experience and information use, were all factors which could be used to explain differences in such understanding. Less thorough readers of the annual report had less understanding of inflation accounting matters than thorough and very thorough readers; the larger the value of the portfolio, the better the respondents' understanding; and the responding groups with less investment or use experience had a higher proportion of members in the above average and average categories than the responding groups with more investment or use experience. Finally, those respondents with understanding of general financial reporting matters (relatively assessed as average or above average) tended to have a better understanding of inflation accounting matters than other respondents included in the survey (Appendix 58).

Thus, it appears that a reasonable understanding of inflation accounting matters such as those surveyed in this study is more likely to be achieved if greater use of annual reports is made, the user is associated with very large investment portfolio values, and has 1-10 years' experience of investment and of using accounting information.

131

Areas of misunderstanding of traditional reporting practice

Finally, given that experience factors were more closely related to knowledge of traditional reporting practices than other characteristics, an attempt was made to identify those areas of traditional reporting practice, knowledge of which was most affected by the respondents' experience. To facilitate the analysis, the same points scores which had been awarded during the construction of the index of comprehension were utilised. Respondents' points score in each of the 5 areas of reporting practices discussed in Chapter 5 were then split into 3 groups, roughly corresponding to the top, middle and bottom thirds. A 6 point scale was divided 6 to 5 (top third); 4 to 3; and 2 to 0; and a 12 point scale was divided 12 to 9 (top third); 8 to 5; and 4 to 0. The evidence provided is of a mixed nature, but can be summarised as follows.

In general terms, the only financial reporting area in which the respondents' levels of understanding could be said to be statistically significantly related to their investment and use experience was that concerned with the nature and content of the main financial statements ($p < 0.01$) — the less experienced respondents revealing greater understanding. In all other areas tested (viz. the general nature of reporting, accounting terminology, accounting valuation bases, and financial ratios), there was evidence that such experiences had no relationship to respondents' understanding.

This general conclusion is supported by the evidence concerning individual reporting items. In the following cases (with $p < 0.05$ in all cases), the less experienced respondents had a significantly better understanding than those with more experience — the directors' report, the profit and loss account, depreciation, and current assets. In several other cases, only one type of experience could be said to be related (again, in all cases, $p < 0.05$) — the balance sheet (those respondents with less use experience comprehending better than those with more experience); the funds statement (those respondents with less investment experience comprehending better than those with more experience); accrued charges (those respondents with more use experience having a better understanding than those with less experience); and dividend cover (those respondents with less use experience comprehending better than those with more experience). In all other cases, there was little or no relationship between understanding of traditional accounting topics and such types of experience.

RESPONDENTS' BACKGROUND

It appears from the evidence of this survey that the understanding of the nature and content of financial statements was inversely related to respondents' use experience and, less frequently, to investment experience — in other words, the less experienced financial experts who were surveyed typically had the best comprehension of these matters. As previously mentioned, these results may indicate that the more experienced respondents could possibly be losing touch with the fast changing world of accounting and financial reporting.[1] In other areas (such as the general nature of reporting, accounting valuation, and financial ratios), however, the evidence is that there was little or no relationship between comprehension of the traditional accounting topics surveyed and experience.

FOOTNOTE

[1] It should be noted in this respect, however, that we conducted similar cross-analyses of respondents' comprehension answers to inflation accounting topics. The evidence is that respondents' comprehension of these relatively new aspects of financial reporting had no significant relationship to their experience. Only in connection with revaluation surpluses (also a traditional accounting practice) was there a significant difference (at the 0.01 level) — respondents less experienced in investment having a better understanding than those more experienced. In considering respondents' overall comprehension of inflation accounting topics (Appendices 55 and 56) it was, however, shown that significant differences between the experience groups did exist.

CHAPTER 12

Summary, conclusions and recommendations

Summary

The purpose of this study was to examine in depth the use and understanding of financial information by financial experts involved in the stock market. Their professionalism and expertise in investment matters, the size of institutional investment, and the apparent widespread acceptance of the existence of an efficient market in securities were each reason for undertaking this study. In addition, this research project complements our earlier studies of the private shareholder and his use and understanding of financial information. Of particular interest to us in this study were:

(a) the thoroughness of the use made of all sources of financial information available to institutional investors and stockbrokers; and

(b) the nature and extent of their understanding of such information.

The following paragraphs summarise how these matters were researched, and what results were found.

(1) *The respondents*

231 financial experts were interviewed, consisting of 136 institutional investors and 95 stockbrokers. The typical respondent usually had: a final say in his firm's investment decision; 6 to 20 years of experience in investment matters and financial information usage; little or no formal accounting training; and direct or indirect responsibility for portfolios of 500 or less items with a total value ranging from £1m to £1,000m.

(2) *Respondents' comprehension*

Nearly all respondents perceived they understood reported accounting information, and very few believed it to be irrelevant to investment decisions. It became important, therefore, to ascertain whether or not their perceived understanding was compatible with their actual understanding and to evidence that they did use available accounting information. Understanding was the first area tested and, so far as traditional reporting practice was concerned, the 5 areas surveyed were the general nature of reporting, the nature of financial statements, accounting terminology, accounting valuations, and financial ratios. The nature of inflation accounting statements, terminology and valuations were also examined.

In relation to traditional reporting practice, the overall levels of understanding were not as high as might have been expected from financial experts. Accounting terminology and financial ratios were particularly disappointing in this respect. Respondents' answers, despite prompting by the interviewers, were characterised by vagueness, with a sizeable number of respondents obviously having a poor or no understanding of many of the topics concerned. Their answers also evidenced group variability in comprehension — for example, 85% had a reasonable understanding of the chairman's report but 64% had a poor or no understanding of the funds statement.

When scores for the respondents' total understanding were computed, the relevant distributions were shown to be skewed by the respondents' understanding in each reporting area tested. In this respect, accounting valuations were best understood, and the general nature of financial reporting was least understood. The points scores, however, re-emphasised the considerable vagueness in many respondents' answers. Ultimately, the scores were used to construct an overall index of understanding to be used for further analysis and which was based on the average understanding of the respondents taken as a whole.

Respondents' understanding of inflation accounting topics was found to be generally poor overall, although, this judgement must be tempered both by the novelty of the concepts and, as with our comments on traditional accounting practice, by the limitations of the comprehension tests used. Generally speaking, the principles of inflation accounting did not appear to be reasonably understood, and only with respect to inflation accounting valuations was there anything like a favourable response to the questions asked. There were indications that some respondents had difficulty in distinguishing between CCA and CPPA.

(3) *Information used by respondents' employing organisations*
A number of questions were asked relating to the general use made of financial information by the organisations in which the respondents were employed. The most useful data appeared to be concerned with

corporate profitability and dividends. Most of the respondents believed their organisation's decision makers made some personal analysis of available information, but there was also evidence that the majority of these decision makers relied on data from internal analysts in their organisations (although a sizeable minority used external analysts). External analysts were more extensively used by institutional investors than by stockbrokers.

Stockbroking firms tended to analyse available financial information about all major companies, with financial institutions interested in analysing data for companies in or potentially in their investment portfolios. On the whole, such analyses were initiated very speedily — that is, either on receipt or within one month of receipt of the relevant information. In this respect, the evidence was that stockbroking firms were quicker than financial institutions at such analyses.

Organisations, typically, appeared to compute their own financial ratios and funds flow statements, despite the existence of these data in many corporate financial reports. Few entities were prepared to rely on such reported data without at least some verification of their computation. The prediction of profitability was usually seen as a major objective of financial analysis, and most respondents believed their organisations' predictions to be reasonably accurate — for example, nearly one-half stated that such predictions were usually within plus or minus 10% of the actual results achieved.

(4) *Use of the annual report*
From the evidence in this study, it is clear that financial experts such as those surveyed make considerable use of corporate annual reports. Few respondents failed to read any part of the annual report, and most respondents read a great deal of it — for example, 9 out of every 10 read thoroughly the profit and loss account and the balance sheet, and 1 out of every 4 read thoroughly all parts of the annual report. The notes to the accounts, the chairman's report, the activities statement, and the funds statements were all extensively read. The poorest use was made of inflation accounting statements and the auditor's report. As well as being read thoroughly, the profit and loss account and the balance sheet were considered by respondents to be the most influential financial statements so far as investment decisions were concerned. The most useful data were considered to be those related to corporate profitability, capital structure, and future prospects.

On the basis of their reading of various sections of the annual report,

136

respondents were grouped for purposes of further analysis. The 3 groups which resulted were a reflection of the extent to which corporate annual reports were used in practice by these institutional investors and stockbrokers — that is, very thorough, thorough, and less thorough readers of the annual report.

The extent of the use made by these financial experts of the annual report is further supported by some additional responses made by the financial experts; for example, 57% of respondents stated that the existing annual report was sufficient for investment decision making purposes, and 79% also stated their confidence in using reported accounting information for such decisions (the reasons given for the latter judgment included (a) accounting standards were of a high quality (28%); (b) financial statements had been audited (23%); accounting information was the best source of information available (13%)). In other words, these respondents gave considerable evidence of the credibility they attached to reported accounting information.

(5) *Other sources of financial information*
Many other sources of financial information other than the corporate annual report were used by respondents, with the majority reading thoroughly every source about which they were questioned with the exception of employee financial reports. The most thoroughly-used sources appeared to be merger and acquisition reports, the financial press, and interim financial statements (in that order). So far as these sources were concerned as influences on investment decisions, however, the ranking order was reversed, with interim financial statements proving to be the most influential.

Corporate profitability and future prospects once again were the main factors for which respondents were looking in their use of these other sources of financial information. Overall, however, none of these sources appeared to be as influential on investment decisions as the profit and loss account and the balance sheet. Additionally, it was discovered that those respondents who were less thorough readers of the annual report did not appear to compensate for this by a thorough use of other sources of financial information — in other words, those respondents who appeared to be less interested than others in a company's annual report made no attempt to supplement their knowledge of the company by greater study of other information about it.

(6) *Company visits*
Only 6% of respondents believed their organisations did not visit

companies. Those organisations which did make such visits were evenly divided between those which made frequent visits and those which visited infrequently. The objects of visits were stated to include the assessment of the ability of corporate management, the provision of a corporate background to financial analysis, and the assessment of future prospects of companies. The first objective stated above was the most popular aim mentioned by 56% of respondents. However, so far as influence on investment decisions was concerned, respondents typically ranked company visits after annual reports and other sources of financial information. Stockbrokers appeared to rank such visits more highly than institutional investors but, overall, annual and interim financial reports were clearly the most influential of all the available sources of information for investment decisions.

(7) *Understanding, reading and background*
Respondents' understanding and reading behaviour were next related to their various background characteristics. Using chi square tests of significance, these cross-analyses revealed few characteristics which could be said to be related either to respondents' understanding or their reading behaviour — that is, rarely could differences in background characteristics be used to explain differences in levels of understanding or in thoroughness of reading the annual report.

More specifically, the following points were evidenced — levels of understanding of traditional reporting practice were not related to thoroughness of reading the annual report (that is, all categories of reader could be found in approximately the same proportions in most of the different levels of understanding); respondents' levels of understanding or their reading of the annual report appeared not to be related to their occupations, portfolio size and valuation, and respondents' accounting experience; but respondents' levels of understanding and reading behaviour were related to their investment experience and information use experience (the less experienced respondents in terms of investment and use information typically having the better understanding of traditional reporting topics and being the more thorough readers of annual reports, compared with those with more experience).

The above findings were more or less repeated when respondents' understanding of inflation accounting topics was cross-analysed with their background characteristics. Once again, respondents' levels of understanding were not significantly related to final say in investment decisions, their occupation, accounting experience and portfolio size. However, comprehension did appear to be related to thoroughness in reading the annual report, portfolio values, investment experience, and information use experience — those respondents who had been classed as more thorough readers were responsible (directly or indirectly) for larger portfolio values; and had less investment and use experiences, typically having a significantly better understanding of inflation accounting topics than, respectively, those who were less thorough readers, had smaller portfolio values, and had more investment and use experiences.

(8) *Areas of misunderstanding*
No reporting area surveyed in this study was found to be consistently well understood by all respondents — that is, in each area, there was at least some variability in the response. This variability was also repeated between the different areas — some being better understood than others. Accounting valuations were best understood (both in traditional and inflation accounting practice), and accounting terminology and the general nature of reporting were least well understood (again, in both areas of practice). This was in contrast to other views expressed — for example, when asked what specific matters they did not understand in financial reporting, 58% of respondents had stated that financial reports were perfectly understandable to them (23% mentioned inflation accounting as a problem area, and 10% taxation matters — but these were the only substantial points of concern); similarly 64% had poor or no understanding of the nature of funds statements but only 3% admitted to not understanding them.

Conclusions

It is difficult to summarise such a complex and long-lived project. Conclusions have, however, been drawn in order to outline the major findings for the reader. We hope, additionally, that the reader will be able to use the contents of this text as a data bank from which other findings can be taken for purposes of other research. Meantime, we offer the following as our main concluding statements.

(1)   The evidence of this study is that institutional investors and stockbrokers made considerable use of many sources of available financial information. The most thoroughly used and influential sources appeared to be annual and interim financial reports and,

particularly, the traditional profit and loss account and its supporting balance sheet. Thus, the work of the reporting accountant appeared to be exceedingly important to these financial experts — a finding at some variance with the popular belief that historical cost-based financial statements are irrelevant for investment decision making purposes. In fact, according to the findings of this study, one of the least used sources of financial information was that concerned with inflation accounting — an area for which there is considerable support as a means of providing investment decision makers with information more relevant than the existing historical cost system. (It should, however, be remembered that the CCA statements were relatively novel at the time of interviewing.)

(2)   The less thorough users of annual reports did not compensate for this under-use by using other sources of financial information more thoroughly — the thorough users of available information tended to use all sources thoroughly, and, conversely, the less thorough users tended to use all sources less thoroughly. By far the majority of users came into the thorough reader category providing an impression of considerable information processing being conducted in their organisations.

(3)   Company visits were made by most organisations — some infrequently, but most mainly to assess management and future prospects. Despite our expectations of the importance of these visits in terms of their influence on investment decisions, respondents appeared to regard them as relatively unimportant — at least to the extent that they were ranked third in influence behind annual reports and other sources of financial information. They were generally regarded as of only considerable to moderate influence in this respect.

(4)   Respondents were very clear in their statements as to one of the main purposes for which information was being gathered in their firms — that is, for predicting company profitability. Interestingly, despite the financial and economic problems afflicting businesses at the time of interview, respondents did not appear to view very highly the assessment and prediction of cash flow.

(5)   The analysis of available financial information by the firms surveyed was consistent with one aspect of the efficient markets hypothesis — that is, institutional investors and stockbrokers

analysed such information very quickly following its receipt. Such analyses, typically, were undertaken internally. Thus, the provision of analysed data by companies in their financial reports, so far as financial experts are concerned, may not be necessary as only a small minority of the organisations surveyed accepted them without some form of verification. On the basis of the evidence from this study, the same may be said for funds statements — many organisations only accepting them after verification.

(6) Nearly all respondents believed they understood reported accounting information, although their actual understanding was characterised by imprecision and variability in many instances. Matters of specific reporting practice (such as valuations) were best understood, whereas matters of principle were least understood. The funds statement was the least understood main financial statement and, coupled with the relatively poor understanding evidenced over inflation accounting statements, warns us that these admittedly recent additions to reporting practice were not as well understood by these financial experts as might have been expected.

(7) In the case of traditional reporting practice, the only factors in this study which appeared to be significantly related to respondents' understanding of it were their investment experience and their information use experience — the less experienced having the best understanding. This finding was largely repeated with the totality of the inflation accounting topics surveyed. The more experienced financial experts in this survey could perhaps have been in the process of losing touch with accounting matters — at a time when these are changing rapidly; and when they admitted making extensive use of accounting reports and, typically, to be involved in the analysis of these reports for investment decision making purposes.

Recommendations

When asked in the interviews as to what measures they would recommend to improve the use and understanding of corporate financial reports, respondents were split as follows — 20% said no additional measures were required; 60% desired more detailed or additional information (on a variety of topics — for example, operational activities

(19%) and inflation accounting (14%); 14% either wanted simpler financial statements or the knowledge of the user improved; and 6% provided no response. Thus, in general, there appeared to be considerable support for expanding the existing financial reporting system beyond its present rather complex state. Confirmation is also given of the previously-mentioned importance of such reports to those financial experts in their investment decision making activities. Consequently, with this and the above conclusions in mind, the following specific recommendations or observations are made:

(1) There appeared to be a considerable and speedy use made of available financial information by institutional investors and stockbrokers. Such experts placed much reliance on such information and its credibility, and also appeared to desire more reported data. Given, however, the vagueness and inconsistency of some experts' understanding of certain aspects of the traditional accounting topics surveyed, there may be a danger of reaching a stage in financial reporting when the meaning of complex and technical accounting messages may not be properly understood even by some financial experts. This may particularly be the case with the more experienced (and thus older) members of the investment community who perhaps may already be losing touch with contemporary accounting matters. In this respect, we would therefore recommend that:

   (a) Attention to be paid within the investment community to any possible weaknesses in its members' understanding of accounting messages, particularly if apparent familiarity with data has caused their meaning not to be questioned.

   (b) The need to update the knowledge of more experienced members of the investment community in matters of a contemporary accounting nature ought to be examined carefully in order to prevent such knowledge becoming obsolete.

(2) The relative lack of attention by institutional investors and stockbrokers to recent additions to annual financial reports was in some contradiction to their demand for more information. Statements of accounting policies, funds statements and inflation accounting statements were not as extensively used as traditional financial statements. The first-named is vital to an understanding

of the profit and loss account and balance sheet — yet did not receive the same attention as the latter statements. Funds statements did not have sufficient credibility to be accepted by many institutional investors and stockbrokers without at least verification or recomputation. Inflation accounting statements appeared to be little used and even less understood by financial experts at a time when they were being introduced to the financial reporting function. These are all matters which should be of concern to accountants, and our recommendations are therefore as follows:

(a) Urgent attention should be given by both the investment community and the accounting standard-setters to finding out why a statement such as the funds statement apparently lacks a certain credibility in its present form and structure; and why vital statements such as the statement of accounting policies (and the auditor's report) are not used more extensively by financial experts.

(b) Equal attention should be paid to the need to improve the use and understanding of inflation accounting statements. This should be a matter of considerable and immediate concern to both accountants and investors, particularly at a time when *SSAP16* is introducing CCA in financial statements.[1] (In defence of the respondents, however, it should be noted that the survey was undertaken at a time when inflation accounting was in a relatively early stage of evolution in the UK and the provisions of *ED18* were in dispute — it would be interesting to ascertain whether or not their comprehension of CCA had improved since the interviews were undertaken.)

(3)   Throughout this study there has been frequent mention of the predominance of company profitability in investment decision making. The search for relevant information by institutional investors and stockbrokers, as evidenced in this project, had, as a major objective, the assessment and prediction of company profits. What was surprising to us was the lesser attention apparently paid to sources of information related to company liquidity and solvency. The term 'cash flow' rarely appeared in interviews, and the one financial statement which ought to be of use in assessing these matters (the funds statement) was less extensively used by respondents than any of the other main

financial statements, and their overall understanding of it was poor. In these circumstances, and given our belief in the importance of investors properly assessing both company profitability and liquidity, we would recommend that:

(a) The investment community should pay attention to the need adequately to predict corporate liquidity and cash flow. We firmly believe that lack of proper attention to such matters may provide an inadequate data base for effective investment decision making.

(b) Accounting standard-setters should also pay attention to the need to provide users of financial statements with information relevant to the assessment and prediction of corporate liquidity and cash flow, thereby providing a more balanced information package for investment decision making.

(4) Company visits by institutional investors and stockbrokers are obviously of importance to them (especially to the latter) in the process of investment decision making. (This is obviously a sensitive matter because of the issue of 'insider' information and we were not unduly surprised at the relatively muted enthusiasm for this source of information apparent in some respondents' answers.) We would, therefore, recommend that the investment community investigate this area with a view to establishing, more clearly than was possible in this study, the nature and purpose of such visits. In particular, it would appear to us to be an area which deserves some official attention, especially in view of the provisions of the Companies Act 1980, with a view to providing institutional investors and stockbrokers with accepted guidelines for such visits — that is, a recognised and agreed code of practice to prevent certain financial experts benefiting from reserved knowledge at the expense of other investors.

(5) Finally, this study has revealed that institutional investors and stockbrokers rated interim financial statements very highly as a source of financial information capable of influencing investment decisions. These statements currently are generally presented in unaudited summary form (with the minimum of disclosure) and are not produced in line with any accounting guidelines or standards. We would therefore recommend to accounting standard-setters that the subject of interim financial statements is a

sufficiently important issue to justify a proper evaluation of their nature, purpose and content.

The above recommendations are offered as positive statements to improve the flow and use of financial information by institutional investors and stockbrokers. On the basis of the evidence of this study, these financial experts cannot be faulted for their extensive use of all available sources of information. These recommendations are designed to improve this use. They also reveal to us the advantages to be gained in the future if the investment community were to be involved in the process of accounting standard-setting to a far greater extent than hitherto. The use made of published accounting statements by the respondents to this survey indicated that there could well be advantages to the investment community accruing from involvement of financial analysts in the production of accounting standards (concerned with disclosure and measurement) both as members of the standard-setting body and as initiators of demands for better reporting practice. Financial reporting is but a service function — its users must make their needs known if it is to succeed in portraying the economic reality of corporate financial performance and position. Financial analysts have a major role to play in ensuring that a correct picture is revealed. If such a goal could be achieved the securities market could well become truly 'efficient'.

REFERENCES

[1] 'Current Cost Accounting', *Statement of Standard Accounting Practice 16*, Accounting Standards Committee, 1980.

APPENDIX 1

Questionnaire sent to non-respondents

Confidential
(Please tick appropriate boxes)

(1) What is the approximate size and value of the portfolio to which your work relates?

	Size	*Value* (State)
1— 100 holdings		
101— 500 holdings		
501—1000 holdings		
1000+ holdings		

(2) What is your background in accounting?

professional accounting qualification
completion of accounting courses
any other experience *(please specify)*
none

(3) How long have you been using accounting information?

0— 5 years
6—10 years
11—20 years
21+ years

(4) How long have you been working in the investment markets?

0— 5 years
6—10 years
11—20 years
21+ years

APPENDIX 2

Interview questionnaire

Note

Most of the questions were pre-coded for purposes of analysis. However, for 14 of the items, the interviewees were given a card specifying the question. This was done because of the complexity of the questions concerned. These are identifiable below. For all other items, the questions only were read out to the interviewees.

(1) *(Show respondent Card 1)*
Which of the following would you regard as being the main approach of your organisation to investment analysis?

the technical 'chartist' approach, emphasising share price, and volume changes and trends *only* (ie making absolutely no use of other available financial information).

the technical 'chartist' approach combined with a minimal use of other available financial information.

the 'fundamental' approach, emphasing the analysis and use of all available financial information other than share price and volume data.

a balanced combination of the 'chartist' and 'fundamental' approaches.

any other *(please specify)*

(If the answer does not include the use and analysis of financial information other than share prices and volume data, omit questions 2 to 26, inclusive, continuing the questioning at question 27. But ask for reasons for rejecting it.)

(2) For what general purposes is available financial information usually used in your organisation?

(If more than one purpose is given, ask the respondent to rank them in order of importance; 1 = most important, 2 = next important, and so on.) (Explain meaning of 'available' to respondent.)

to provide background detail when:

   making predictions for investment decisions

   monitoring previous investment decisions

to provide primary data when:

   making predictions for investment decisions

   monitoring previous investment decisions

any other *(please specify)*

(3) Which particular pieces of available financial information are found to be of the greatest assistance in your organisation's investment activities?

(Ask the respondent to indicate the accounting system to which his answer(s) applies, and to rank in order of importance if more than one item is given: 1 = most important, 2 = next important and so on.)

	HCA	CPPA	CCA	CCA/CPPA	DK
earnings per share					
price-earnings ratio					
dividend per share					
dividend yield					
dividend cover					
any other *(please specify)*					

149

(4) *(Show respondent Card 2)*
Is reported financial information

	Annual reports	Interim reports
read, analysed and used by the investment decision makers in your organisation?		
read and analysed by investment analysts who then report to investment decision makers, all within your organisation?		
read and analysed by external investment analysts who report to the investment decision makers in your organisation?		

(5) *(Show respondent Card 3)*
In general terms, for which companies is reported financial information read and analysed in your organisation?

	Annual reports	Interim reports
for all major companies		
only for companies in its existing portfolio		
only for companies which you are interested in adding to its existing portfolio		
only for companies in its existing portfolio plus potential additions to it		

(For stockbrokers: for 'its' read 'clients')

(6) *(Show respondent Card 4)*
On average, when is reported financial information read and analysed in your organisation?

	Annual reports	*Interim reports*
as soon as it is reported		
as soon as time permits		
as soon as it is required for investment purposes		
any other *(please specify)*		

(7) *(Show respondent Card 5)*
On average, and again in your organisation, how much delay is there between receiving reported information and analysing it?

	Annual reports	*Interim reports*
none		
less than 1 month		
between 1 and 3 months		
between 4 and 6 months		
more than 6 months		

(8) In general terms, what form of analysis of reported information is usually undertaken in your organisation (or is undertaken on its behalf)?

	Figures taken without further analysis	Financial ratios prepared		Funds flow prepared		Any other (please specify)
		his-toric	pre-dicted	his-toric	pre-dicted	
no comparison made						
comparison of current and previous years' data						
for one company only						
for several companies only						
for one company and its industry						
for several companies and their industry						
comparison of several years' data						
for one company only						
for several companies only						
for one company and its industry						
for several companies and their industry						
any other (please specify)						

(9) *(Show respondent Card 6)*
Which parts of company annual financial reports do *you* read and to what extent?

	Not read at all	Read briefly for interest	Read thoroughly
chairman's report and review of operations			
report of directors			
statement of accounting policies			
profit and loss account			
balance sheet			
notes to the accounts			
auditor's report			
source and application of funds statement			
supplementary CPPA statement			
supplementary CCA statement			
statistical information			
composition of activities statement			
any other (please specify)			

(10) *(Show respondent Card 7)*
When financial ratios and/or funds flows are provided in financial reports, it is your organisation's practice to:

	ratios	funds flow
ignore them and compute its own		
accept them without verification		
accept them after verification		

(11) Do the analysts employed by your organisation use reported financial information to make predictions of company financial results?

yes ▢
no ▢

(If 'no' to question 11, skip to question 14)

(12) *(If 'yes' to question 11)* Which financial results are predicted?

(Ask the respondent to indicate to which accounting system his answer(s) relates.)

	HCA	CPPA	CCA	CCA/CPPA
earnings per share				
price-earnings ratio				
dividend per share				
dividend yield				
dividend cover				
any other *(please specify)*				

(13) *(If 'yes' to question 11)* On average, how accurate do you find the predictions you indicated in question 12? Indicate the degree of accuracy by a ± percentage of the prediction to its actual equivalent.

(Again ask the respondent to indicate to which accounting systems his answer(s) relates)

	HCA	CPPA	CCA	CCA/CPPA
earnings per share				
price-earnings ratio				
dividend per share				
dividend yield				
dividend cover				
any other *(please specify)*				

154

(14) *(Show respondent Card 8)*

What ranking of importance does your organisation give to the following parts of the company annual financial report? (1 = most important, 2 = next important, and so on). What degree of influence does each source have in relation to investment decisions made in your organisation? (1 = maximum, 2 = considerable, 3 = moderate, 4 = slight, 5 = none.)

	Importance	*Influence*
chairman's report and review of operations		
report of directors		
statement of accounting policies		
profit and loss account		
balance sheets		
notes to the accounts		
auditor's report		
source and application of funds statement		
supplementary CPPA statement		
supplementary CCA statement		
statistical information		
composition of activities statement		
any other *(please specify)*		

(15) What particular data contained in any of the previously-indicated parts of the company annual financial report does your organisation find particularly relevant? *(Specify part of report as well)*

Data specified | *Part of report specified*

155

(16) *(Show respondent Card 9)*
Which of the following sources of financial information about companies do *you* read and to what degree?

	Not read at all	Read briefly for interest	Read thoroughly
three or six-monthly financial reports			
financial press reports			
company reports to employees			
occasional acquisition of merger reports			
Moodie's or Extel cards			
stockbrokers' reports			
industry data and reports			
economy data and reports			
any other *(please specify)*			

(17) What particular data contained in any of the previously-indicated sources of information does your organisation find particularly relevant?
(Specify source as well)

Data specified	Source specified

(18) *(Show respondent Card 10)*

What ranking of importance does your organisation give to the following sources of financial information? (1 = most important, 2 = next important and so on). What degree of influence does each source have in relation to investment decisions made in your organisation? (1 = maximum, 2 = considerable, 3 = moderate, 4 = slight, 5 = none).

	Importance	*Influence*
three or six-monthly financial reports		
financial press reports		
company reports to employees		
occasional acquisition or merger reports		
Moodie's or Extel cards		
stockbrokers' reports		
industry data and reports		
economy data and reports		
any other *(please specify)*		

(19) *(Show respondent Card 11)*

To what extent are visits made by your organisation to companies in which it has invested (or is about to invest)?

	Infrequently	*Frequently*
in every case		
only in selected cases *(please specify)*		
not at all		

(If the answer to question 19 is 'not at all', ask why, then omit questions 20 to 22, inclusive).

(20) What companies does your organisation visit?

existing investments

potential investments

both existing and potential
investments

(21) For what purposes are such visits made?

to assess future prospects

to learn of new projects

to assess management

to monitor progress

to maintain good relations

to learn of managerial changes

any other *(please specify)*

(22) With whom are relevant matters discussed on such company visits?

with the chairman or managing director

with the finance director

with other directors *(please specify)*

with the chief accountant

any other *(please specify)*

(23) *(Show respondent Card 12)*
What ranking of importance is given by your organisation to the
following? (1 = most important, 2 = next important, and so on).
What degree of influence do the following have in relation to investment decisions made in your organisation? (1 = maximum, 2
= considerable, 3 = moderate, 4 = slight, 5 = none).

	Importance	Influence
formal accounting information from companies		
other information about companies and their industries		
company visits		

(24) On the whole, do you believe the financial information provided in the present type of company annual financial report is sufficient for institutional investors (stockbrokers)?

yes

no

do not know

(25) Do you feel confident in using reported accounting information for investment decisions? Why do you hold this view?

yes

no   *(reason)*

(26) Is there any additional information which you think institutional investors (stockbrokers) would benefit from in company annual financial reports?
(If more than one is given, rank in order of importance; 1 = most important, 2 = next important, and so on)

budgets

profit forecasts

CPPA statements

CCA statements

CCA/CPPA statements

replacement cost statements

net realisable value statements

employment reports

value-added statements

government transaction statements

cash flow statements

human resource statements

any other *(please specify)*

159

(27) What is (or are) the main purpose(s) of the financial statements contained in the company annual financial report? Which is the most important one? *(Indicate by a * the most important if there is more than one.)*

to make company directors
accountable to shareholders

to provide information for the
Inland Revenue

to give shareholders an indication
of the value of the company

to give shareholders an indication
of the market value of their shares

to give shareholders data of use
for investment decisions

to justify the dividend payments
proposed by the directors

any other *(please specify)*

do not know

(28) Who is (or are) legally responsible for providing company annual financial reports to shareholders?

company chairmen

boards of directors

financial directors

company secretaries

company accountants

auditors

any other *(please specify)*

do not know

(29) What do the following terms mean to you?
profit
price-earnings ratio
dividend yield
dividend cover

(30) Can you describe briefly the kind of information you would expect to find in the following parts of a company annual financial report?

chairman's report
report of directors
profit and loss account
balance sheet
auditor's report
source and application of funds statement
supplementary CPPA statement
supplementary CCA statement

(31) Can you describe briefly what you would understand by the following terms used in company annual financial reports?

(a) *In present HCA financial statements*
depreciation
equity capital
current assets
reserves
accrued charges

(b) *In proposed CCA financial statements*
revaluation surpluses and deficits
cost of sales adjustment
statement of change in shareholders' net equity interest after allowing for the change in the value of money

(32) What is the proposed CCA basis of valuation for the following items often included in company annual financial reports?

plant and machinery
raw materials stocks
specific contract work-in-progress
quoted investments

(33) What is the traditional basis of valuation used to determine the following items often included in company annual financial reports?

	OC	OC-D	RC	NRV	Other*	DK
plant and machinery						
stocks and work-in-progress						
quoted investments						

*please specify

(34) (Show respondent Card 13)
Do you consider the HCA financial results which are reported annually to you by companies to be:

an accurate reflection of their financial progress and position

an approximation of their financial progress and position

an inaccurate reflection of their financial progress and position

any other (please specify)

do not know

(35) *(Show respondent Card 14)*
Which of the following statements correspond most closely to your impression of company annual financial reports?

you are able to understand the information contained in such reports and it is of considerable relevance and use to you with regard to investment decisions

you are able to understand the information contained in such reports but find it irrelevant or of little use to you with regard to investment decisions. *(State reason for its irrelevance)*

you are unable to understand the information contained in such reports sufficiently for it to be of use to you with regard to investment decisions. *(State reason for non-understanding)*

any other *(please specify)*

(36) Is there anything in particular in the present company annual financial report which you do not fully understand? *(Specify briefly)*

(37) What measures do you feel are necessary to improve your use and understanding of company annual financial reports? *(Specify briefly)*

(38) What is the approximate size and value of the portfolio to which your work relates?

Size Value (state)

   1— 100 holdings
101— 500 holdings
501—1000 holdings
1001 + holdings

(39) Do you have a final say in investment decisions?

yes — completely independently in every case

yes — as part of a committee decision in every
case

yes — completely independently in some cases only

yes — as part of a committee decision in some
cases only

a mixture of the above

no

(40) If no, do you report to an individual or committee which makes the
decision?

individual

committee

(41) Sex

(42) Accounting qualifications?

professional qualification

accounting courses

any other *(please specify)*

(43) Experience in using accounting information?

0— 5 years

6—10 years

11—20 years

21 + years

(44) Experience in institutional investment?

0— 5 years

6—10 years

11—20 years

21 + years

(45) Name of Respondent   Organisation

(46) Does he require summary of results?

yes

no

Interviewer's signature .... Date of Interview ....

APPENDIX 3

Estimated portfolios for which survey respondents were responsible

£	%
100,000— 250,000	5
250,001— 500,000	-
500,001— 1,000,000	2
1,000,001— 10,000,000	3
10,000,001— 25,000,000	3
25,000,001— 50,000,000	5
50,000,001— 100,000,000	5
100,000,001— 250,000,000	6
250,000,001— 500,000,000	7
500,000,001—1,000,000,000	3
'Do not knows'	28
'Over 1,000,000'	33
	100

APPENDIX 4

Final say in investment decisions

	%	%
Yes:		
completely independently in every case	27	
as part of a committee decision in every case	5	
completely independently in some cases only	9	
as part of a committee decision in some cases only	4	
a mixture of the above situations	15	60
No:		
report instead to an individual	8	
report instead to a committee	5	
report instead to a client	3	
reporting functions not specified	19	35
'Do not knows' and 'no answers'		5
		100

APPENDIX 5

Accounting and related experience or knowledge of survey respondents

	%	%
Significant experience, etc.		
Possession of an accounting qualification	19	
Substantial courses in accounting	6	25
Little experience, etc.		
Short courses in accounting		16
No experience, etc.		59
		100

APPENDIX 6

Type of survey respondent and perceived relevance of accounting information

TYPE OF SURVEY RESPONDENT	PERCEIVED RELEVANCE			
		Understand and find relevant	*Understand and find irrelevant or only sometimes relevant*	*Total*
	n*	%	%	%
Institutional investors	135	87	13	100
Stockbrokers	88	93	7	100

(Not statistically significant at the 0.05 level)

*5 respondents gave no indication of perceived relevance; and 3 respondents stated they did not understand accounting information.

APPENDIX 7

Number of shareholdings and perceived relevance of accounting information

NUMBER OF SHAREHOLDINGS HELD BY SURVEY RESPONDENTS		PERCEIVED RELEVANCE		
		Understand and find relevant	Understand and find irrelevant or only sometimes relevant	Total
	n*	%	%	%
1—100	55	85	15	100
101—500	75	87	13	100
501 +	20	90	10	100

(Not statistically significant at the 0.05 level)

*78 respondents did not know how many shareholdings for which they were responsible; 5 respondents gave no indication of perceived relevance; and 3 respondents stated they did not understand accounting information. This has meant the omission of 81 respondents in total from this analysis.

APPENDIX 8

Value of portfolios and perceived relevance of accounting information

VALUE OF PORTFOLIOS		PERCEIVED RELEVANCE		
		Understand and find relevant	*Understand and find irrelevant or only sometimes relevant*	*Total*
£	n*	%	%	%
100,000— 100,000,000	51	90	10	100
100,000,001—1,000,000,000 +	36	92	8	100

(Not statistically significant at the 0.05 level)

*64 respondents gave 'do not know' or 'no answer' responses regarding portfolio values; 75 respondents were unable to specify portfolio value sufficiently accurately; 5 respondents gave no indication of perceived relevance; and 3 respondents stated they did not understand accounting information. This has meant the omission of 144 respondents in total from this analysis.

APPENDIX 9

Final say in investment decisions and perceived relevance of accounting information

FINAL SAY IN INVESTMENT DECISIONS	PERCEIVED RELEVANCE			
		Understand and find relevant	*Understand and find irrelevant or only sometimes relevant*	*Total*
	n*	%	%	%
Yes	133	88	12	100
No	80	94	6	100

(Not statistically significant at the 0.05 level)

*12 respondents gave 'do not know' or 'no answer' responses regarding final say; 5 respondents gave no indication of perceived relevance; and 3 respondents stated they did not understand accounting information. This has meant the omission of 18 respondents in total from this analysis.

APPENDIX 10

Investment experience and perceived relevance of accounting information

INVESTMENT EXPERIENCE (years)	PERCEIVED RELEVANCE			
		Understand and find relevant	Understand and find irrelevant or only some-times relevant	Total
	n*	%	%	%
1—10	131	89	11	100
11 +	88	91	9	100

(Not statistically significant at the 0.05 level)

*5 respondents gave no indication of perceived relevance; 3 respondents stated they did not understand accounting information; and 4 respondents had no investment experience. This has meant the omission of 12 respondents in total from this analysis.

APPENDIX 11

Experience of using accounting information and perceived relevance of accounting information

USE EXPERIENCE (years)	PERCEIVED RELEVANCE			
		Understand and find relevant	*Understand and find irrelevant or only some-times relevant*	*Total*
	n*	%	%	%
1—10	107	88	12	100
11 +	116	91	9	100

(Not statistically significant at the 0.05 level)

*5 respondents gave no indication of perceived relevance; 3 respondents stated they did not understand accounting information; and 1 respondent had no experience of using it. This has meant the omission of 8 respondents in total from this analysis.

APPENDIX 12

Accounting experience and perceived relevance of accounting information

ACCOUNTING EXPERIENCE		PERCEIVED RELEVANCE		
		Understand and find relevant	*Understand and find irrelevant or only some-times relevant*	*Total*
	n*	%	%	%
Significant	57	90	10	100
Little	37	89	11	100
None	129	90	10	100

(Not statistically significant at the 0.05 level)

*5 respondents gave no indication of perceived relevance; and 3 respondents stated they did not understand accounting information.

APPENDIX 13

Actual understanding of legal responsibility for annual financial statements

	%	%
Reasonable understanding		
Board of directors		79
No or poor understanding		
Finance directors	1	
Company secretaries	13	
Auditors	4	
Other answers (including 'do not knows' and 'no answers')	7	25
		104*

*8 respondents (3% of 231) indicated 2 responsibility groups; and 1 respondent (0% of 231) indicated 3 responsibility groups.

Note:
9 respondents (4% of 231) indicated an incorrect category in addition to the 'board of directors' category, and were re-designated for purposes of Table 15 as having a vague understanding.

APPENDIX 14

Actual understanding of the objectives of annual financial statements

	%	%
Reasonable understanding		
Accountability to shareholders	19	
Data for investment decisions	10	29
Vague understanding		
Justification for dividends	1	
Vague answers indicating accountability	59	60
No or poor understanding		
Indicate value of company	15	
Indicate market value of shares	4	
Fulfilling a legal obligation	11	
Indicate plans for future	2	
Other answers (including 'do not knows' and 'no answers')	2	34
		123*

* 32 respondents (14% of 231) indicated 2 objectives; 6 respondents (3% of 231) indicated 3 objectives; and 3 respondents (1% of 231) indicated 4 objectives.

Note:

21 respondents (9% of 231) gave a reasonable answer coupled with an incorrect one, and were redesignated for purposes of Table 15 as having a vague understanding. A further 30 respondents (13% of 231) gave a vague answer coupled with an incorrect one, and were re-designated for purposes of Table 15 as having poor or no understanding.

APPENDIX 15

Actual understanding of the accuracy of reported accounting information

	%	%
Reasonable understanding		
Annual accounting information gives an approximation of financial progress and position		51
No or poor understanding		
Annual accounting information gives:		
An accurate reflection of financial progress and position	27	
An inaccurate reflection of financial progress and position	19	
'Do not knows' and 'no answers'	3	49
		100

APPENDIX 16

Actual understanding of contents of chairman's report

	%
Contents of chairman's report stated to include:	
a review of past year's results and a statement of future prospects (§)	84
a review of past year's financial results	10
a statement of future prospects	2
a statement of future policy	3
a review of major events and developments during past year	9
comments relating to the economic, political and/or taxation environment	9
comment on labour relations	2
Other answers	4
'Do not knows' and 'no answers'	4
	127*

*41 respondents (18% of 231) gave 2 content items; 9 respondents (4% of 231) gave 3 content items; and 1 respondent (0% of 231) gave 4 content items.

Note:

For purposes of Table 16, all of the above-mentioned specific items were classified as correct answers, and all of the 'other answers' were also classified as correct. *Reasonable understanding* was attributed to those respondents who either gave item (§) or who gave 2 or more of the other correct items. *Vague understanding* was attributed to those respondents who either gave only one correct item or gave two correct and one incorrect item. The remaining respondents were classified as having *no or poor understanding.*

APPENDIX 17

Actual understanding of contents of directors' report

	%
Contents of directors' report stated to include:	
a review of past year's financial results	23
information regarding:	
directors	23
issues of new capital	3
changes in assets	6
dividends and retentions	6
turnover and profit of different classes of business	13
principal activities of company and subsidiaries	10
employees	14
Other answers	6
'Do not knows' and 'no answers' (§)	35
	139

* 45 respondents (19% of 231) indicated 2 content items; 21 respondents (9% of 231) indicated 3 content items; and 1 respondent (0% of 231) indicated 4 content items.

(§) including 60 respondents (26% of 231) who replied 'statutory information' only, despite prompting from the interviewer.

Note:

For purposes of Table 16, all of the above-mentioned specific items were classified as correct answers, and certain of the 'other answers' were also classified as correct. *Reasonable understanding* was attributed to those respondents who gave 2 or more correct answers and no incorrect ones. *Vague understanding* was attributed to those respondents who either gave 1 correct answer and no incorrect ones or gave 2 correct and 1 incorrect items. The remaining respondents were classified as having *no or poor understanding*.

APPENDIX 18

Actual understanding of contents of profit and loss account

	%
Contents of profit and loss account stated to include:	
sales or turnover	49
revenue and expenses	5
expenses required legally to be disclosed	4
profit or trading results	37
trading profit and expenses required legally to be disclosed (§)	36
profit, sales and trading expenses (§)	2
dividends and/or profit retentions	34
Other answers	9
'Do not knows' and 'no answers'	6
	182

* 61 respondents (26% of 231) gave 2 content items; 63 respondents (27% of 231) gave 3 content items; and 1 respondent (0% of 231) gave 4 content items.

Note:

For purposes of Table 16, all of the above-mentioned specific items were classified as correct answers, but all the 'other answers' were classified as incorrect. *Reasonable understanding* was attributed to those respondents who either gave item (§) or who gave 2 of the other correct items, in both cases with no incorrect answers given. *Vague understanding* was attributed to those respondents who either gave 1 correct item and no incorrect one or gave 2 correct and 1 incorrect items. The remaining respondents were classified as having *no or poor understanding*.

APPENDIX 19

Actual understanding of contents of balance sheet

	%
Contents of balance sheet stated to include:	
assets	3
liabilities and/or share capital	5
details of liquidity or working capital	3
assets and liabilities (§)	28
assets, liabilities and net worth (§)	46
financial state of company at a point in time	4
Other answers	8
'Do not knows' and 'no answers'	4
	101*

* 2 respondents (1% of 231) gave 2 content items

Note:
For purposes of Table 16, all of the above-mentioned specific items were classified as correct answers, and certain of the 'other answers' were also classified as correct. *Reasonable understanding* was attributed to those respondents who gave either of items (§), provided no incorrect item was also given. *Vague understanding* was attributed to those respondents who either gave 1 of the other correct items, with no incorrect item, or gave 2 correct and 1 incorrect items. The remaining respondents were classified as having *no or poor understanding.*

APPENDIX 20

Actual understanding of contents of auditor's report

	%
Auditor's report stated to be a reporting that:	
the financial statements have been verified and are satisfactory (**)	10
the financial statements show a true and fair view (**)	49
the financial statements are in accordance with accounting principles (**)	6
proper books and records have been kept	2
the financial statements are correct	3
Audit qualifications only mentioned	11
Other answers	6
'Do not knows' and 'no answers' (§)	14
	101*

* 2 respondents (1% of 231) gave 2 content items

(§) including 21 respondents (9% of 231) who stated 'statutory requirement' only despite prompting from the interviewer

Note:

For purposes of Table 16, all of the above-mentioned specific items were classified as correct answers, and certain of the 'other answers' were also classified as correct. *Reasonable understanding* was attributed to those respondents who gave one of items (**), provided no incorrect item was also given. *Vague understanding* was attributed to those respondents who either gave 1 of the other correct items and no incorrect one or gave 2 correct and 1 incorrect items. The remaining respondents were classified as having *no or poor understanding.*

APPENDIX 21

Actual understanding of contents of funds statement

	%
Contents of funds statement stated to include details of:	
particular sources of finance only	6
particular uses of finance only	1
sources and uses of finance (**)	21
changes in working capital	11
Other answers (§)	36
'Do not knows' and 'no answers'	32
	107*

* 16 respondents (7% of 231) gave 2 content items.

(§) including 62 respondents (27% of 231) who gave answers indicating a belief that funds statements were pure cash flow statements.

Note:
For purposes of Table 16, all of the above-mentioned specific items were classified as correct answers. All other items were classified as incorrect. *Reasonable understanding* was attributed to respondents who gave item (**), provided no incorrect item was also given. *Vague understanding* was attributed to those respondents who either gave one of the other correct items and no incorrect one or gave 2 correct and 1 incorrect items. The remaining respondents were classified as having *no or poor understanding*.

APPENDIX 22

Actual understanding of term 'profit' in financial statements

	%	%
Reasonable understanding		
Surplus from trading revenue after deduction of various expenses	7	
Surplus available for distribution and retention	8	15
Vague understanding		
Sum or surplus remaining after deducting expenses	39	
Cash produced from trading	8	47
No or poor understanding		
Incorrect answers	11	
'Do not knows' or 'no answers'	27	38
		100

APPENDIX 23

Actual understanding of term 'depreciation' in financial statements

	%	%
Reasonable understanding		
Amount written off fixed assets over time or life of assets concerned		23
Vague understanding		
Amount written off assets	34	
Loss in value of assets; wear and tear on assets	6	
Answers suggesting depreciation is a means of replacing fixed assets	29	
Other vague answers	1	70
No or poor understanding		
Incorrect answers	3	
'Do not knows' and 'no answers'	4	7
		100

APPENDIX 24

Actual understanding of term 'equity capital' in financial statements

	%	%
Reasonable understanding		
Ordinary shareholders' capital, interest, or funds		29
Vague understanding		
Shareholders' (unspecified) capital, interest, or or funds	54	
Risk capital	5	
Other vague answers	1	60
No or poor understanding		
Incorrect answers	6	
'Do not knows' and 'no answers'	5	11
		100

APPENDIX 25

Actual understanding of term 'current assets' in financial statements

	%	%
Reasonable understanding		
Stock, debtors, cash, etc. (any 2 or more of these items)		56
Vague understanding		
Stock, debtors, cash, etc. (any 1 of these items)	7	
Liquidity or readily realisable assets	24	
Other vague answers	2	33
No or poor understanding		
Assets held at date of reporting	2	
Other incorrect answers	5	
'Do not knows' and 'no answers'	4	11
		100

APPENDIX 26

Actual understanding of term 'reserves' in financial statements

	%	%
Reasonable understanding		
Past profits not distributed but available for distribution	46	
Capital and revenue reserves mentioned	4	50
Vague understanding		
Funds set aside for contingencies and/or specific purposes	6	
Other vague answers	6	12
No or poor understanding		
Money set aside for contingencies and/or specific purposes	7	
Equity minus share capital	15	
Other incorrect answers	7	
'Do not knows' and 'no answers'	9	38
		100

APPENDIX 27

Actual understanding of term 'accrued charges' in financial statements

	%	%
Reasonable understanding		
Expenses or charges due but not yet paid		45
Vague understanding		
Specific accrued charges mentioned	2	
Other vague answers	1	3
No or poor understanding		
Incorrect answers	16	
'Do not knows' and 'no answers'	36	52
		100

APPENDIX 28

Actual understanding of traditional plant valuation bases

	%	%
Reasonable understanding		
Original cost less depreciation		62
Vague understanding		
Original cost		29
No or poor understanding		
Original cost and replacement cost		
or realisable value	2	
'Do not knows' and 'no answers'	7	9
		100

APPENDIX 29

Actual understanding of traditional stock valuation bases

	%	%
Reasonable understanding		
Original cost	29	
Lower of cost and net realisable value	52	81
Vague understanding		
Original cost less depreciation		3
No or poor understanding		
Realisable value	4	
Replacement cost and realisable value	1	
Directors' valuation	3	
'Do not knows' and 'no answers'	8	16
		100

APPENDIX 30

Actual understanding of traditional quoted investments valuation bases

	%	%
Reasonable understanding		
Original cost	16	
Original cost with market value given as a note	<u>51</u>	67
Vague understanding		
Directors' valuation		1
No or poor understanding		
Realisable value	26	
'Do not knows' and 'no answers'	<u>6</u>	32
		100

APPENDIX 31

Actual understanding of term 'price-earnings ratio'

	%	%
Reasonable understanding		
Definitions relating share price to earnings per share		47
Vague understanding		
Answers indicating the ratio involved earnings and share prices		45
Poor or no understanding		
Incorrect answers	4	
'Do not knows' or 'no answers'	<u>4</u>	8
		100

APPENDIX 32

Actual understanding of term 'dividend yield'

	%	%
Reasonable understanding		
Dividend as a return on current share price		13
Vague understanding		
Dividend as a return on the price paid for the shares	9	
Vague answers indicating some form of return on investment	71	80
Poor or no understanding		
Incorrect answers	5	
'Do not knows' and 'no answers'	2	7
		100

APPENDIX 33

Actual understanding of term 'dividend cover'

	%	%
Reasonable understanding		
Number of times dividend is covered by available profit	56	
Number of times dividend is covered by net profit	12	68
Vague understanding		
Amounts of profit available to pay dividends	1	
Dividend paying potential	9	
Other vague answers	16	26
Poor or no understanding		
Incorrect answers	4	
'Do not knows' or 'no answers'	2	6
		100

APPENDIX 34

Understanding scores for financial reporting matters

UNDERSTANDING SCORE	General nature of reporting[a]	Nature of financial statements[b]	Accounting terminology[c]	Accounting valuation bases[d]	Financial ratios[e]
	%	%	%	%	%
0	3	3	2	6	2
1	9	1	2	2	2
2	13	1	1	5	5
3	25	4	4	9	17
4	18	3	9	16	30
5	22	4	13	21	40
6	10	11	15	41	4
7		11	18		
8		18	14		
9		14	13		
10		15	5		
11		9	4		
12		6	—		
	100	100	100	100	100
Mean	3.52	7.83	6.61	4.52	4.06
Standard deviation	1.56	2.72	2.33	1.76	1.20
Skewness co-efficient	−0.25	−0.83	−0.44	−1.23	−1.22

Maximum possible scores: a = 6; b = 12; c = 12; d = 6; e = 6; total = 42

APPENDIX 35

Actual understanding of contents of current purchasing power accounting statement

	%
Contents of CPPA statement stated to include:	
unspecified purchasing power adjustments	12
purchasing power adjustments to profit	7
purchasing power adjustments to monetary items	4
purchasing power adjustments to assets,	
liabilities, and profits (§)	9
Answers implying an accounting for inflation	21
Other answers	17
'Do not knows' and 'no answers'	30
	100

Note:

For purposes of Table 24, all of the above-mentioned specific items were classified as correct answers. All other answers were classified as incorrect. *Reasonable understanding* was attributed to respondents who gave item (§). *Vague understanding* was attributed to those respondents who gave one of the other correct items. The remaining respondents were classified as having *no or poor understanding*.

APPENDIX 36

Actual understanding of contents of current cost accounting statement

	%
Contents of CCA statement stated to include:	
adjustment to current cost of sales	3
adjustment to current cost depreciation	2
adjustments to profits in terms of value to business or replacement cost	10
adjustments to assets in terms of value to business or replacement cost	6
adjustments to assets and profits in terms of value to business or replacement cost (**)	7
Other answers (§)	45
'Do not knows' and 'no answers'	28
	101*

* 3 respondents (1% of 231) gave two content items.

(§) including 78 respondents (34% of 231) who stated CCA was a form of accounting for inflation or current purchasing power.

Note:
For purposes of Table 24, all of the above-mentioned specific items were classified as correct answers. All other answers were classified as incorrect. *Reasonable understanding* was attributed to respondents who either gave item (**) or who gave 2 of the other correct items, in cases where no incorrect answer was given. *Vague understanding* was attributed to those respondents who either gave 1 correct item and no incorrect item or gave 2 correct and 1 incorrect items. The remaining respondents were classified as having *no or poor understanding*.

APPENDIX 37

Actual understanding of term 'revaluation surpluses'

	%	%
Reasonable understanding		
Differences between assets at historical cost and current valuation	31	
Increases/decreases arising on asset revaluations	26	57
Vague understanding		
Changes in asset values because of inflation	4	
Other vague answers	2	6
No or poor understanding		
Surplus on adjustment of assets and liabilities	1	
Answers specifying current purchasing power accounting adjustments	4	
Other incorrect answers	9	
'Do not knows' and 'no answers'	23	37
		100

APPENDIX 38

Actual understanding of term 'cost of sales adjustment'

	%	%
Reasonable understanding		
Adjustment of cost of sales from historical cost to replacement cost	18	
Adjustment for holding gain on stock consumed	1	19
Vague understanding		
Adjustment of costs to bring them in line with inflation	5	
Adjustment to remove stock profit	7	
Adjustment on stock	14	
Adjustment to historical cost of sales	6	
Adjustment for inflation on stock	6	38
No or poor understanding		
Answers specifying current purchasing power adjustments	3	
Other incorrect answers	9	
'Do not knows' and 'no answers'	31	43
		100

APPENDIX 39

Actual understanding of statement of change in shareholders' net equity interest

	%	%
Reasonable understanding		
Comparison of current cost accounting net asset values and equity capital on a current purchasing power basis		2
Vague understanding		
Assessment of change in shareholders' real stake in the business	7	
Current purchasing power accounting adjustment to opening shareholders' capital	4	
Measure of the effect of inflation on shareholders' capital	29	
Current purchasing power adjustment to current cost accounting figures	2	42
No or poor understanding		
Incorrect answers	18	
'Do not knows' and 'no answers'	38	56
		100

APPENDIX 40

Actual understanding of CCA plant valuation bases

	%	%
Reasonable understanding		
Value to the business	6	
Replacement cost	51	57
Vague understanding		
Cost adjusted for inflation	10	
Current market price or value	5	15
No or poor understanding		
Realisable value	1	
Other incorrect answers	2	
'Do not knows' and 'no answers'	25	28
		100

APPENDIX 41

Actual understanding of CCA raw materials stock valuation bases

	%	%
Reasonable understanding		
Value to the business	1	
Replacement cost	46	47
Vague understanding		
Cost adjusted for inflation	7	
Current market price or value	9	16
No or poor understanding		
Historical cost	6	
Realisable value	2	
Other incorrect answers	2	
'Do not knows' and 'no answers'	27	37
		100

APPENDIX 42

Actual understanding of CCA specific contract work-in-progress valuation bases

	%	%
Reasonable understanding		
Value to the business until date of consumption; thereafter, actual cost		1
Vague understanding		
Historical cost	15	
Other vague answers	1	16
No or poor understanding		
Replacement cost	7	
Realisable value	1	
Cost adjusted for inflation	4	
Current value	2	
Other incorrect answers	7	
'Do not knows' and 'no answers'	62	83
		100

APPENDIX 43

Actual understanding of CCA quoted investment valuation bases

	%	%
Reasonable understanding		
Current market price	55	
Realisable value	5	60
No or poor understanding		
Replacement cost	1	
Historical cost	3	
Other incorrect answers	7	
'Do not knows' and 'no answers'	29	40
		100

APPENDIX 44

Understanding scores for inflation accounting matters

UNDERSTANDING SCORE	Nature of inflation accounting statements and adjustments[a]	Inflation accounting valuation bases[b]
	%	%
0	18	21
1	10	3
2	9	8
3	14	5
4	13	18
5	15	8
6	12	28
7	4	8
8	2	1
9	3	
10	—	
	100	100
Mean	3.39	3.77
Standard deviation	2.41	2.46
Skewness co-efficient	0.17	− 0.40
Maximum possible scores: a = 10; b = 8; total = 18		

APPENDIX 45

Respondents' view of the relative importance of the sections of the company annual financial report to their organisation

RANKING	PART OF ANNUAL REPORT	DEGREE OF IMPORTANCE RELATIVE TO OTHER SECTIONS OF THE ANNUAL REPORT*												Total*	Mean
		1	*2*	*3*	*4*	*5*	*6*	*7*	*8*	*9*	*10*	*11*	*12*		
		%	%	%	%	%	%	%	%	%	%,	%	%	%	
1	Profit and loss account	57	19	9	5	4	1	1	1	—	1	—	2	100	2.11
2	Balance sheet	39	32	17	5	3	2	1	—	—	—	—	1	100	2.21
3	Chairman's report	23	9	14	19	10	8	8	3	·	1	1	1	100	4.04
4	Notes to accounts	15	9	18	13	12	8	4	8	1	2	1	9	100	4.92
5	Source and application of funds statement	10	2	10	11	15	10	11	9	6	1	4	11	100	6.19
6	Composition of activities statement	7	3	4	8	15	10	11	8	8	6	4	16	100	7.05
7	Statement of accounting policies	9	3	4	9	8	7	13	9	11	7	8	12	100	7.17
8	Directors' report	3	3	2	8	9	13	18	8	11	8	4	13	100	7.40
	Statistical information	3	—	2	5	8	10	13	13	14	7	6	19	100	8.05
10	Supplementary CCA statement	2	1	1	4	6	12	10	10	15	13	10	16	100	8.32
11	Supplementary CPPA statement	1	1	1	2	5	8	8	9	15	13	15	22	100	9.07
12	Auditor's report	8	1	1	1	3	4	8	5	8	11	11	39	100	9.27

*n = 211; the 3 respondents who did not read any section of the annual report; and the 2 respondents who used a chartist approach to investment analysis were not asked the question. Those respondents (15) who did not answer any part of the question have been omitted from the analysis. Respondents who did not rank any particular section of the report were deemed to have considered it to be of the least importance (rank 12). The rank correlation between 'no answers' and 'rank 12' was 0.88. With one slight exception (rank 11) this was considerably higher than the rank correlation of 'no answers' and the other categories of response.

APPENDIX 46

Annual report reading patterns of defined reader groups

READER GROUP*	n	CR %	DR %	SAP %	PL %	BS %	NA %	AR %	SAF %	SI %	CAS %
Reader group 2(a)											
Read thoroughly		75	47	49	100	100	86	22	65	46	72
Read briefly		24	47	43	—	—	13	56	32	48	25
Not read		1	6	8	—	—	1	22	3	6	3
	142	100	100	100	100	100	100	100	100	100	100
Reader group 2(b)											
Read thoroughly		14	—	—	100	100	14	—	43	14	14
Read briefly		86	57	14	—	—	86	—	29	57	72
Not read		—	43	86	—	—	—	100	28	29	14
	7	100	100	100	100	100	100	100	100	100	100
Reader group 3											
Read thoroughly		93	36	14	36	22	29	—	29	36	29
Read briefly		7	50	72	57	64	50	43	43	14	28
Not read		—	14	14	7	14	21	57	28	50	43
	14	100	100	100	100	100	100	100	100	100	100
Reader group 4											
Read thoroughly		—	—	—	—	50	50	—	—	50	—
Read briefly		100	50	50	100	—	—	—	50	50	—
Not read		—	50	50	—	50	50	100	50	—	100
	2	100	100	100	100	100	100	100	100	100	100
Reader group 5											
Read thoroughly		—	—	—	—	—	—	14	—	—	14
Read briefly		100	71	57	100	100	71	29	86	71	57
Not read		—	29	43	—	—	29	57	14	29	29
	7	100	100	100	100	100	100	100	100	100	100

(The header spanning "CR DR SAP PL BS NA AR SAF SI CAS" is titled PART OF ANNUAL REPORT)

*2 respondents who used a chartist approach to investment analysis were not asked the question.

CR = chairman's report; DR = directors' report; SAP = statement of accounting policies; PL = profit and loss account; BS = balance sheet; NA = notes to accounts; AR = auditor's report; SAF = source and application of funds statement; SI = statistical information; CAS = composition of activities statement.

APPENDIX 47

Defined reader groups' reading of supplementary inflation accounting statements

READER GROUP*	n	CCA STATEMENTS %	CPPA STATEMENTS %
Reader group 1			
Read thoroughly		93	93
Read briefly		7	7
Not read		—	—
	54	100	100
Reader group 2(a)			
Read thoroughly		33	23
Read briefly		56	58
Not read		11	19
	142	100	100
Reader group 2(b)			
Read thoroughly		14	14
Read briefly		43	29
Not read		43	57
	7	100	100
Reader group 3			
Read thoroughly		7	7
Read briefly		43	43
Not read		50	50
	14	100	100
Reader group 4			
Read thoroughly		—	—
Read briefly		50	50
Not read		50	50
	2	100	100

Cont. on page 201

READER GROUP*	n	CCA STATEMENTS %	CPPA STATEMENTS %
Reader group 5			
Read thoroughly		—	—
Read briefly		57	57
Not read		43	43
	7	100	100

*2 respondents who used a chartist approach to investment analysis were not asked the question.

APPENDIX 48

Survey respondents' views of the relative importance of sources of financial information other than the annual report in their organisations' investment decisions

RANKING	SOURCE OF INFORMATION	DEGREE OF IMPORTANCE RELATIVE TO OTHER SOURCES OF INFORMATION									
		1	*2*	*3*	*4*	*5*	*6*	*7*	*8*	*Total**	*Mean*
		%	%	%	%	%	%	%	%	%	
1	Three or six monthly financial reports	50	10	15	8	6	5	2	4	100	2.51
2	Financial press reports	16	23	19	16	13	9	2	2	100	3.33
3	Stockbrokers' reports	25	11	12	8	7	7	15	15	100	4.21
4	Occasional acquisition or merger reports	15	11	13	17	11	11	13	9	100	4.30
5	Industry data and reports	5	15	19	16	18	12	8	7	100	4.33
6	Economy data and reports	12	6	16	12	15	21	9	9	100	4.57
7	Moodies or Extel cards	12	8	5	12	12	16	15	20	100	5.11
8	Company reports to employees	—	—	2	4	7	12	23	52	100	7.04

*n = 212; the 2 respondents who used a chartist approach to investment analysis were not asked the question. Those respondents (17) who did not answer any part of the question have been omitted from the analysis. Respondents who did not assess the importance of any particular source of information were deemed to have considered it to be of least importance (ie rank 8). The rank correlation between 'no answers' and 'rank 8' was 0.57. The correlations between 'no answers' and 'ranks 6 and 7' were marginally higher than 0.57 but, in all other cases, were considerably lower — the correlations with ranks 1 to 4 were negative.

APPENDIX 49

Respondents' views of the relative importance of various sources of financial information about companies

RANKING	SOURCES OF INFORMATION	DEGREES OF IMPORTANCE RELATIVE TO OTHER SOURCES				
		1	*2*	*3*	*Total·*	*Mean*
		%	%	%	%	%
1	Formal published account-ing information from companies	64	25	11	100	1.46
2	Other sources of informa-tion about companies and their industries	36	35	29	100	1.93
3	Company visits	26	26	48	100	2.22

*n = 218; the 2 respondents who used a chartist approach to investment analysis were not asked the question. Those respondents (11) who did not answer any part of the question have been omitted from the analysis.

APPENDIX 50

Reading of annual report and level of understanding of inflation accounting matters of survey respondents

READING OF ANNUAL REPORT		LEVEL OF UNDERSTANDING					
		Much above average	*Above average*	*Average*	*Below average*	*Much below average*	*Total*
	n*	%	%	%	%	%	%
Very thorough readers	54	9	20	52	6	13	100
Thorough readers	142	8	19	54	10	9	100
Less thorough readers	33	3	9	39	21	28	100

*2 respondents have not been included in the readership analysis.
($p < 0.05$)

APPENDIX 51

Type of survey respondents and level of understanding of inflation accounting matters of survey respondents

TYPE OF SURVEY RESPONDENT		LEVEL OF UNDERSTANDING					
		Much above average	Above average	Average	Below average	Much below average	Total
	n	%	%	%	%	%	%
Institutional investors	136	7	17	55	12	9	100
Stockbrokers	95	7	19	48	8	18	100

(Not statistically significant at the 0.05 level)

APPENDIX 52

Number of shareholdings and level of understanding of inflation accounting matters of survey respondents

NUMBER OF SHAREHOLDINGS FOR WHICH SURVEY RESPONDENTS RESPONSIBLE		LEVEL OF UNDERSTANDING					
		Much above average	Above average	Average	Below average	Much below average	Total
	n*	%	%	%	%	%	%
1—100	56	5	13	55	14	13	100
101—500	75	5	16	57	12	10	100
501 +	22	4	14	50	9	23	100

*78 respondents did not know the number of shareholdings for which they were responsible
(Not statistically significant at the 0.05 level)

APPENDIX 53

Value of portfolios and level of understanding of inflation accounting matters of survey respondents

VALUE OF PORTFOLIOS		LEVEL OF UNDERSTANDING					
		Much above average	Above average	Average	Below average	Much below average	Total
£	n*	%	%	%	%	%	%
100,000— 100,000,000	54	—	11	50	15	24	100
100,000,001—1,000,000,000 +	37	13	14	60	8	5	100

*64 respondents gave 'do not know' or 'no answer' responses; and 76 respondents did not specify portfolio values sufficiently accurately.

($p < 0.05$)

APPENDIX 54

Final say in investment decisions and level of understanding of inflation accounting matters of survey respondents

FINAL SAY IN INVESTMENT DECISIONS		LEVEL OF UNDERSTANDING					
		Much above average	Above average	Average	Below average	Much below average	Total
	n*	%	%	%	%	%	%
Yes	138	8	15	54	11	12	100
No	81	7	24	53	7	9	100

*12 respondents gave 'do not know' or 'no answer' responses.

(Not statistically significant at the 0.05 level)

APPENDIX 55

Investment experience and level of understanding of inflation accounting matters of survey respondents

INVESTMENT EXPERIENCE (years)	LEVEL OF UNDERSTANDING						
		Much above average	Above average	Average	Below average	Much below average	Total
	n*	%	%	%	%	%	%
1—10	135	8	18	59	8	7	100
11 +	92	6	19	44	14	17	100

*4 respondents who had no investment experience have been omitted from this analysis.

(Not statistically significant at the 0.05 level. On suitable aggregation horizontally the resultant data were found to be significant at the 0.01 level.)

APPENDIX 56

Experience of using accounting information and level of understanding of inflation accounting matters of survey respondents

USE EXPERIENCE (years)	LEVEL OF UNDERSTANDING						
		Much above average	Above average	Average	Below average	Much below average	Total
	n*	%	%	%	%	%	%
1—10	109	6	15	65	8	6	100
11 +	121	9	21	41	12	17	100

*1 respondent with no experience of using accounting information has been omitted from this analysis.

($p < 0.01$)

APPENDIX 57

Accounting experience and level of understanding of inflation accounting matters of survey respondents

ACCOUNTING EXPERIENCE		LEVEL OF UNDERSTANDING					
		Much above average	Above average	Average	Below average	Much below average	Total
	n	%	%	%	%	%	%
Significant	58	10	22	50	9	9	100
Little	37	11	30	43	8	8	100
None	136	5	13	55	12	15	100

(Not statistically significant at the 0.05 level.)

APPENDIX 58

Respondents' understanding of general financial reporting topics and their understanding of inflation accounting topics

UNDERS ANDING OF GENERAL FINANCIAL REPORTING		UNDERSTANDING OF INFLATION ACCOUNTING			
		Above average	Average	Below average	Total
	n	%	%	%	%
Above average	61	33	62	5	100
Average	113	29	56	15	100
Below average	57	5	35	60	100

(p<0.01)

Bibliography

The following items represent the published works which have resulted to date from this research project, currently financed by The Institute of Chartered Accountants in England and Wales.

T. A. Lee, 'Using and Understanding Financial Information', *The Investment Analyst*, April 1976, pp5-10.

T. A. Lee and D. P. Tweedie, 'Accounting Information: An Investigation of Shareholder Usage', *Accounting and Business Research*, Autumn 1975, pp280-91.

T. A. Lee and D. P. Tweedie, 'Accounting Information: An Investigation of Shareholder Understanding', *Accounting and Business Research*, Winter 1975, pp3-17.

T. A. Lee and D. P. Tweedie, 'How Well Used Are All Those Figures?', *Accountants' Weekly*, 7 November 1975, pp11-12.

T. A. Lee and D. P. Tweedie, 'The Private Shareholder: His Sources of Financial Information and His Understanding of Reporting Practices', *Accounting and Business Research*, Autumn 1976, pp304-14.

T. A. Lee and D. P. Tweedie, *The Private Shareholder and the Corporate Report*, The Institute of Chartered Accountants in England and Wales, 1977.

T. A. Lee and D. P. Tweedie, 'Subjectivity in Research into Shareholder Behaviour', *The Accountant's Magazine*, July 1978, pp295-8.

D. P. Tweedie, 'The Corporate Report: Evolution or Revolution?', *The Accountant's Magazine*, October 1975, pp343-6.